# TESTIM

"Never Fight Alone is like a Bible for te...
er of She is Sacred

"Shelomo is on a great mission and knows what he is doing. You can apply these concepts to overcome adversity in your day-to-day life." **~ Will Holdren**, teenage entrepreneur, host of the WillPower podcast, author of Becoming the Best

"This book is way ahead of its time. It does a great job of collaborating with others to provide practical tips, strategies, and personalized stories on how to become more confident in your teenage years." **~ Arman Chowdhury**, founder of Armani Talks

"We need someone who relates to teens and is living proof that it does get better. I am glad someone stepped up and put this all together." **~ Nyah Jones**, TikTok influencer with over 800,000 followers

"I had a lot of hardships when I was younger. If I had something like Teenage Impact, I would have avoided some of those hardships, and my success would have come a lot sooner." **~ Laura Egocheaga**, CEO and founder of Viral Growth Media

"Shelomo has interwoven stories of healing and transformation from real people around the world in a genuine way. This book will help so many young lives." **~ Francesca Rose**, founder of Francesca Eats Roses

"Shelomo is built to succeed because his intent is helping others. He is professional, competent, ethical, and responsible, and he sets a great example for young people to achieve in their careers." **~ Joe Yazbeck**, CEO of Prestige Leadership Advisors

"You made me believe in myself to work harder and never give up, just like you. Thank you very much." **~ Anonymous** high school student

"I recommended my friends to follow you. Shelomo, you literally have the best Instagram page to follow." **~ Anonymous** high school student

"Thank you for being a grown-up who takes into full consideration that teenagers' moods fluctuate. Thank you for creating a platform and a book for us to share your kindness." **~ Anonymous** high school student

1

# NEVER FIGHT ALONE

### 51 Inspiring Interviews to Help Teens Overcome Their Struggles & Improve Their Mental Health

Never Fight Alone/Shelomo Solson — 1st edition

ISBN: 9780578762999

Editing and typesetting by Kevin Miller (www.kevinmillerxi.com)

Proofreading by Sue Shea

Cover design by https://99designs.ca/profiles/meella

# NEVER FIGHT ALONE

### 51 Inspiring Interviews to Help Teens Overcome Their Struggles & Improve Their Mental Health

## SHELOMO SOLSON

# CONTENTS

# ACKNOWLEDGMENTS

I wouldn't be where I am without my close relationships with people, both the positive and negative experiences in life, and the mentors who guided me. I might not say it enough, but I genuinely appreciate everyone in my life. I wouldn't be the man I am today without you. Names are not listed (you know who you are). In no particular order, I would like to thank:

- My parents
- My siblings, their spouses, and their children
- My girlfriend
- My fraternity brothers and my childhood friends
- My mentors
- The people who I have interviewed
- My followers, fans, school administrators, and youth organization leaders
- People I have met at some point and experiences that I have faced
- Myself
- God

# INTRODUCTION

I felt hopeless and tired and wanted to fast-forward to finishing school. I was tired of being bullied year after year, tired of not fitting in, and tired of the pressure from teachers, parents, coaches, and the rest of society. *Give me a break,* I thought. *No one really understands me.*

People think that teenagers who entertain such thoughts are rebellious or too emotional, and adults think discipline is the only way to teach such young people a "lesson." That couldn't be further from the truth. Teenagers who are struggling just want someone to understand and genuinely care for them. So much goes on behind closed doors that people don't see. Teens want to express how they feel, but they're afraid of being judged or someone telling them to "suck it up." The teenage years are some of the toughest and most unfair years of our lives. Teens' brains are still developing. They experience hormones and go through puberty. They have to balance school with their family life, social life, extracurricular activities, and a part-time job on top of the mess that is going on inside their heads. This leads to experimentation with:

- Drugs
- Sex
- Rebellion
- Bullying
- Our personality
- Our wardrobe
- Friends
- Relationships with the same or opposite sex

Teenagers often feel that no one understands them. They want to fulfill the basic human need to be accepted by their teachers, friends, and family members, but this is often more difficult than it sounds. All of this is going on while they experience daily struggles that have the potential to shape who they are for the rest of their lives—if they let them. Some of the most common struggles teenagers experience include:

- Anxiety
- Depression
- Suicidal thoughts
- Confidence/self-esteem issues
- Bullying
- Troubles at home
- Loved ones passing away
- Health problems
- Mental health disorders
- Relationship problems
- Drug or alcohol addiction
- Social media addiction
- School problems
- Physical and/or sexual abuse
- Friendship problems
- Feelings of failure
- Being in foster care
- Fear of disappointing others
- Lack of a support network/mentors
- Absentee parents
- Have too much going on and can't handle it
- LGBTQ and being judged for it
- Cross-cultural problems due to emigrating from another country

If you have struggled with at least one of the above issues, then this book is for you.

When I was a teen going through these problems, I wished I had someone I could relate to and who would come to my rescue. I was afraid to talk about my problems to my friends and adults. I thought no one would understand, and I would be a burden. I thought I was the only one battling these issues. Several times I couldn't control my tears in front of my friends due to everything going on in my life, and they ridiculed me. I vowed I would never cry in front of my friends. I thought men should never cry because it was a sign of weakness.

During my fifth year of college, four of my closest fraternity brothers were killed in a car accident (more on that in the final chapter of this book). That's when I discovered counseling existed. Although my counselor didn't solve my problems, it was an avenue for me to share what was going on inside instead of bottling up my feelings.

As the years went by after college, I realized I wasn't the only one with problems. Many friends vented to me about their struggles. Why? Because I would listen without judging. I also observed others who had problems and why they turned out the way the way they did. Their past struggles shaped who they became.

We are all unique. We all have strengths and weaknesses because of what we've experienced. Instead of judging, we should strive to understand one another. If we dig deep into the past, we will find we have more in common with each other than we think. Name any problem or challenge you face, and I guarantee you can find thousands if not millions of people around the world who have faced something similar. This is exactly why I wrote this book: to let you know that you are not fighting alone. I consider myself fortunate, but even I had my fair share of struggles.

## WHO SHOULD READ THIS BOOK?

If you are between the ages of thirteen to nineteen and are struggling with any of the challenges I mentioned earlier and feel trapped, this book is for you.

If you are a parent who has at least one teenager or kids who are almost teenagers, you should also read this book.

If you deal with teenagers on a daily or weekly basis, whether as a teacher, school staff member, youth pastor, or as part of a youth organization, you should read this book.

This book will give teens a perspective on how to overcome various challenges. It will also help adults become more aware of these challenges and the unique pressures facing young people today.

We are human. We want to read stories about people who have gone through the same things or who have overcome whatever challenges we are facing. We want to know we are not alone. Reading about other people's experiences and how they overcame their situations provides us with a sense of hope.

Hope that one day we will overcome the struggles we are facing.

Hope that one day we will make a difference in our community.

## WHAT WILL YOU LEARN FROM THIS BOOK?

- How other people overcame adversity
- Coping methods to deal with mental health struggles
- Actionable steps you can take today to make your life worth living
- Ways to be happier and more positive

- Ways to overcome daily challenges
- Life lessons from successful people

## HOW IS THIS BOOK OUTLINED, AND HOW SHOULD YOU USE THIS BOOK?

This book contains interviews with fifty-one people. These people are a combination of teens and adults who provide a variety of perspectives on various problems. These people are facing the problems listed above right now or have overcome them in the past.

Each chapter contains:

- A title that summarizes the chapter's main point
- An introduction to the person being interviewed
- The person's social media handles or websites (if you want to connect with them)
- An outline of the struggles mentioned in their chapter
- Their story about dealing with various challenges and how they overcame them or are working to do so
- Tips for those facing the same struggles
- Top takeaways from the chapter
- My favorite takeaway for each chapter (italicized)

The interviews were long and included some points that wouldn't make sense if they were transcribed completely. I have trimmed the interviews significantly to extract the most important parts from each interview and rephrased them in a way that will make sense to you.

Everyone I interviewed has faced or is facing a range of challenges. Some were suicidal, and some didn't realize they were facing significant struggles until it was almost too late. I have included people from all walks of life to provide a variety of perspectives.

I don't expect everyone to read all fifty-one interviews. Think of this book like Chicken Soup for the Soul by Jack Canfield and Mark Victor Hansen or Tribe of Mentors by Tim Ferris. This book is not meant to be read from cover to cover unless you want to. I encourage you to find the people you relate to the most. In the beginning of each interview, I mention their struggles and a short bio. If you want to read about a particular person, then continue reading. If not, move on to the next person or skim through the key points at the end of the chapter. You can also reference the table of contents if you want to jump to certain parts of the book.

I am super grateful that you picked up this book and allowed me to be part of your journey. I hope you enjoy this book and take away at least one tip that will change your life forever. If you see a phrase, story, or tip that you like, write it down, highlight it, or share it on social media and tag me @ShelomoSolson.

## DISCLAIMER

This book will not solve your problems. It provides stories, tips, and specific strategies on what has worked for certain people. To see similar results, you must take action and implement the tips shared within. The strategies in this book have worked for other people, but they may not work for you. This book does not provide you with all the strategies that exist. However, this book is a good start and one of many books you should read. Neither I nor anyone else featured in this book bears any responsibility for loss or damages caused directly or indirectly by the information enclosed in this book.

## TRIGGER WARNING

When reading this book, you may feel triggered. This book talks about sensitive information like suicide, self-harm, anxiety, depression, abuse, sexual assault, addiction, and mental health challenges that may trigger certain emotions. If you are thinking about self-harming or committing suicide, please dial the National Suicide Prevention Line: 1-800-273-8255. If you need immediate medical attention, please dial 911 or visit your local emergency room.

If you are not in a good state of mind, seek help. You probably have been told that before, but I am telling you again: Don't take matters into your own hands. You are better off telling a trusted adult what you are going through. Asking for help is not a sign of weakness. In fact, doing so requires courage. The trusted adults will give you what you need to help you recover.

If a friend or a loved one has opened up to you about self-harm or suicide or has shown signs of it, take that person seriously. Consult a trusted adult immediately even if the person told you to keep it a secret. You could save a life.

## DON'T TAKE OFFENSE

If I or anyone I have interviewed offends you, we apologize. Everyone has a different viewpoint on overcoming certain challenges in life. Some of us use different terminology when talking about mental health. The terminology I use in this book is what I am comfortable using, and I don't mean to offend anyone. Please look past the viewpoints and terminology. The sole purpose of this book is to help people.

## IT'S THE MESSAGE THAT MATTERS

Depending on when you read this book, some things have changed in the interviewees' lives. If I have listed out an age, grade level, company name, social media info, or their current status in their life, it may have changed. At the time of the interview, that's what it was, and as time goes by, people evolve. So, there may be some inaccuracies because time has passed. Don't focus on the minor details; focus on the message.

## WE ARE NOT MENTAL HEALTH PROFESSIONALS

The sole purpose of this book is to share our struggles with you and to explain what has worked for us to overcome those problems. I wrote this book to help as many teenagers and adults who work with teenagers. I hope this book is a catalyst for change in your life and help you open up about some of the challenges that you are facing. I also hope this book helps adults understand the struggles that you face daily and how important it is for them to display empathy.

I believe this book can be a life changer if you are open to change. This book took over a year to create, but it will be worth every minute of it if you implement just one of the tips it contains and use it to change your life or the life of someone you love.

Everyone is on a different path. Some are further along the journey, and some are further behind. Don't compare your journey with others. Your journey is your journey, so be grateful for the path that you're on. Everyone faces different struggles, which is part of what makes us unique.

Finally, remember, I love you all. I hope you enjoy this book and find it not only educational but also life-changing!

Respectfully,

Shelomo Solson

# 1
# HOW TO BUILD CONFIDENCE

*Arman Chowdhury*

Arman is a communications expert and coach. He helps people all over the world build their confidence in public speaking and social dynamics. He has been a good friend of mine for nine years. We are in the same fraternity. Back in college, he was the fraternity's social guy. He helped bring other people to events and was good at recruiting students to the fraternity.

We have grown closer over the past few years. Arman and I started doing side hustles right after graduating from college. He got into the personal development phase after I introduced him to Toastmasters (a public speaking organization). Then he told me about starting a Twitter account that provided communication and public speaking advice. Within a year, he's gained over 20,000 followers on Twitter. Some may call it luck, but I call it a determination to make a difference. As you'll read in his story, he wasn't always social and confident.

## CONTACT:

- Website: www.armanitalks.com
- Twitter: @ArmaniTalks
- YouTube: Armani Talks

## STRUGGLES INCLUDED IN THIS CHAPTER:

- Social and speech anxiety
- Lack of confidence/self-esteem
- Coming from another country
- People-pleaser
- Parents put too much pressure on him
- Skinniest kid in class

## COMING TO AMERICA FROM BANGLADESH

**Arman Chowdhury:** I came from Bangladesh when I was five years old. When I was in Bangladesh, the most popular language was Bangla. We would read and write English, but we wouldn't speak it. When we moved to America, over the next few years, I had to learn how to speak English. It was a tough time for me. I was often mocked and ridiculed for my accent. I spent years being "that shy kid."

I was also ridiculed for being skinny. Typically, Bengali parents want their children to be healthy. For them, being bigger is better than being smaller. They would ask me, "Why are you so skinny? You don't eat?" Kids at school also made fun of me for being skinny.

## ONLY THE COOL KIDS WERE IN THE BACK OF THE BUS

**AC:** One day I got on the bus, and someone was sitting in my assigned seat. I didn't know where to sit; I took assigned seats seriously. As I looked around, I saw one open seat all the way in the back of the bus.

I didn't know what to do because that wasn't my seat. All the cool kids were in the back of the bus, and I wasn't one of them. Not knowing what else to do, I walked slowly to the back. The other "non-cool" kids stared at me in shock, but I kept walking. The cool kids in the back also stared at me, wondering why I was back there. I put my backpack in an open seat and sat down.

As soon as I did, the cool kids asked my name. When I didn't reply, they started to make fun of me. Before that moment, the cool kids didn't even know I existed. Once I entered their territory, I became visible in their eyes, and I became their target for the rest of the school year. It made it tough for me because the bus ride was a big part of my school day.

## ARMAN'S SOCIAL ANXIETY

**AC:** When you don't know much about something, your brain starts thinking in a chaotic way, and that gives it a negative label. I didn't know what social anxiety was back then. The main reason I didn't like social events was because I was shy. Being around all these people seemed out of the ordinary for me. Even on days leading up to the social event, I started asking myself, "What if this goes wrong? What if everyone's watching me?"

**Shelomo Solson:** Was there a moment where you froze up in middle school or high school?

**AC:** I wouldn't freeze up, but I would have trouble saying something. If several people were contributing to a conversation, I thought I would have the perfect thing to say, but I kept trying to get the sentences perfect in my head before I said them.

## STOP CHASING THE "A" SO MUCH

**SS:** Did your parents ever yell at you for doing poorly?

**AC:** Yes, they yelled at me for not studying hard enough. My parents came from a different country and were here mainly for the education. If I didn't do well in school, I felt like I was letting them down.

**SS:** What advice would you give to someone who has it engraved in their head that they must please their family by getting good grades, or their family won't accept them?

**AC:** I recommend gaining some perspective from books. What kept me motivated was hearing about people who succeeded after many failures. For me, being poor at tests was good in terms of doing well in business.

**SS:** Why?

**AC:** Because failure is normal when you get into the real world. That's the only way I learned. Instead of focusing so much on a grade in order to get acceptance, focus more on exercising your work ethic.

If I were to give my younger self advice, I would say, "Arman, stop chasing the A so much. Just work as hard as you can. Design a structured plan. Keep following it day in and day out." These are all tips that you can apply in the real world. Keep working hard every day, and good grades will be a byproduct.

## HOW ARMAN STARTED FEELING MORE CONFIDENT

**AC:** Joining the fraternity played a big role in building my confidence. Once I joined the fraternity, I was exposed to more social events than ever before. I had to make the decision to speak up; there was no way around that. Later, I joined Toastmasters. I thought to myself, *Hmm, this may seem bold, but what if I could become a public speaker?* If I could speak in front of fifty people, then having a one-on-one interaction would be a piece of cake.

**SS:** I still remember your first speech when I brought you to Toastmasters. I was the president of Toastmasters back then. One of my mentors came up to me afterwards and said, "Your friend, Arman, is going to need some work. He kept on saying ums, like, and ahhs." Look how far you've come.

**AC:** I think that was the second time that I went to Toastmasters. The first time I got called onstage, and I didn't say a word. When I said, "um," "ah," and "like," many times, it was bad, but at least I spoke in front of an audience. It was progress. The next time my goal was to get rid of the filler words. Then I was able to cut down on that. I kept on giving speeches and talking in front of people. I started feeling more confident when I decide to turn my biggest pain into my greatest strength.

## BECOMING LESS OF A PEOPLE PLEASER

**AC:** The people-pleasing stopped once I made a huge mental shift. Instead of competing with other people, I decided to focus more on myself. Instead of going external, I went internal, and I focused on developing one goal. Once I shifted my mentality toward this goal, I no longer attempted to please other people.

Once you get one goal, it creates an avalanche of goals. The first goal was to get up on stage. My second goal was to get up on stage and speak. I said a bunch of words, but a lot of them were filler words. My third goal was to speak without saying so many filler words. My fourth goal was to go from improv speaking to planned speeches. Once I kept going from goal to goal, eventually, I was giving presentations. My next goal was to volunteer for leadership positions in Toastmasters. Once you go into self-development for your life, you're going to get an avalanche of these different goals. The more you invest yourself in that avalanche, other people's opinions become a waste of time. Who cares what they think about you?

## TURN SOCIAL/SPEECH ANXIETY INTO SOCIAL/SPEECH EXCITEMENT

**AC:** My perception toward social anxiety changed as I grew older. Instead of calling it social anxiety, I called it social excitement. Humans are creatures of energy. With any interaction, there will be tension. The question is, how do you perceive it? Before getting on stage to speak in front of five hundred people, I feel a level of tension, similar to right before I get on a roller coaster.

You might view it as speech anxiety, but I view it as excitement. I did have anxiety before when speaking, but now I focus on it being a good thing. Imagine if we didn't get these feelings before doing something exciting.

## HOW CAN TEENAGERS BECOME MORE CONFIDENT AND SOCIAL?

**AC:** Once you start developing yourself, confidence will be a byproduct. Pick one thing that you are curious about. Many times you will find your answers behind your pain. I had speech anxiety, which was the one thing that I needed to focus on. Instead of trying to overcome it in one day, I did it piece by piece. The more challenges that you overcome, the more confidence you will have with subsequent challenges. The more confident you become, the easier it is to go up to different people and start interacting with them.

**SS:** At a social gathering, did you find one person to sit with, or would you find a group of people who looked more receptive and then try to join that table?

**AC:** I recommend trying both. While growing up, I would find one person because I didn't want to approach a group. It felt too daunting. If you identify with that, I recommend taking it one person at a time. Eventually, you will feel more comfortable approaching more than one person.

**SS:** You are with a group of people and sometimes; you don't know what to say. How do you overcome that?

**AC:** Do a micro acknowledgement. Imagine if you and I are having a conversation, and you finish talking. I don't know what to say, but I can nod, which indicates to your subconscious mind that you should keep talking. You'll be surprised how often you get more information out of another person through such actions.

Also, when you think too much, you become self-conscious. When you say the first thing that comes to your mind, conversation can flow naturally. It all comes down to framing. If you think your social skills can't be improved, they won't be. If you view everything as a muscle that simply needs to be worked out, it will be improved.

Focus on your mindset. Tell yourself that it will improve. Fight through the discomfort, and keep pushing forward. The more goals you tackle, the more you're going to build your confidence.

## TOP TAKEAWAYS:

- Step outside your comfort zone.
- Gain some perspective from books.
- Don't focus too much on results, such as your grades; focus on your work ethic.
- *Turn social anxiety into social excitement.*
- When you pursue a goal that you are passionate about, you will forget about what other people think of you because you are too busy pursuing that goal.
- Once you start developing yourself, confidence is a byproduct.
- If you don't have anyone to sit with at lunch, find someone else who is sitting alone.
- When conversing with someone, don't overthink things. If you don't

23

know what to say, do a micro acknowledgement, or say whatever comes to your mind to keep the conversation flowing.
- If you view social skills as a muscle that simply needs to be worked out, you can improve them through daily "exercise."

# 2
# THE POWER OF CHOOSING JOY

*JACK SERNETT*

Jack Sernett has had several bumps in his life, both in his teen years and as an adult. Jack survived a suicide attempt, had an eating disorder, and suffered from depression and anxiety. He was in the hospital almost every week from age twenty-two to twenty-five battling stage-three chronic kidney disease, for which he had twelve surgeries in eighteen months. One day he decided to change his mindset and transformed himself into Mr. Peace. His mission is to empower individuals, the community, and the world to live a calm, stress-free life by learning how to overcome adversity.

## CONTACT:
- Website: www.jacksernett.com
- Instagram: @IAmJackSernett

## STRUGGLES INCLUDED IN THIS CHAPTER:
- Anxiety
- Depression
- Eating disorder
- Low self-esteem
- Suicidal thoughts
- Afraid of disappointing others
- Put a lot of pressure on himself
- Too much stress and worry
- Hospitalization

## SELF-INFLICTED PRESSURE

**Jack Sernett:** My anxiety was the catalyst for all the other struggles that I ended up experiencing up until age twenty-five.

My first memories of having anxiety are associated with school. One was a spelling test in first grade. Also, one time I was playing kickball in school. I hit a home run, kicking the ball the farthest. I received positive reinforcement from my friends, and I started to become known as the best athlete. From that point on, I believed I needed to be the best at everything, and I put pressure on myself to do so for many years. I had an image I wanted to live up to, to be the best in everything and to be known as the perfect student and the perfect athlete. It all started back when I was six.

I didn't know what to call it at first, but my anxiety got worse and worse over the years. I didn't know how to tame it. At about age thirteen, my anxiety started to cause me a lot of stress. By the time I was fifteen or sixteen, I started to feel very depressed, though I didn't realize it at the time. I didn't know what those terms were until I started receiving treatment for it later. I was a high achiever during my teenage years. School was the most important thing in the world to me. My goal to be perfect in school became very unhealthy. I had straight A's my entire life, and I used to get frustrated if I got 98 percent. I was mad I didn't get 100 percent. My parents didn't put that pressure on me; it was completely self-inflicted. I couldn't control my thoughts, my emotions, or my reactions.

I also became controlling about what I ate. That led to an eating disorder. I ended up losing a bunch of weight. I was strict with my food, and I wouldn't eat as much as I should have. I was too worried about my body image, too hard on myself. There were many days when I wouldn't look at myself in the mirror when brushing my teeth. I always brushed my teeth with the light off. I spent about four years brushing my teeth in the dark because I couldn't stand looking myself in the face. It was rough. I was half the weight that I am now.

When I was seventeen, I had to drop out of high school for the last three months of my junior year because I was too unhealthy. I was having suicidal thoughts, and I was getting sick. I had to go to the hospital sometimes. The only hope I had was going to a residential facility in Wisconsin (I was living in Kansas at the time). I spent three months there, which helped with my anxiety and depression. I was getting better. I stopped putting so much pressure on myself. That place saved my life. It completely turned things around. When things in your life go in a downward spiral, you must change something.

## YOU ARE ONE OF A KIND

**JS:** I used to care way too much about what other people thought about me. I was always a muscular kid, and I was doing sports all the time. In first grade, my nickname was "Six-pack Jack."

26

From then on I thought I needed to maintain a perfect physique and live up to that name. In third grade I would suck my stomach in, thinking I had to look skinnier. The way I got over it was someone told me to treat myself like someone I loved. I thought, *Gosh, I'm such a bully to myself.* The way I looked at and talked about myself when I was younger, I would never do that to anyone. It was a mean thing to do. I realized that when I was in public, a lot of people weren't thinking about me even though I was paranoid they might be. I also realized it was impossible to be perfect.

Immediately, I started developing the habit of being kind to myself. Every day I wrote down three things that I liked about myself. At least one of them had to be a physical thing. The way we learn is through repetition. It's the same as learning how to ride a bike. You must repeat it constantly. How do you learn how to hit a baseball? Practice. It's the same thing with positive self-talk. I practice being nice to myself and writing down things I like about myself. I would be honest when I had bad thoughts about myself and then reverse them. I would always have a couple of affirmations in my mind to help reverse negative thoughts about myself.

How can you ever love someone else if you can't love yourself? If you are not comfortable in your own skin and lack self-esteem, know that you are one of a kind. There's never been another person with your brain chemistry, your thoughts, your characteristics, your emotions, your triggers, or your positive attributions in the history of humankind, and there never will be in the future. No other person will ever be like you.

An African proverb says, "If there's no enemy within, the enemy outside can do us no harm." That could not be truer. When you are good with yourself, no one will be able to hurt your feelings or get you down. Don't give them that power.

## IF YOU ARE THINKING ABOUT SUICIDE, HOLD ON TO THAT SILVER OF HOPE

**JS:** There were many nights when I prayed that I wouldn't wake up in the morning. The one thing that helped me was knowing that tomorrow there was a chance that my life would be slightly better. It's like that picture of two miners digging a tunnel, but one of them quits when he is three inches away from reaching diamonds. It would be unfortunate to commit suicide when the next day your entire life could have changed. I always hold on to that sliver of hope that something will change soon.

Many people need a wake-up call before they change. My wake-up call was on March 6, 2015, when I attempted to commit suicide, and I survived. I realized I had been given a second chance, and I completely turned my life around. A survey was done on people who survived suicide attempts. Most people regretted it the second they tried. For me the second I woke up from blacking out, I totally regretted it and felt like I had made a mistake. Suicide is a permanent response to a temporary problem.

Have faith, not hope. Hope is wishing. Faith is confidence that your life will get better. There's always an opportunity to turn your life around.

## DITCH THE EGO, AND ACCEPT HELP

**JS:** Your ego is your worst enemy. The way I got better was by asking for help. I threw my ego out the door. I knew I couldn't get better alone. If you're self-aware enough to realize you have suicidal ideations, you need to have a plan to get to a safe environment or reach out to someone you trust when you are in that dangerous state of mind. It's different for everyone. Call a suicide hotline (1-800-273-8255). I know people who have gone straight to the ER and told the doctors they need help.

No great person has ever done anything great alone. I wouldn't be here if it wasn't for a team around me and a support system to help me. Throw your ego out the door. It's OK not to be OK. You don't have to tell the whole world. For many years in high school, only a couple of people—my counselor and the school psychologist—knew I was suicidal. There should be no stigma around asking for help. It's a health struggle. No one will look at you poorly because you went for help.

## YOU ARE NOT AT THE MERCY OF WHAT HAPPENS TO YOU

**JS:** Many people live at the mercy of their circumstances. Their emotions and their mood are dictated by what happens to them from moment to moment. I used to be that way, but now I have a good grip on how to handle negative things that happen to me.

First, I break down what I have control over. The only thing we have control over is our attitude and actions. I also focus on a couple of things at a time, not fifty or a hundred. If you bite things off little by little, your personality, your habits, and your life will change for the better.

Consider my health, for example. I was doing everything the doctor told me, but I was still getting sicker, and I was getting more surgeries. Finally, the chronic kidney surgeries forced me to become a master at controlling what's between my ears. If you can't control your mind, you will have a tough time and be at the mercy of what happens to you. Being negative all the time is not a fun way to live.

One day during my third or fourth time in the hospital with a short period of time, I thought, There has to be a better way to do this. If this is as miserable as I'm going to be, there's no way I'm going to handle things. The meds they had me on made my vision blurry. I couldn't watch television, and I couldn't go on my computer. I was there with my thoughts. Wow, this is going to really suck if I don't get better at handling what pops into my head, I thought. I asked myself what I could do to get better. In that moment, I became self-aware, which means I quit lying to myself.

I had lied to myself for years. I was in denial. I didn't admit my faults or my weaknesses. What you resist will persist. If you can't handle adversity, your life will be one big rollercoaster of emotions. That's not a fun way to live. The only way to handle adversity is to be honest with yourself.

## IT'S GOING TO TAKE TIME

**JS:** The way I started thinking more positively was through constant repetition. The first couple of months I tried to get less stressed. It wasn't that great. It was like watching professional athletes, many of whom aren't very good in the beginning. But don't quit if things don't get better in the beginning. It's a lifelong journey.

Every day is a constant battle, but it's a good battle. The word "battle" has a negative connotation to it, but it shouldn't. The old Jack still creeps up from time to time, but now I have ways to handle him and reverse that way of thinking. Life is not about what happens to you. The only thing that matters is how you respond to what happens to you.

## TOP TAKEAWAYS:

- If you are self-conscious and critical about yourself, write things you like about yourself every day.
- There's never been another person with your brain chemistry, your thoughts, your characteristics, your emotions, your triggers, or your positive attributions in the history of humankind, and there never will be anyone like you in the future.
- *An African proverb says, "If there's no enemy within, the enemy outside can do us no harm."*
- Suicide is a permanent response to a temporary problem.
- Many people who survive a suicide attempt regret having tried it.
- Throw your ego out the door, and ask for help.
- We can't control everything, but we can control our attitude and actions.

- Become self-aware, and stop lying to yourself.
- You don't get good at anything on the first try.
- Every day is a battle, a good battle. The term "battle" should not have a negative connotation.

# 3
# HOW TO FEEL COMFORTABLE IN YOUR OWN SKIN

*SHINJINI DAS*

Shinjini was born in Kolkata, India. As a kid, she was super shy. She had a hard time socializing with other kids, especially at birthday parties. Eventually, her parents stopped taking her to such events because she would make a scene.

At age five she moved to Malaysia, then to New Jersey at age nine and Georgia at age eleven. When she moved to the United States, she felt out of place and lacked confidence. She kept to herself and stuck to a small crowd. At times she was insecure, especially about never having a boyfriend. She was also made fun of for being Indian and because of her culture.

She fell in love with public speaking in high school and won multiple competitions right away. Eventually, she went to the nationals of the Future Business Leaders of America speech competitions with nine other people. When she graduated from Georgia Tech, she gave a commencement speech to thousands of people.

Now she is building a brand where she inspires people around the world to be comfortable in their own skin and become go-getters. Even though she lacked confidence, she was always proud of who she was. This led her to write a memoir by age twenty-six called *Unapologetically Shinjini*.

## CONTACT:
- Website: www.unapologeticallyshinjini.com
- Twitter: @SpeakerShinjini
- Instagram: @SpeakerShinjini

## STRUGGLES INCLUDED IN THIS CHAPTER:

- Social anxiety
- Low self-esteem
- Insecure about never having a boyfriend
- Shyness
- Coming from another country

## NO ONE WANTED TO INVITE HER TO BIRTHDAY PARTIES

**Shinjini Das:** Whether you call it social anxiety, coming out of your shell, or growing up, I had a hard time going to birthday parties. The parents hung out by themselves, and they wanted the children to play together. I didn't do that, and I created problems during that time. It was painful for my family, and I still hear the stories today.

The other parents would eventually stop inviting me to birthday parties because I was too afraid to play with the other kids.

I am super grateful for my parents' sacrifices. It was definitely a team effort to make sure that I grew up knowing how to socialize normally.

## NOT FITTING IN WHEN COMING TO THE UNITED STATES

**SD:** When I was nine, our family moved to New Jersey from Malaysia. I felt left out because we moved near the end of the year. I wondered why we would do that while I had two months left of the school year and while standardized testing was taking place. I also felt unwelcome among my new peers and teachers in the United States. No one asked me to join their circle, and they didn't know anything about my culture. No one even knew where Malaysia was.

My third-grade teacher asked me why I didn't know what a poem was. I never wrote poems in Malaysia. She also asked me why I didn't know what the currency was. I had a different currency in Malaysia. It seemed like a very ignorant question to me.

When I was in Malaysia, I was part of the expat community, which is defined as a community of people who were born in other countries. I used to hang out with them, so I was used to a more diverse friend group.

When I came to the United States, there were Indians my age, but many of them were born in the United States, which was completely different. When I talked about India and Malaysia, no one understood. Their mentality was, "We're in America now." I felt different, but I was also proud to be etāic. I never wanted to be like everyone else.

## WANTED TO BECOME POPULAR

**SD:** Throughout my life I've been the smart kid. My mental barrier was if I was smart and nerdy, I couldn't be popular.

I questioned why I could be the eighth-grade valedictorian, but I couldn't be the most popular. Why couldn't I be a girl with values and morals and still be popular? My goal has always been to influence and inspire, but I questioned whether I was enough.

## COMFORTABLE IN HER OWN SKIN AND CULTURE

**SD:** I was always "fresh off the boat." I'm obsessed with Indian movies, music, and the culture. I got made fun of so much for growing up in America. A lot of Indians I knew who were born in America didn't watch Bollywood movies growing up. They didn't appreciate them as much as I did. For me such movies are a beautiful way of expression.

I love how Indian movies empower women. She's singing, she's dancing, she's beautiful, she's talking. That was the image I saw growing up, and it was my influence. I was always proud and comfortable in my own skin even though I got made fun of for it.

## GUYS SAW HER AS A FRIEND

**SD:** I always focused on school and work in high school. I had no time even to think about boys. I never had a guy friend up until college. I didn't know what I would talk to them about.

At the time, Georgia Tech was almost 80 percent males. I knew I should talk to guys even though I didn't know what I would talk about. I couldn't just talk about homework all the time.

It was my first time away from home. I grew up sheltered. I never went to camps or overnight sleepovers. Being in a dorm for four years was a big move for me.

I had to practice how to talk to boys as friends. My goal during my freshman and sophomore years was to talk to them as friends. I didn't have time to date, and that was never my goal. I started by asking guys to grab breakfast or lunch.

For teens who are trying to get over opposite-gender anxiety, I think it's easy to start off as friends first.

Slowly, I started realizing that I was an interesting person, and guys genuinely liked talking to me. They said I was so passionate. What bothered me was they didn't see me as anything more than a friend. I was too busy to worry about it, but part of me felt a little hurt. I asked them how they saw me. They told me I was like one of the guys because of the energy that I gave off. Other girls came off as "girls," and I came off as a "guy."

At the end of college, I can say my goal was met. I left college with a lot of good guy friends. At times I had more close guy friends than girlfriends.

My irritation was at age twenty-three when the media discovered me. I thought, *Why don't any of these guys think of me as more than a friend?* To be honest, it hurt. I wanted to be a potential girlfriend, so I started working toward that.

One thing I am proud of was that I never blamed myself. I told myself, *There's nothing wrong with you.* Just because boys didn't see me as a potential girlfriend didn't mean I was ugly or not sexy. I had some packaging work to do though. I needed to change up my energy a bit as well as my style, but I never viewed it in a negative way.

Now I laugh to myself because guys always tell me that I'm the perfect girl. I'm the same person who no one looked at as a girlfriend. What I have worked on is myself, my image and my feminine energy.

Ironically, I didn't do this to attract a guy. I had to fix my image a bit because I was building a media company. Guys see that I'm not trying hard to attract them. I'm being myself and not apologizing for it. I believe the right guy will come along. I won't have to work so hard because he will like me for who I am.

## FROM SHY TO PUBLIC SPEAKING CHAMPION

**SD:** I realized I loved public speaking at age fourteen. I was discovered in eighth grade and nominated as the eight-grade graduation speaker.

By age fifteen, I won my first competition. At age sixteen, I was the state champion. Then at age seventeen, I was one of the top ten national finalists. Winning is fun, but it takes a lot of work. I loved it. I had over twenty competitions at my school. These competitions went all day on Saturdays. I would wake up at 5:00 a.m., the competition would start at 8:00 a.m., and end at 8:00 p.m. Awards went till 11:00 p.m. That's an eighteen-hour day!

Anyone doing it had to enjoy it. There's no way that someone could force me to do that because the competitions were too long. I had to study and prepare before and afterwards in addition to doing my schoolwork.

**SS:** How did you realize you had that talent?

**SD:** I'm very truth conscious. A lot of the things that I preach about are universal. For example, integrity is good, and lying is bad. I'm trying to get us back to our roots, back to where we come from. That's because immigrants make America great.

I'm shy, but these things that I was saying when I took the mic were my authentic self. I was spreading the truth about what I believed. I was focused on the message. I was fascinated with sharing the truth.

I also gave a commencement speech at Georgia Tech in front of 10,000 people. That was a struggle. I was trying to pave the way for other etāic women. I had to find the person who oversaw naming the commencement speaker and consistently email that person until they finally gave me a shot to present myself to them.

My hard work paid off when I graduated. I worked full-time for a couple years before I went full-time into building my brand. I didn't know how I was going to monetize my brand, but I was determined. Now I have people asking me to speak in different countries. Recently, a woman told me that I inspired her to quit her job to pursue medicine. Nothing beats that.

## GO AFTER YOUR GOALS

**SD:** It's important to invest in yourself. Get out there, and go after your goals. It takes a lot of effort to achieve your objectives. To be a top-ten national finalist for the Future Business Leaders of America speech competition and a commencement speaker, I worked hard consistently.

You also become happier, more confident, and sexier when you pursue what you love to do versus what you are told to do.

It helps to write your goals down. Make them achievable daily goals. When you make your goals, make sure you use metrics to track how far you are from achieving them.

I want you to be in control of your life and decide who you want to become. You shouldn't become something to impress your friends or your parents. Your success is in your hands.

## TOP TAKEAWAYS:

- Be proud of your heritage and background.
- *Don't try to be someone you're not just to impress other people.*
- The right guy or girl will like you for who you are, not someone you are trying to be.
- Work hard. Your goals will not be handed to you.
- Pursue what you love to do, not what someone else wants you to do.
- Write your goals down, and make them achievable.
- When giving a speech, focus on the message, not yourself.
- Hold yourself to a higher standard.
- No one can make you happy except you.

# 4
# HOW TO TURN YOUR LIFE AROUND FROM A NEGATIVE EXPERIENCE

*CASEY ADAMS*

Casey is a nineteen-year-old entrepreneur. Before beginning his entrepreneurial life, he was an average fifteen-year old kid. He played football in high school and aspired to continue playing football afterwards. He also associated himself with the wrong friend group who would often do drugs and alcohol. During the season when he was fifteen years old, he was involved in an injury that almost paralyzed him. He was diagnosed with interspinous ligament damage and was in a neck brace for about six months. His football aspirations went down the drain and were temporarily negative. During that time, he read *How to Win Friends and Influence People* by Dale Carnegie. That book changed his life. Then he was mentored by well-known entrepreneur Tai Lopez. He decided to learn about business. Over the past four years, he's interviewed over a hundred world-class entrepreneurs, including Gary Vaynerchuk, Grant Cardone, Tai Lopez, Jay Shetty, and Larry King for his podcast, *Rise of the Young*. He also published a book called *Rise of the Young*. He is inspiring many young people around the world.

**CONTACT:**
- Website: www.caseyadams.com
- Instagram: @Casey

**STRUGGLES INCLUDED IN THIS CHAPTER:**
- Toxic friends
- Serious high school football injury
- Couldn't accomplish his original goals

- Temporarily felt hopeless and depressed

## CASEY'S INJURY STORY

**Casey Adams:** I remember the day so vividly. It was the first day of football practice, and I was going into my sophomore year of high school. We were on the field doing something called the B drill. It's when you go head to head with one person, and you see who can take the other to the ground. Long story short, I was doing this drill, and the other guy ended up spinning me. I smacked my head on the ground. My helmet was loose in the first place, so it was falling off my head when I hit the ground.

I couldn't move right away, and I had massive neck pain. I thought I would lie there for a couple minutes, get back up, and be a little sore for a couple days. A few minutes later, I took off my pads, and my neck was still hurting so badly that I could hardly move my head right or left. The next morning is what altered the next six months of my life.

I was in deep pain, and I couldn't move my head at all. My mom took me to the doctor. They did an X-ray, and then we sat in the room for ten or fifteen minutes. I was mad that I couldn't go to practice, thinking it was only a minor injury and at the worst I wouldn't be able to play in that week's game. However, one of the quotes I live by is, "Expect the unexpected."

When the doctor came in, he asked, "Do you want to hear the good news or the bad news?" I told him that I wanted to hear the good news. "The good news is you're not paralyzed," he said. "The bad news is you have interspinous ligament damage. You'll have to be in a neck brace for about six months, and you can never play football again due to the mobility of your neck, and you could be paralyzed if you get hit a certain way."

In that moment, everything changed. Over the next twenty-four hours, I was uncertain about the future. Little did I realize that moment would set me along a path of learning online social media marketing, becoming an entrepreneur, and starting a podcast, altering the next three years of my life.

## HIS DEPRESSION AFTER HIS INJURY

**CA:** When I got injured, I fell into a depression because I was reliving my past. Things had been great. I was going to high school, playing football on a great team, crushing the workout, and then suddenly, I couldn't do any of that. Being injured was my new reality. Thankfully, I had a great support system. I could talk to my mom or my dad.

We all define depression differently. I believe depression is dwelling on the past and what we would have done differently. We get depressed about what we can't change. That was my reality. I would see my friends post about football on Instagram, and I would get depressed because I was trying to relive what my reality used to be, not what it was at the moment. Eventually, I reached a point where I didn't get bogged down with what I couldn't change and started taking control of what I could change, which was my mindset and my actions. That is what set me along the path toward entrepreneurship.

## MENTALITY SHIFT

**CA:** Steve Jobs once said, "You can't connect the dots looking forward; you can only connect them looking backwards." My injury was a dot. I didn't realize that the neck injury would eventually lead me to speaking about it on stages, doing podcasts, and moving from Virginia to Arizona at age eighteen to run a company. That all happened because I took one step forward every single day.

I heard a beautiful speech at an event that I was speaking at. It was insane because the guy had just started his speaking career. He had sold a company for high eight figures, and he said he got himself out of his deepest depression by taking one step every day, even though he couldn't see the entire staircase. To use another analogy, it's not about the sprint across the football field to see how far you can go. You must be able to develop your character and enjoy life along the way.

I wanted to read one book at a time, do one podcast at a time, and travel to one city at a time. I grew up in a household where I never went on a plane until I could afford to pay for it myself. At a young age, I wanted to travel and meet people. I've read fifty books over the past year. I've started to build my brand online from 2,000 followers to over 220,000 people, and I'm connecting with a lot of new people.

The philosophy of one step at a time helped me pivot my mentality and not think about the past.

## EVERYONE HAS A STORY

**CA:** If you're at a point where your life is going one way and then suddenly you have to stop and go a completely different way, that can affect you in a good or a bad way. For me, I couldn't play football. For you, it might be a loss in the family. It could be that you're caught up in drugs, and now you finally realize you need to make a change. Remember, everyone has a story. You must realize what phase of the story you're in.

I've sat down with so many successful people. They talk about their pivotal moments. They talk about the times when they were broke, when they couldn't afford a bus pass or they had to be in survival mode. Having no other options can cause you to change. I used to dedicate eight hours a day to football. After my injury, I had to spend my time differently. I pivoted toward reading books and surrounded myself with good people. It was part of my story.

## HANDLING TOXIC PEOPLE

**CA:** I was exposed to partying early on. In ninth and tenth grade, my friends were partying every weekend. They would go out, party, do drugs, and gossip about people. Before my injury, those were the people I was surrounding myself with. Some people were even carrying around guns like they were iPhones. In one Tai Lopez video, he says, "You are who you associate with." He learned that from a successful entrepreneur. I started to think about altering my network and the people I hung out with if I wanted to change.

If you know someone in your life is not good to be around, either eliminate that person from your life or minimize how much time you spend with them. If they start to ask why you aren't hanging out with them, simply tell them, "Our goals don't align. I want to surround myself with people who are pushing me forward, and every time we're together, we're blank."

It's about cutting people off, blocking people on social media, and not talking to them. A word of warning though: if you do that, you'll get lonely. But if you're surrounding yourself with people who are not moving you forward, you need to slowly remove them from your mental space. Replace them with people who lift you up or align with your goals.

I didn't wake up one day with amazing people next to me. It happened through sending direct messages on Instagram, starting a podcast, having a reason to sit down with people, going to business events, and investing in plane tickets to network. I was doing all the little things that added up over time. You must understand your goals first.

Remove toxic people from your life, and surround yourself with people who align with you and your goals. You are who you associate with.

## TOP TAKEAWAYS:

- You are who you associate with.
- Surround yourself with people who can help you grow.
- Cut toxic people from your life, or distance yourself from them.
- All successful people have a story. Leverage the bad things that happen in your life instead of looking down on them.
- "You cannot connect the dots looking forward, you can only connect them looking backwards."

- Expect the unexpected.
- *Create positive change in your life based on your pivotal moment.*
- Take one step at a time.

# 5
# HOW TO DEAL
# WITH ANXIETY

*DENNIS SIMSEK, A.K.A. THE ANXIETY GUY*

From the outside, Dennis Simsek looked like he had it all. He started doing world tours in his teenage years and winning junior tennis championships. On the inside, he put an unhealthy pressure on himself that led to anxiety. Around age twenty-two, he slowed down his involvement in tennis, and by age twenty-five his anxiety was so bad that he couldn't leave the house. He planned his suicide, but he decided not to go through with it after his child was born. Life worked in his favor. He read a book and received a mentor who changed his life. Nine years later, he's helping other people with anxiety all around the world. The Anxiety Guy brand has received over 7 million views and counting. He specializes in helping people overcome anxiety.

## CONTACT:
- Website: www.theanxietyguy.com
- YouTube: The Anxiety Guy
- Instagram: @TheAnxietyGuy

## STRUGGLES INCLUDED IN THIS CHAPTER:
- Anxiety
- Depression
- Family put too much pressure on him
- People pleaser
- Feared being a disappointment
- Put a lot of pressure on himself
- Always stressed
- Wanted to commit suicide

## THE START OF HIS ANXIETY

**Dennis Simsek:** My anxiety started at a young age. At age three, I was introduced to tennis. It was an on-and-off a passion for me. Being so young, I was told to go to the backboard because nobody wanted to play with a little kid. I was at the backboard every day, hitting the ball against the wall and trying to figure things out. I was enjoying myself and developing a skill. Starting at age six, I started to enter tennis tournaments. I thought it was cool. Prior to the match, my dad would give me suggestions. It didn't take long for the fun part of it to leave. Things got serious quickly.

Starting around age eight, when the school day was over, I saw my friends playing on the playground. They were having a great time and laughing. Then there was me. I had an after-school routine. I remember driving away from school, looking back to see the kids having a great time while waiting for their parents, but I had to go to practice. Things were becoming so serious that I wasn't sure if I was enjoying it or not.

Starting at age ten, I began playing and winning nationals. I also traveled around the world. I wasn't sure if it was my passion or my dad's. Sometimes I was really into it, but there were days where I didn't enjoy it, just like any professional athlete.

My dad was very controlling and going through his own anxiety disorder (we rekindled our relationship later in life). I vividly remember him forcing me to throw my trophy out of a moving car. We were driving over the Lions Gate Bridge in Vancouver, BC, and my dad told me to throw the trophy out because I didn't give as much effort as I could have.

As children, we take everything in. We develop thinking patterns, belief systems, and emotions that say we're not good enough no matter how hard we try. We adopt a perfectionist mentality. If we don't, we think we have no chance in this world and no chance to gain self-love.

There was a five-year span where I didn't take even one day off. Sundays didn't mean anything. Saturdays were the same as Mondays. Winning was nice though. When I won, I wanted to do more of it. When I lost, I wanted to do less of it. I reached a point in my life where, after the hundreds of tournaments that I played, there was no real difference between winning and losing. In the beginning stages it was fun, but later I realized my passion wasn't there anymore. I took it up more of as an avid tennis player as I moved on in life.

Despite how hard it was at times, I have no regrets. My experience with tennis led me to my true purpose in this world, which is to serve others by helping them overcome their anxiety disorders.

## HIS DARK PERIOD AND PLANNING HIS SUICIDE

**DS:** At age twenty-five, I was hit with a massive anxiety disorder, to the point that I couldn't leave my house, and I couldn't socialize with people. That was a dark place in my life. Not only did I stop playing tennis, I stopped everything. I put everything on the shelf.

When I woke up in the morning, I couldn't wait to close my eyes at night. I would worry about waking up in the morning with a potential panic attack that was going to take me out of this planet, and I would die. I dreaded the feeling of having to face the physical symptoms that were going on in my body. I was fearful of eating food in case I choked. I was afraid of going into a new environment in case I was judged or labeled.

I started to weigh the differences between staying on this planet and leaving it. I asked myself, "Am I going to experience more pain committing suicide or living out the rest of my life in this state?"

I planned it out perfectly. I parked my car on the side of the road. I was going to drive it over a bridge. Don't ask me exactly how I was going to do that, but I had worked out a formula to get my car over the bridge.

Not only was I dealing with my own battles, my child had just been born. I was supposed to be a good father and a good fiancé. There was a lot of pressure on me. It started piling up, and suicide felt like a valid option. The one reason why I didn't follow through with committing suicide was I had a big enough reason to stay here. If my child had not been born, I might not be here right now.

I decided to give it another day. That day passed, and I wanted to give it another day. Then more days passed. Over time, everything started to align. I found a book on the beach that I picked up and read. Then a mentor called me out of the blue.

For a long period, I believed I needed to fight through my day, to hustle through everything, to compete with everybody. All of that came to a standstill, and it was incredible. The word "flow" came to me all the time. I realized I could live with a tremendous amount of flow, just as we see in nature. Those were the beginning stages of what you see today with the Anxiety Guy. That was at around age thirty-three.

## TECHNIQUES TO OVERCOME ANXIETY

**DS:** One of the best tecāiques that helped me overcome my anxiety disorder was the word "reframe." For me, that means changing the way I view emotionally traumatic experiences that are still living in my body. In the old *Ghostbusters* movie, they would move into a room and zap a ghost. When they zapped the ghost, it went into a box. Zap! Another ghost into another box. Then those little boxes went into a much bigger box. If we think of those ghosts as the things that worry us and cause anxiety, the question is, what happens when that big box starts to overflow?

David Snyder, who is a neuroscience linguistics programming expert, uses this analogy. When the "big box" starts to overflow, your body and your emotions start to let you know that something is out of balance. Reframing was the number-one tecāique that I used each day to deal with this.

In the beginning, I needed to be guided toward safely reliving past experiences that caused the snowball of anxiety. I reframed experiences like when I was in the car with my dad and throwing the trophy out the window. When I think about that experience now, it doesn't affect me. Between being bullied at school, getting an F on a test, the tennis days, I had to reframe many different events. Thinking about them positively shaped who I am. I have reframed my past emotional traumas thousands of times.

Also, I listen to my thoughts in a different manner. I began to listen to my thoughts from thirty meters away as if I couldn't hear them. If you do that, after a certain amount of time, you start to become disinterested in the thought. I started to listen to my negative thoughts through the voice tones of Barney, Daffy Duck, or Bugs Bunny. You can't take those guys seriously.

I also got more specific about who I wanted to be. Before, I just wanted to be happy, which was so general. Now I know exactly what I want out of life.

## TAKE CONTROL OF THE FIRST TWENTY MINUTES

**DS:** Even during a chaotic time in your life, you can create balance within. Take control of the first twenty minutes of your day. That's when your subconscious mind opens and asks you what direction you want to go that day. You might be getting up and running to school or figuring out how difficult the day is going to be. This is a habit of emotional distress that is present every day. You can do many different things to take control the first twenty minutes of your day. One of the best things you can do is slow down. Get up twenty minutes earlier, and do everything that you have to do, like showering, brushing your teeth, and eating breakfast. Take your time while doing those activities. Open your mind to perceiving things in a different way as you go about your day.

## QUESTION YOUR BELIEFS

**DS:** You need to question your beliefs. In fact, question everything. Don't allow yourself to succumb to the ideas that are floating in your head that are coming from the outside. Your core beliefs are engraved in your subconscious mind, and these beliefs run the show, often without you realizing it. That's why you need to identify them and question them.

Feelings are attached to beliefs at a deeper level. A feeling could be related to you saying something at the cafeteria with your friends and then asking yourself if they are going to judge you. How much of this is going to matter five years from now?

Very little.

How important are these people in your life at a deep level?

Very little.

Are you doing the best that you can each day?

Yes.

If you do this, you're going to begin questioning each feeling. When you question the feeling, you begin to alter your core beliefs because now you're responding rather than reacting. No longer are you succumbing to habits. You're taking control of your mind, your emotions, your body, and your imagination. By questioning the feelings in your body and questioning your core beliefs, you're painting different pictures in your mind. When you paint different pictures in your mind, you begin to change the way you see everything in the outside world. Nothing on the outside changes, but the way you see things inside does. Therefore, your emotional state will change. You won't feel like you must be a part of the crowd.

## DON'T BE AFRAID TO LET OTHER PEOPLE DOWN

**DS:** The temporary pain of letting other people down is OK in the long run because you're going to begin opening yourself up to what you're truly meant to do. Have a talk with yourself. During that talk, ask yourself how passionate you are about what you're currently doing. If the level of passion, love, and happiness for what you're doing isn't there, it's important to take a step back. When you take a step back, you can begin to evaluate everything that's going on. Many times athletes get so caught up in the sport and the expectations and what they need to do next. It's a rapid, habitual way of living and we never take time to pause, step back, and evaluate what's going on. When you take a step back, you will learn how to think. When you learn how to think, you can begin to widen your perspective on your life and what's going on inside.

I used to have a talk with myself, and then I had to go through the temporary pain of letting people know that I didn't want to do a particular thing I didn't enjoy anymore.

If you enjoy what you're doing, fantastic; keep doing it. You may succeed, or you may fail. Either way, there really is no such thing as failure because you'll learn lessons that you'll be able to be able to apply toward your family and to teach other people.

## TOP TAKEAWAYS:

- Have no regrets about the negative experiences in your life.
- Get specific on who you want to be.
- Don't commit suicide. Live another day because things will eventually start working in your favor.
- Live in a flow state.
- Reframe past emotional traumas.
- Play your negative thoughts in a funny voice that you can't take seriously.
- *Take control of the first twenty minutes of your day, and don't rush getting ready.*
- If you feel pressure from other people to perform, have a talk with yourself to see if that is what you really want.

# 6
# HOW TO ESCAPE A TOXIC HOME TO DO WHAT YOU LOVE
## *TYLER BRADY*

Tyler isn't your typical twenty-year-old. He grew up with an abusive dad. After a long, stressful day, he got into a heated argument with his father, and it escalated fast when Tyler stabbed him. As a result, he was sent to juvenile detention for three weeks. He escaped from his father's home and hopped around other homes. He was even homeless for a period. He discovered his passion for graphic design, and now he uses it as a positive creative outlet, serving clients around the world.

## CONTACT:
- Website: www.designwithphoenix.com

## STRUGGLES INCLUDED IN THIS CHAPTER:
- Abusive parents
- Imprisoned for a violent crime
- Homeless
- Lack of money
- Death of a loved one

## STABBING HIS DAD

**Tyler Brady:** My dad couldn't hold onto any jobs. He had a job after not having a job for eight years and then lost it again. Then he would be upset with whoever about it.

One day my grandmother, my dad, and I were fixing up a rental property to make it available for the next tenant. It had been a long, hard day.

49

Cutting the grass, cleaning out stuff, and cleaning out a 2,000-square-foot home was difficult. Sometimes it would take us a month to clean the house. People would leave it that messy after they had only been in it for five months. One time we had somebody who was in there for three months. They made it a complete pigsty, and we had to clean it all.

That day things got heated between my father and me. I was flustered and wanted to end things right then and there. I grabbed a knife and stabbed him. The knife shattered into a million pieces. Then he pinned me to the ground, choking me. He was on stimulants, which gave him more energy. I was having a hard time breathing. My grandmother was the one who called the cops. It took them three hours to even think about coming to the house. My dad survived, but I ended up serving three weeks in juvenile detention as a result.

## GETTING INTO HIS PASSION FOR GRAPHIC DESIGN

**TB:** It started with a curiosity about Photoshop. My grandmother had worked as a designer in the past, and she had some older versions of the program. I played around with them, starting with the basics.

I did some homeschooling courses with some other families. One of my teachers saw talent in me, and he looked at me as the chosen child in the classroom. He put me to work designing some of his graphics. He even paid me to do it.

He helped me with understanding design language and gave me a foundation of what good design was. There was a lot of synergy between us. Funny story: One day he left his computer unlocked in Photoshop. I saw a design project, and I finished it for him on his computer while he wasn't there. He loved it!

## LEAVING HOME AND HOMELESS

**TB:** My dad was abusive, so why would I want him in my life? My mother had never been in the picture; I never knew her. I also had family in a trailer park in Orlando. It was not a good situation.

Other family members were in different states, like Georgia and Maine. It wasn't easy for me to find an alternative living situation. They saw me as an ugly, uncontrollable kid, even though I had gone through some healing and had been doing better. I don't think they cared enough to let me stay. My grandmother was one of the only people to make me feel happy and loved.

One of my last resorts was to live at my brother's home, but that soon became toxic. There was no structure, cleanliness, or communication in the house. He lived on his own terms. If he didn't want to get up for two days, he didn't. Finally, I left. Unfortunately, my grandma passed away while I was at my brother's place.

At age eighteen I lived in a homeless shelter for six months. It was rough during the first month, but I got used to it. It's like moving to a new state; you get used to it.

Eventually, I got a job. That allowed me to get into an apartment. I also qualified for Section 8, which provided financial help for housing. I lived in my apartment for three or four months. I got fired from my job within the first two weeks of being in my apartment. I kept spending my paychecks on tech items, furniture, and food, so I couldn't pay the rent. Section 8 helped me with 50 percent of my rent, and my church paid $300, so I was able to stay. I should have been evicted during the first month, but I wasn't. It was rough though. I was sleeping on the floor.

Once I lost my apartment, I started going through the list of friends who I met at the homeless shelter. They had their own apartments. Seven decent people were kind enough to let me stay with them for a couple of months. Finally, I found someone to share an apartment with.

## LIVING DAY BY DAY

**TB:** For a time I was living day by day. Food stamps helped me get through that period. Now all I need is a Starbucks close by and my laptop to get my design work done. Right now I am only doing small gigs for fifty or a hundred dollars. Eventually, I want to charge hundreds and thousands for my work because I believe I'm that talented. I'm being positive about it. I have a cool mentor, a roof over my head, and I get to eat every day. I'm happy.

## FOCUS ON WHAT YOU HAVE, NOT ON WHAT YOU DON'T HAVE

**TB:** Focus on what you have, not what you don't have. It's about being positive. It's like gazing up at the sun. If you focus on that, the sun will be too bright, and then it's going to be hot. If you tell yourself that the sun feels good, you will enjoy the sun. If you are in a negative situation, and you express gratitude, the negative situation won't feel as bad. That's how I've been thinking. Even though my life is not where I want it to be, I'm happy, and I'm thankful for how it is.

## TOP TAKEAWAYS:

- Remove toxic people from your life.

51

- Always look on the positive side.
- Take your problems day by day.
- Focus on what you have, not what you don't have.
- Find a cool mentor.
- Utilize all your resources and/or the people you have met.
- *Find your passion project, and work toward it every day.*
- Go above and beyond for people.
- Just because you are charging a little now doesn't mean you can't charge more later.

# 7
# DIAGNOSED WITH ADHD TO BOOKSTAGRAM INFLUENCER

*MATT HUTSON, A.K.A. BOOKMATTIC*

At seven years old, Matt was diagnosed with attention deficit hyperactivity disorder (ADHD) and then rheumatoid arthritis at age ten. As a result, he was put in a lower-than-average class at school. He took control of his focus and got good grades, but in high school, he was still put in a below-average class. That made him feel dumb. He was a happy kid but didn't feel "normal" because of the classes he was put in. Therefore, he felt awkward around others who were in higher classes. He was insecure and was overly focused on what others thought of him.

Now he manages one of the top nonfiction Bookstagram accounts and websites, BookMattic. He's inspiring people to read more and receive more knowledge in order to put what they learn into a plan and take action. He also leads personal development workshops and an online course called The 6 Principles of Lifelong Learning.

## CONTACT:
- Website: www.bookmattic.com
- Instagram: @BookMattic
- YouTube: BookMattic

## STRUGGLES INCLUDED IN THIS CHAPTER:
- Attention deficit hyperactivity disorder (ADHD)
- Easily distracted
- Low self-esteem
- Problems articulating himself

- Worried too much about other people's opinions
- Didn't do well under pressure
- Used to be awkward

## HIS ADHD CAUSED HIM TO BE IN LOWER CLASSES

**Matt Hutson:** Looking back at my teen years, I was not as confident as I am now. The school system put me in a lower class because I was diagnosed with ADHD. They kept me in it all the way through high school, even though by then I had figured out how to deal with my ADHD. I learned how to focus more on my homework and during class. The classes that I was in were way too simple for me, I was passing with straight A's, and I had a 3.98 GPA. It made me feel bad because I was looking at all the kids who were in advanced classes or regular classes who were given fun reading assignments. Being in a lower class decreased my confidence. My parents tried to put me in higher classes, but the administrators wouldn't budge. I questioned why I couldn't be in a "regular" class because I had the ability for it.

My past is a perfect testament of overcoming learning challenges and making a business and brand out of it. Reading is my passion now, and I didn't let the struggles I faced in my childhood define my ability as an adult.

## WORRIED TOO MUCH ABOUT OTHER PEOPLE'S OPINIONS

**MH:** When I was a child and then a teenager, I couldn't articulate myself very well. My speech was slower, and I felt awkward talking to people. I didn't talk a lot to other people except for my close friends, in band, and in cross country. I was worried about what other people thought about the way I talked or the way I acted. It stopped me from talking.

I worried too much about what other people thought about me. Eventually, I learned I needed to stop worrying about what other people thought of me because they were going to continue thinking what they thought no matter what I did. I had to live my own life.

## DIDN'T DO WELL UNDER PRESSURE

**MH:** I did not like change. If the teacher sprang a pop quiz on us, my thought was, *Oh my gosh, I'm not even prepared,* and just like that, I would feel stressed out. I like to have my daily routine, which may have something to do with my ADHD.

I have many routines, and I try to follow them, but if I want to change them a bit, I can. Having a routine can help you stay on track, but if you have a routine that's broken, don't feel stressed about it. Get back on track, and do the best that you can, even if you fall behind a bit, whether it's on an assignment or some other project. Just try your best.

## PASSION BRINGS FOCUS

**MH:** I believe I still have ADHD. Sometimes I can't get work done as fast as I should because my brain is all over the place. Back then was the same issue. If I had to write a five-page paper, it would take me twice as long compared to other students. Reading a book took me a long time. Just to read one page might take me four minutes because the ADHD disrupted my focus.

When I do something I love, I focus as much as I can on it. I believe it was the same back then. Whenever I played in band, band was my major focus. I was into playing my trombone, playing in the jazz band, and playing in the orchestra. Any time I got a chance, I would play. That was my love and my passion. I did enjoy other subjects. I liked creative writing class. Writing has always been one of my passions. I love writing my blog. I also love writing posts on Instagram, Facebook, and Twitter. Writing has been a huge part of my life. Any time I would write or learn history, I would completely focus. In math, I would lose focus because I hated it. Doing something that you love allows you to remain focused even if you have ADHD.

## OVERCOMING CONFIDENCE ISSUES

**MH:** I didn't start to gain confidence until I was in college, but I did see a bit of progress by the end of high school. I started making new friends outside of class and putting myself out there. The one thing that I've learned more recently is to conquer the fear of doing. Whatever you're afraid of, get out there and do it. You're going to be afraid of doing it at first. Once you experience that fear for the first time and you don't completely freeze up or faint, it becomes much more comfortable. The second time will still be tough, but you can do it. The third time will be much easier. Practice, practice, practice.

**SS:** How did you start building your confidence in college?

**MH:** I got involved in communities. I was still taking some band classes, and I was a music major for a while. I also joined the Japanese student society. We had Japanese kids coming in from abroad, and we would converse in Japanese and English. We shared each other's cultures. I also got involved in other international communities where people from all over the world gathered for coffee, ate food, and chatted. I got involved in an entrepreneurship organization too. That planted a seed in my mind that I wanted to take the entrepreneurial route. Those organizations and communities helped me to meet new people, break out of my shell, and express myself in an authentic way. I didn't have to worry about what someone else was going to think. If they didn't like me, they didn't like me. They could go off and make friends with someone else. If the person liked me, then I could be the best loyal friend to them.

## YOUR CIRCLE MATTERS

**MH:** Entrepreneur and author Jim Roā once said, "You're the average of the five people you spend the most time with." If you want to be a successful businessperson, you should surround yourself with people who are motivated to become better, not people who just sit and watch Netflix all night long.

## READ WHAT YOU LOVE

**SS:** I was like you when I was younger. I was always getting bad grades in my reading assessments, and I was always the slowest reader in class. Now I love reading, and I read all the time. It proves that it doesn't matter how well you do when you're in elementary, middle, and high school in reading because eventually, you're going to enjoy reading based on what you like to read, not what they provide you to read.

**MH:** Those school assignments might be a drag. They may not be something that you want to read. They can destroy your love of reading because they make you read stuff that you don't want to read. Pick up something that you think you might enjoy. If you really don't like reading, I recommend audiobooks. I went from hating reading to reading thirty-two books last year.

## TWENTY MINUTES OF STUDYING, TEN-MINUTE BREAK

**MH:** I have this condition for a reason. I don't necessarily like the fact that I have it, but I feel it has helped me to narrow my focus on building up my Bookmattic brand. If it weren't for my ADHD, maybe I would be doing something completely different. If you have trouble focusing because of ADHD, develop a routine. I would always do the same things every day at the same time with some variants to keep it interesting. If you create a routine and give yourself time to study, give yourself time to relax. Break up your study into twenty-minute intervals. It will change things up a bit. Sometimes people with ADHD have a hard time focusing. That will help you get less tired or frustrated. Twenty minutes of study, ten-minute break, twenty minutes of study, ten-minute break.

## BUILD STRONG FRIENDSHIPS WITH A FEW PEOPLE

**MH:** I know how important friends are in high school. Once you graduate from high school, you all go off to separate places. Some of your friends will go to the same college, and some will go to other places. Friendships are important, but in the end, most people go their separate ways. Try to be yourself, and find at least a few people who you get along well with. The memories that you create with those few people will last for the rest of your life.

I have a friend from elementary school who I still keep in touch with. I still talk with him on the phone, even though I'm all the way in Indonesia. We can be ourselves around each other. That's the only best friend that I've kept in touch with from my childhood.

Build strong friendships with those few people to help create a foundation. It's OK to make more friends after that. Don't worry about what other people think about you. Just build those friendships, and create those memories.

## DO YOUR BEST

**MH:** Stay strong. Whatever struggle that you are facing right now, realize that it is not the end of your world. You can make it to the next day, and always try to do your best. You can't do more than your best. If you're doing less than your best, try harder. If you're doing your best, then great; keep on doing that. But if you're stressing yourself out and trying to do more than your best, you're going to burn out. The next day will be better if you keep trying. Rely on the people who are close to you. Life becomes better, and you become stronger as you learn from bad experiences.

## TOP TAKEAWAYS:

- Don't worry about what others think about you; live your own life.
- Create a routine, but be flexible in case something throws you off.
- Find what you're passionate about because that will bring you focus.
- Step outside your comfort zone to build confidence.
- *Hang out with people who allow you to be yourself.*
- Read what you love.
- Use your ADHD or whatever else you are struggling with to your advantage.
- Don't try to have many friendships. Build a few strong friendships, and create memories with those people.
- Do your best, and stay strong.

# 8
# HOW TO OVERCOME THE STRUGGLES OF YOUR FAMILY NOT HAVING ANY MONEY

*LAURA EGOCHEAGA*

Laura has been facing struggles since she was seven years old, including her mom leaving and remarrying, her father's struggle to accept her sexuality, and her own insecurities. Laura was so insecure that she bullied others, so they wouldn't bully her. She wanted to get a car at age sixteen, but her family struggled financially, so she took matters into her own hands. She learned about online marketing and made her first $20,000 at sixteen years of age, which allowed her to buy a brand-new car. Now she is the founder of Viral Growth Media and speaks around the world about online marketing.

## CONTACT:
- Website: www.viralgrowthmedia.com
- Instagram: @LauraEgocheaga

## STRUGGLES INCLUDED IN THIS CHAPTER:
- Low self-esteem
- Parents divorced
- Poverty
- Dyslexia
- Judged for being a lesbian
- Not good in school and felt dumb
- Parents never around

## THE HEARTBREAK FROM HER MOM LEAVING HER

**Laura Egocheaga:** My mom told my dad and me that she was going on vacation. Three days later, my dad found out she have gotten remarried. When it happened, my grandma (my dad's mom), came here from Peru to take care of me.

I used to misbehave and treat my grandma badly. My father thought that I felt like he was trying to replace my mom or my grandma from my mom's side. I was close to my grandma from my mom's side of the family. My mom didn't raise me; my grandma from my mom's side raised me. My biggest heartbreak was when my parents left each other, and my dad kept me from my mom's side of the family.

I was hurting so much that I tried to make other people hurt along with me. I didn't get bullied; I bullied other people. People thought I was happy because I always had a smile on my face, but when I look back on it, I was in so much pain.

When sixth grade hit, I knew I was a lesbian. I wasn't insecure about being a lesbian; I was more insecure about people coming up to me thinking I was a boy. It made me feel uncomfortable, but eventually, I became numb to it.

## THE STRUGGLES OF BEING A LESBIAN AND DYSLEXIC

**LE:** I have always dressed differently, even when I was a kid. With my mom out of the picture, I got to choose how I wanted to express myself. When I was fourteen, my dad started putting his foot down, telling me I could no longer dress like that. He would throw my clothes away. He called my mom after seven years of telling her she couldn't see me to tell her to take me. It was the first time I was able to see my mother, all because I came out.

I also have issues with reading. I'm dyslexic. I have a learning disability, but that doesn't mean I'm stupid. My teachers would bully me, and some of them were homophobic.

In grade seven, one of my teachers would make fun of my looks in front of the whole class. Everyone would laugh. It was super sad.

One time I came home crying. "What happened?" my dad asked. When I explained to him, he was ready to go to the school and complain. I had to talk to him out of it.

## YOUR WEAKNESSES DON'T HAVE TO LAST FOREVER

**LE:** I can read a book if it's good. At school, people who have learning disabilities are put in remedial classes. The reality is, what they're learning is probably boring. Teachers aren't making it entertaining enough for them.

**SS:** So true. For the longest time I had trouble focusing and reading, even though I was good at everything else. I was good at math, but I always did poorly on the Florida Reading Assessment. I was put in remedial reading classes. In the past few years after college, I read over sixty books while many people who received good reading assessment scores haven't read a single book after graduating.

**LE:** I would fail the language arts portion in English classes, and now I'm a copywriter. I write copy that convinces people to purchase products. That's what I do for a living. In college, I failed my public speaking class. Now I travel the world and talk to people for a living. You still have time to get better at your weaknesses.

## SHE MADE $20,000 IN SIX MONTHS AT AGE SIXTEEN

**LE:** I was fourteen years old in 2008/2009 when the economic recession happened. That's when I realized my family had no money. We were probably at the bottom of the totem pole. My dad took on massive debt to make sure I was in a better school district. I didn't see any of my friends suffering. I also saw my friends getting brand-new Mercedes and brand-new BMWs. I wasn't even allowed to get the new Xbox or new Xbox games because we didn't have enough money. My dad was always telling me that he didn't have money. I thought if I didn't ask anything from him for the next two years, he would have enough money to buy me things. I didn't comprehend how money worked.

I turned sixteen years old, and I hadn't asked for anything; I'd been a good girl. So, I asked my dad, "Where's my car? I'm getting a car, right?"

"What?" he replied. "I don't have any money."

"What do you mean?" I asked. "I haven't asked you for anything." I was so upset. I felt like a failure, a loser. I felt embarrassed of my family situation, my own situation. I decided to call my mom. "Mom," I said, "I haven't seen you in seven years, but you can make it up to me by buying me a car. I won't hold a grudge." She laughed and told me she couldn't afford a car.

I end up going onto Google and looking up how to make money online. I found an affiliate marketing company, and I made $20,000 in six months. I bought my first car in cash. It was a 2002 Honda Civic XE, fully loaded with a sunroof. My dad was super proud of me because I was able to pay for the car, and I was able to pay for years of insurance up front.

## HER ENTREPRENEURSHIP JOURNEY

**LE:** The company I did affiliate marketing for shut down. It ended up being a Ponzi scheme, and it was shut down by the government. Once the company shut down, I didn't know how to make money. The company already had websites, copy, and a product to sell. They just needed traffic, and I helped get that traffic to sell their product. When I didn't have that anymore, I had to reverse engineer what they were doing and figure out how I could do it for myself. I taught myself how to build websites, I learned about search engine optimization (SEO) and analytics, and I started creating several streams of income. Soon I was working on several websites as a freelancer.

You can get paid to do whatever. I was bidding on projects, and I realized my competition was people in countries where they value every single dollar. Getting ten dollars is a lot to people in certain countries. I realized I was underselling my services. I saw an ad on YouTube that said, "Make money by selling to local business owners." That was the light bulb, and that's when I realized I should start my own agency. The biggest issue was that I didn't know how to sell. I didn't know how to convey a message on how valuable something was to business owners and convince them to purchase. That was an uphill battle. I failed miserably when I first launched. Then I got a sales job at Nissan, and that's where I learned how to sell.

Now I'm speaking everywhere. Last year, I went back to Peru, where I spoke with Congress. It wouldn't have happened if I didn't make the choices that I did in my life.

## BUILDING MORE CONFIDENCE

**LE:** I went semi-viral on YouTube when I was in sixth grade. I had a video that had over 65,000 views, and the comment section was bad. That is when I experienced online bullying.

I made a parody video, and people bashed that. Some of the comments were, "Are you a boy or a girl? You lesbian and dyke." They said these harsh words.

I didn't love myself until the last three years. Everyone thought I was already confident. I portrayed confidence, but I didn't believe it.

**SS:** How did you get that inner confidence?

**LE:** When my great-grandma died, I had to check my lifestyle. I was addicted to drugs, I was doing bad things, and I was in a very toxic relationship. One day after my great-grandma died, I had a dream about her. We were sitting in her dining room, and she was holding my bag of drugs—pounds of weed and a whole bunch of other drugs. On the table was my laptop. "You don't need to do this," she said. "Go back and focus on what you love to do."

After I graduated from high school, there were two or three years when I was really lost. I was super depressed. My best friend robbed me at gunpoint. I think I lost a total of $10,000. Another best friend set me up to get jumped.

I woke up one day, and I broke up with my girlfriend because she was holding me back from working hard. I decided to change my life. Slowly but surely, I lost a lot of weight. Then I started focusing on perfecting my skill sets.

My business took off in 2017. I went from zero to six figures in seven months. And that was only because a year before that, I was working at a car dealership where they hired Grant Cardone to teach us how to sell.

That is when my confidence started to skyrocket. Now there are months where I am making $100,000.

## IF YOU COME FROM A FAMILY WITH NO MONEY

**LE:** Wake up! It's nobody's fault but yours. If you feel trapped, there's a reason for it, and you need to overcome that. There's no excuse. You need to learn a high-income skill, especially now with automation taking our jobs. Learn copywriting, learn how to make people money; that's what you need to learn.

People call me because they know I can make them money. It's going to cost them, but it's an investment.

## BE PROUD OF YOUR SEXUALITY

**LE:** Do you want people in your life who judge you based on your sexuality? I don't. Why do I have to fake who I am? I'm against that. Don't hide yourself for any reason. Be who you are, period. You deserve that. You have one life to live, so why hide anything? Be who you are. They're not really your friends if they don't like it.

## TOP TAKEAWAYS:

- Find what you are passionate about, and pursue it.
- If your family doesn't have money to buy you nice things, figure out how to make money yourself.
- Surround yourself with people who you can trust and who accept you for who you are.
- If you are off track right now, it's OK. Get back on track and focus.
- Be confident in who you are.
- If your partner doesn't push you to become better, that person might not be the one for you.
- Learn a high-income skill.
- *Be comfortable with your sexuality.*
- Don't let what others say about you bother you.

# 9
# HOW TO LOOK AT THE BRIGHTER SIDE AFTER BEING DEALT THE WRONG HAND

*AUSTIN REYNOLDS*

Austin Reynolds was born with dwarfism. He had fifteen surgeries by age fifteen. One surgery left him paralyzed and in a wheelchair. Most people look at this as an unfortunate circumstance, but Austin always looks at the brighter side. He started getting into personal development and basketball. He recently got a job with the Miami Heat and is a true inspiration. He is building an influential brand on Instagram and is working on a documentary.

## CONNECT:
- Instagram: @AustinxReynolds

## STRUGGLES INCLUDED IN THIS CHAPTER:
- Dwarfism
- Paralyzed from the waist down
- Always stressed
- Worried too much about people's opinions

## BORN WITH DWARFISM AND PARALYZED FROM THE WAIST DOWN

**Austin Reynolds:** I was born December 28, 1994, in Norwalk, Connecticut. My parents wanted to name me Forrest because they were working for a rainforest and animal foundation at the time. Probably about five weeks before I was born, *Forrest Gump* came out, and in the movie, he had special needs. Seeing as they knew I had dwarfism, they decided against that name because they thought I would be bullied for it.

Up until age fifteen, I was in and out of doctors' offices. I had a bunch of surgeries in Baltimore, which is about a two-and-a-half hour flight from South Florida, which is where I live. I had about fifteen surgeries by age fifteen. They were extensive and gruesome. One of the surgeries took fourteen hours. They didn't hold me back though. I played a lot of sports. I'm a sports junkie. I grew up watching sports, and I loved playing them.

Right before I went into high school, I was supposed to get a simple surgery. Unfortunately, the day before it happened, January 27, 2010, was the last time I would walk unassisted.

The recovery time was supposed to be four to six weeks, but during the fifth to sixth month, we started seeing some red flags. We were on the phone with doctors trying to see what was going on. I went into high school walking with assistance by riding my Segway. I didn't fathom in my head that I would never be able to walk again. I went to the doctor in November that year after they deemed that I had spinal compression. They had to do another surgery. Imagine my spinal cord as a carpet. When you go to a new home, and you move your old couch from that old carpet, it's still indented. Imagine my spinal cord being the carpet and pressure being on the spinal cord. The doctors essentially moved the couch, and the carpet began levitating back up, but the nerve endings were too compressed to allow feeling in my legs.

## WHAT WENT THROUGH HIS MIND AFTER THE NEWS?

**AR:** All I was thinking about after the surgery was, "Why me? Why is this happening?" I'd already been dealt the wrong hand. One of the most crucial points of my life was middle and high school, trying to fit in. I was down. I wouldn't say I was depressed; I was just upset. I always knew at the end of the day that things would get better. I was lucky to have a good core group of friends who went to the same middle and high school as me. Other than that, it was mentally challenging, but I have been dealt this card my entire life. I've learned that things don't always go my way. I've always been overly prepared for negative situations because I always expect the unexpected. I had a good head on my shoulders, but there were definitely some bad days with good days.

## LIFE WAS DIFFICULT, BUT AUSTIN NEVER CONSIDERED SUICIDE

**AR:** Luckily, I'm a man of faith, and I could never commit suicide. I would never want to put anyone else through that situation because of my mistakes. I've come to realize that life is difficult, but nothing's more difficult than losing someone. I never experienced someone close to me die, but I've seen death affect a lot of my close friends. Life is tough, but even on the worst days, you can turn on a light. If you have clothes on your body, you're richer than someone else.

Being in and out of the hospital, I've seen kids go from walking in as my hospital roommate to never being able to sit or talk again. Anytime I felt weak or vulnerable, instead of asking, "Why me?", I thought of people who had it worse than me, and it changed my mindset to "What can we do to make each other happy? How can we do the things that better each other?" My dad put this in perspective and told me that it sucks what happens to me, but there is always someone who has it worse. Negativity will eat you alive if you let it. If you have negativity in your life, you're not going to be happy.

## WORRIED TOO MUCH ABOUT WHAT OTHERS THOUGHT OF HIM

**AR:** I'm a noticeable guy and an approachable person. It's a blessing and a curse. It's nice to know that a lot of people care about me. On the other hand, I don't know how people will perceive me. Growing up, I never wanted to go out because I didn't want to be that kid with the wheelchair taking up too much space or needing a ramp. Eventually though, I had to break my comfort barrier, or else I'd never do it. There were plenty of times when I felt nervous and didn't want to do the uncomfortable, but I forced myself to get outside my comfort zone and came up smiling almost every time. If you want to get outside of your comfort zone, it's as simple as just doing it. If you're in a situation where you feel complacent, and you don't know how to handle it, don't ask your mom, dad, brother, sister, best friend, or uncle. Look at yourself in the mirror to say, "I've got this," and then go do it.

## HOW AUSTIN GOT A MORE POSITIVE MINDSET

**AR:** I read a lot. I looked at motivational social media posts and bought the authors' books. Gary V was a big influence in my life. I would listen to him. I would also find the music and sports I loved the most. I started listening to podcasts. I would look up TED talks on YouTube, and I would play video games. I would gain new skills and pursue what I am passionate about. You should also do the things that you enjoy.

## GET OUT THE HOUSE WITH A SMILE

**AR:** I always socialize. Whether it's calling people, hanging out with them, or being out on the street. I always have a smile on my face. I always say hello, and I always make myself approachable because you never know who you're going to meet. It doesn't hurt to smile; it can make someone's day. A smile can go a long way. You must be comfortable with where you are in life. You can't let anything define who you are. You can't let people who are talking about you get to you. Just let it go in one ear and out the other. Otherwise, it's going to eat you alive, and you'll never be happy.

## TIPS FOR OTHERS WITH DWARFISM OR WHO ARE PARALYZED

**AR:** Don't listen to people who say you can't do something. If you want something to happen, put in a lot of work, and eventually, it'll happen. There's nothing in this world that can't happen without the power of will and without the power of money. I know money isn't convenient for everyone. There are plenty of websites like GoFundMe where you can put your dream online for people to contribute to. If you are truly passionate about it, that will be contagious to others. There are lot of ways to help people in this world.

I finally got my dream job of working for the Miami Heat and building my Instagram influence by making an impact on others. If I can do it, so can you. Now I have over 10,000 followers.

## APPRECIATE THE STRUGGLE

**AR:** If you're going through something, and it feels like the weight of your world is on your shoulders, you must take that weight off. At the end of the day, you create your legacy. Everyone has a great story. I read something very interesting recently: "Spend time appreciating everything bad that's happened in your life. Nobody ever clocks in the middle of the movie. Your story isn't over yet. When it's all said and done, everyone will clap because of the scenes you are living today. Appreciate the struggles. They are perfectly designed to be an Academy award-winning film in your life." That resonated with me because it made me realize that if a movie were to have all good things, it would probably get a bad rating. A story is about the struggle, the build-up, the climax, and the happy ending. At the end of the day, everyone should look at the obstacle that they are trying to overcome and understand that this is supposed to happen. Don't get frustrated; everyone faces obstacles. Every day is something new. You can't let it faze you or take you down. If you let it take you down, you're letting your emotions win.

## TOP TAKEAWAYS:

- Life doesn't always pan out your way, but that's OK.
- Perspective is key.
- Don't put anyone else through pain by committing suicide.
- Get outside your comfort zone.
- Read books to help you grow, and watch motivational videos.
- Socialize and smile. You never know who you can impact.
- Don't let others tell you that you can't do something.
- Create your legacy.
- *"Spend time appreciating everything bad that's happened in your life. Nobody ever clocks in the middle of the movie. Your story isn't over yet. When it's all said and done, everyone will clap because of the scenes you are living today. Appreciate the struggles. They are perfectly designed to be an Academy award-winning film in your life."*

# 10
# UNMASKING YOUR FEELINGS
## *MATT G, A.K.A. UNWASTED MIND*

Matt's sister died when she was seven from epilepsy and cerebral palsy. He was eleven years old when this happened. Two years later, his parents got divorced, and he felt neglected. In high school, he rebelled against all adults and anyone who tried to help him. He experimented with drugs and alcohol to escape his problems. When he and his girlfriend broke up, he fell in a deep depression. He had to call the suicide hotline, so they could talk him out of killing himself. Now he has a brand with over 38,000 followers on Twitter around spirituality, mental health issues, and personal development. Most importantly, he is recovering.

## CONNECT:
- Twitter: @FireFromWithin

## STRUGGLES INCLUDED IN THIS CHAPTER:
- Anxiety
- Depression
- Death of a loved one
- Parents' divorce
- Wanted to commit suicide
- People pleaser
- Got in trouble a lot
- Parents never around

## HOW THE DEATH OF MATT'S SISTER AFFECTED HIM

**Matt G:** I was eleven years old when my sister died at age seven. She was born with epilepsy and cerebral palsy, so she couldn't walk or talk.

She had been in a wheelchair since she was a toddler. Two years after my sister died, my parents got divorced.

At age eleven, I didn't think my sister's death was that big of a deal, but only because I didn't understand it. I assumed it was a part of life, and she already had physical disabilities before that. I saw how it affected my parents, and I was more concerned about them. I didn't understand how it affected me until later in life when I went to therapy. It helped me recognize insecurities and the abandonment feeling that I have deep down. It started with my sister's death. I buried it and didn't touch it until last year.

As a result of my pain, I developed people-pleasing behaviors. I didn't want people to look at me and judge me, especially with my parents being divorced. I grew up around a bunch of kids who seemed well-rounded or had families that were well off. I didn't want to talk about what was going on in my life.

I became a rebel after my parents divorced. I rebelled against every authority that I could: teachers, parents, parental figures, mentors, and anyone who was older. I didn't want anybody to tell me what to do with my life, and I did whatever I wanted. At age sixteen, I got into drinking. That's also when I started experimenting with smoking weed. Within a couple of years, I started experimenting with more hardcore drugs.

I became emotionally detached and anti-authoritative. By the time I was a senior in high school, I was sent to the principal's office every week. Any after-school detention I had, I would blow it off. If they tried to reach my parents, they couldn't because my parents were going through their own problems. My parents were neglectful. I felt like no one cared. I would blow it off like it wasn't a big deal. I convinced myself that I didn't need to follow any rules because I thought my parents didn't care. I thought, *These teachers and the principal can't do anything to me after I graduate.* I became uninvolved with school.

## DISGUISING HIS FEELINGS

**MG:** I grew up in a conservative town in West Texas where nobody likes to talk about the things that are going on beneath the surface when it comes to their families and their lives. Everything is focused on the external, like how much money your parents make, their profession, how big your house is, anything that signifies social status. My family didn't have a nice house or a nice car. I felt like an outsider all the time. I tried to hide it because I didn't want others to exclude me from their social functions. Being popular was important to me, like it is to all kids.

I also tried to hide the fact that I was struggling with anxiety and depression in high school because I was afraid of how I'd look. I'd mask it in any way that I could, usually with arrogance, cockiness, or attitude. I masked it so that others wouldn't see that I was hurting deep down. Suppressing my feelings affected me in a big way ten years later.

I only talked about how I was feeling with close friends. There was not much they could do except allow me to lean on them emotionally. Kids only open up to other kids, and they don't want to talk to anybody who has any type of authoritative influence. They're so afraid of how authority figures might see them, or they don't know how to open up. They only know how to open up to people who they can trust and relate to. That's what I did when my sister passed away, I relied on my close friends. They could only do so much seeing as they were going through their own struggles. I wish I had opened up about it to adults.

## CREATING UNWASTED MIND

**MG:** I discovered more of who I was because I got involved in music. I was one of those anti-nine-to-fivers. I didn't want to work in an office or a cubicle and do things that didn't interest me. I didn't know where my future was headed, so I left college for a while. I got into music, and I pursued that for a while until it connected me with my passion, which ended up being writing. That leads me to where I am now, podcasting and multimedia. I'm still an avid dream chaser. I am a proponent of following your dreams and pursuing your passions.

It was my path through music, writing, and spirituality that got me into social media. I connected with an extended network of people through Twitter, and we're all trying to spread these messages of enlightenment, awareness, and spirituality.

It started in social media in 2014. This group had started a website built around spirituality, awareness, enlightenment, and elevated levels of consciousness. After that group disbanded three years later, everybody went their separate ways. I wanted to take that and keep doing it somehow. Over time, I came up with the concept of the "Unwasted Mind." My thought process was, "Unwaste your mind, unwaste this beautiful, beautiful part of who we are that is capable of doing so much." Too many of us are wasting our time, our energy, our minds, our hearts, and our spirits on things that aren't giving us any value. How can I help develop new solutions and understandings to help people overcome whatever they're struggling with? I started that brand a couple of years ago, and I have been building it ever since.

## SUICIDAL THOUGHTS

**MG:** I've felt low so many times in my life. It started when I was a teenager. There were times when I was pushing music, and I felt like it was never going to take off. Anytime life didn't steer in the direction I wanted it to go, I felt down. After my breakup a year ago, that's when everything came to a head. That's when I was at my worst, and I realized I needed to do something about this. If I kept feeling this way for the rest of my life, I didn't know if I'd make it.

**SS:** How did you get over the hurdle of not committing suicide?

**MG:** I was in my car with my friend, and Linkin' Park came on. That was a little after Chester Bennington committed suicide. "I don't understand suicide," my friend said.

"Maybe you've just never been that low before," I replied. He looked at me because he knew he had tapped into a subject that he wasn't sure if he was prepared to go into. "I understand if you don't get it," I said. "But honestly, man, I understand it because I have been that low before."

I realized I had fallen into a deep, dark depression and all the things that come with it: loneliness, anxiety, heartbreak, trauma, past abuse, and abandonment. It was paralyzing. It drops you to your knees to the point where you're immersed in pain, and you can't see a way out. Every single day is bad. It's the worst feeling anyone can experience.

When I wasn't getting better, I did the only thing that I figured I would help me, which was call the suicide hotline. That led me to start seeking professional counseling and looking up resources for mental health counseling. I scheduled a talk with a few of their staff members. They had resources available for me to seek different types of professional help.

I went ahead and started emailing everyone who I thought might be able to help me. I had a few friends who motivated me to do that. They said, "Hey, dude, if you feel like this is becoming too much for you to handle, and you're going down this path, we would hate to lose you. Please, for your own sake and for the sake of staying with us, get some help if this is getting that bad." I got into counseling, and I also started getting into personal development. I started reading more material that was dedicated to that subject, listening to podcasts, and watching YouTube videos. I also realized after talking to many people that I wasn't alone.

## ELIMINATE WHAT'S HOLDING YOU BACK

**MG:** Eliminate the things that are holding you back, whatever they may be: drugs, drinking, toxic relationships, negative behavior and thoughts, and negative things in your environment. You must change everything about what you're doing in your life if you want to change how you feel. Analyze all of it. It doesn't matter who is involved. If you ignore it, those vices will continue to take away from what you're trying to do. Doing this will also help you get out of whatever rut you've fallen into.

I've connected with a lot of great people over the last six months since I launched the podcast. A lot of them have also come out of a rut. Once you are out of the rut, you do everything to stay out of it.

This process looks different for everybody. Some do it with a gratitude journal, and some listen to motivational YouTube videos, read development books, or listen to podcasts. Others talk to their close friends.

The most important thing is to form strong bonds with the people who are closest to you, the people you trust. Come up with one to three people who are the closest to you—friends, mentors, loved ones, a family member—open up to them and say, "Hey, I need somebody in my corner pushing me every step of the way because I can't do this on my own." That way, they can help you through that time. That's what people did for me. These people will remind you that you matter to somebody, and you can count on them to be there whenever you need them.

I always had somebody in my corner who I could talk to about my struggles and update about how I felt and what my goals were. When someone is dealing with depression or suicidal ideation, talking about goals is a major key.

## START TALKING TO ONE PERSON

**MG:** Start with one person. It only takes one. If you don't have anybody close to you, start with a stranger online. Social media can help with this. Even if you don't know that person, he or she can be a mentor from afar.

Once you start sharing your story with that person, you'll become more open. You will start finding others who you can relate to and who may be in your area. It's a step-by-step process. It takes that bold first step, that first message you send to somebody on Instagram or Twitter. Take it moment by moment.

## HOW TO HAVE MORE GOOD DAYS

**MG:** If you are someone who falls into a funk all day, every day, try not to be in a funk for the next hour. If you can't do an hour, do the next five minutes. I had to do it in five- to ten- or fifteen-minute intervals. If you can get through the next five minutes, you can turn that into a half an hour. Then you can turn that into two hours and eventually half a day and then a full day and then two days, and eventually you'll discover that you can go half of your week feeling OK, and then you will be having more good days than bad.

## USE THE SUICIDE HOTLINE IF NECESSARY

**MG:** Speaking from experience, the suicide hotline is your best bet if you feel like you have nobody. Those people are trained professionals, and this is what they do every day. There's nothing you can tell them that they haven't heard before. It will open you up in ways that you can't imagine. Other youth services are available too, such as the YMCA, churches, and nonprofit organizations that are focused on helping people just like you. You should never fight alone.

## TOP TAKEAWAYS:

- Pursue your passion.
- Eliminate what's holding you back from your potential.
- Get out of your toxic environment.
- Find your own way to stay out of your rut.
- If you don't feel like you have someone to talk to, start with social media.
- *Use the suicide hotline if necessary: 1-800-273-8255.*
- Join outside communities, like the YMCA or a church.
- Don't be afraid to open up and talk to people.

# 11

# OVERCOMING CYBERBULLYING AND SHYNESS

## *ALEXA CARLIN*

Alexa Carlin always felt left out of the group. It got worse when rumors spread about her on AOL Aim, which was a chatting service back in the day. She found her confidence when she got involved in student government in high school and became the first junior student body president. Now she is the founder and CEO of Women Empower X. She empowers women from all over the world and conducts her own speaking tours.

## CONNECT:
- Website: www.alexacarlin.com
- Instagram: @AlexaRoseCarlin

## STRUGGLES INCLUDED IN THIS CHAPTER:
- Lack of confidence/self-esteem
- Autoimmune disease with 1 percent chance of living
- Worried too much about people's opinions
- Wanted to find new friends
- Social exclusion
- Cyberbullying
- Put too much pressure on herself

## HOW HER LACK OF CONFIDENCE STARTED

**Alexa Carlin:** I was living in Boca Raton, Florida, and then we moved to Wellington, which is a little bit north. I was going into sixth grade, not knowing a single person. It was hard. I was always changing who I was in order to fit in. I was shy because I was afraid people would judge me, and I was afraid of people looking at me. Back then, I was so shy that I wouldn't even raise my hand in class, and now I'm a public speaker. I think most of my insecurity came from comparison or from an inner belief of not feeling worthy enough.

It stemmed from my younger years. I used to have curly hair. I was always the girl who couldn't brush her hair. I already felt like I didn't fit in during preschool and elementary. Then in middle school I started being bullied. I had a lot of hard times with being bullied. I was always thinking that I was not good enough, based on what other people told me.

## HER EXPERIENCE WITH CYBERBULLYING

**AC:** When I was in school, the kids would talk through AIM, which was a popular instant messaging service back then. One time someone stole my username and then started messaging everyone in the school, pretending they were me, ruining my reputation by being horrible to people. Suddenly, I was getting all this hate, and I wondered where it was coming from.

That was a horrible time. I was scared and crying, so I got my mom involved. She got other parents involved because it was bad. It was cyberbullying. I found out that the people who did it were my "friends," people who I was flirting with and dating. I was no longer friends with those people. I found a new group of friends. I had to remove myself from that situation. It was hard.

## SELF-CONSCIOUSNESS

**AC:** I became self-conscious. I never felt pretty enough, smart enough, or popular enough. The other girls were way more outgoing and popular than me. I thought I had a good group of friends, and then suddenly I found out they were going to the movies and didn't invite me. That happened a lot. I was always the person who was friends with everyone, but for some reason, I was always left out. I'd be invited to the bigger parties, but if they were having a sleepover, it was four of them and not me. I didn't know why that was because they were nice to my face. I would always question myself.

## FROM BEING SUPER SHY IN MIDDLE SCHOOL TO BECOMING THE FIRST JUNIOR IN HIGH SCHOOL TO BECOME STUDENT BODY PRESIDENT

**AC:** In middle school, I was super shy. I was the person who would hang out with a group but didn't add to the conversation. For example, in middle school, I wanted to become part of the National Junior Honor Society. I wanted to run for vice president because I was a determined, motivated person, and I cared about my grades. However, I was accidentally added to the roster as running for treasurer. I was so shy that instead of correcting them, I just ran for treasurer.

The shift came in high school. One of my friends from middle school was running for freshman class president. She asked if I wanted to run as her vice president. I didn't know what it was, but I agreed. I ran, and I ended up getting elected, which meant I got into a class called Student Government. That was the first time I was introduced to leadership. The student body ran the entire school of 3,000 students. I felt more passionate about stepping into that leadership role, and I fell in love with it. I was still shy, but I had a good group of friends.

When I was a sophomore going into junior year, my student government advisor, the teacher who I looked up to as a mentor, saw I had been working hard over the past couple of years. She saw something in me that I didn't see. She told me I should run for student body president. I had been planning to run for junior class president, not for the whole student body. But I looked up to her, and she believed in me, so I went for it. It was scary and tough, but when I saw my name on the ballot, I was super excited. I thought, If I can do this, what else can I do? It was achieving something that was bigger than me, something that was meaningful to me, that made an impact. I cared more about the impact that I was making and less about what people thought about me.

## HER OPPONENT WRITING A PETITION

**AC:** I was the first junior ever to be elected student body president. The person who lost against me was a senior. She decided to write a petition and get all the seniors to petition against me.

She created the petition because the student body president always spoke at graduation; that was part of the job. The person who lost didn't want me, a junior, speaking at graduation, even though it was just the welcome speech. The senior class president would still speak, as would the valedictorian.

It was difficult because most of the senior class signed the petition, but the administration staff still wanted me to speak. I was brought into the principal's office almost every day during that time.

I asked myself what I should do: stand my ground, listen to the administration staff, and speak because I deserve it, or let the seniors have what they wanted? It was difficult. I thought about how I would feel up on stage speaking and how I would feel afterwards. I would feel so scared and unwanted. That didn't make me feel happy or excited. It made me feel like I was putting myself in an extremely stressful position. I forgot about what the seniors wanted and what the administration wanted, and I asked myself what I wanted. I didn't want to put myself in that situation. It wasn't about standing my ground. I didn't deserve to put myself in that situation. I decided not to speak.

Afterwards, the group that started the petition came up to me and apologized. They told me it was just the welcome speech and that I could have spoken.

It wasn't such a big deal, but at the same time, I took the higher road. I ended up getting re-elected as student body president during my senior year, and I spoke at my own graduation.

## INSPIRATION TO BECOMING AN ENTREPRENEUR AT AGE SEVENTEEN

**AC:** I was always passionate about making a difference, especially once I got into leadership. I wanted to make a difference in at least one person's life every day, and that is still my mission today. I saw a company that was using fashion to build schools in Africa to make villages self-sustaining. I was passionate about working in the fashion industry, so I reached out to the company about this idea to design jewelry for them, and they went for it. I became a licensee and started to turn my ideas into reality. I donated a percentage to help fulfill their mission of building schools. It was a passion project that I thought I was going to do through my student government, thinking it was a great idea to raise money through the school. It ended up taking a year to sign the contract and find a factory to manufacture the bracelets and get the product made. It ended up becoming my own thing. I started running this business, and I fell in love with the process of turning an idea into reality. The reason I got into it was because I wanted to make an impact.

After high school, I went to the University of Florida, where I continued to run my business from my dorm room. I would go to class, come back, ride my bike ride to the post office, and ship out orders. I did that every single day.

Word-of-mouth marketing didn't work as well for me in college as it did in high school. I taught myself how to sell and how to code a website. I started marketing my website, and I got the company to put my bracelets on their website, which had way more traffic. I ended up getting sales through drop shipping. It was an organic process. I had to figure everything out.

I did it for about three years until I sold out of the designs. Then the company went in a different direction.

## THE INSPIRATION BEHIND WOMEN EMPOWER X

**AC:** Women Empower X was the product of a blog. The blog was called *Hello Perfect*. It's mission was to instill confidence in young girls and women because I went through my own fair share of low confidence. I saw how confidence is imperative to success in any field. I wanted to help women and young girls have confidence. After a few years of running the blog in college, I started putting on events and then sharing my story.

I also went through a near-death experience while I was in college that changed my life.

When I was twenty-one, I was in a coma for a while and had a 1 percent chance of survival. Six months after that, I was diagnosed with an autoimmune disease, which is something I still live with. There is no cure for it.

After that, I had a new sense of meaning, a feeling that I was meant to do more than just work in the fashion industry or run a blog. I needed to share my story about why this happened for me and not to me. That's what led me to speaking publicly about my story and then starting Women Empower X.

I had a mental shift. I was always a positive thinker, and I always believed in being optimistic and the law of attraction. It taught me so much. It showed me the power of my mind. It showed me how much my mind and thoughts affect my reality. It taught me to focus on things I can control because there are a lot of things that we can't control. We can't control other people, we can't control our health all the time, and we can't control the past. This experience taught me about focusing on what I can control, which gave me more freedom. It gave me the courage to be myself in front of others, because it's scary sharing things that you're going through. Courage is doing something despite the fear you feel. That's what helped me because I didn't want to continue feeling how I felt. Instead of thinking I needed to get healthy before I did the things I loved, I pursued them anyway. I also shared about my struggles, which is scary, but courage is what got me started on my journey.

## ADVICE TO THOSE STRUGGLING WITH SELF-CONFIDENCE

**AC:** What's more important, someone else's opinion of you or your dreams and goals? I know that's a tough question, but if you truly want to become the person who you dream of being, if you truly want to achieve anything that you can think of, you must ask yourself what's more important. The more you focus on other people's opinions of you, the less energy you will have to put toward the things that are meaningful. Continue to focus on that question when the tough times come, when the bullying comes, when low confidence comes. Most of the time, you'll realize your dreams are more important, and you'll put your energy toward them.

## TOP TAKEAWAYS:

- You are good enough even though people might tell you that you're not.
- If you are being cyberbullied, get adults involved.
- Even when you don't see something valuable in yourself, someone else will.
- When you feel like people are pulling you in different directions, ask yourself what you truly want.
- Find a way to make an impact.
- Fall in love with the process of making an idea into reality.
- *Focus on what you can control, not what you can't.*
- Have courage despite fear.
- When you find yourself worrying about what others think, ask yourself what's more important: other people's opinions of you or achieving your dreams?

# 12

# HOW TO USE YOUR EXPERIENCE OF BEING BULLIED TO YOUR ADVANTAGE

*TANIA SPEAKS*

Tania Speaks was named among *Time* magazine's top twenty-five teen influencers in 2018 and was also featured in *Forbes*. She got called nasty names for her bushy eyebrows, got tired of it, and shaved off her eyebrows in elementary school. They grew back deformed, and she still got made fun of. Eventually, she found an organic solution that helped make her eyebrows more manageable. Soon enough, her classmates wanted her solution, and she created a business out of it.

## CONNECT:
- Website: www.taniaspeaks.com
- Instagram: @Tania.Speaks

## STRUGGLES INCLUDED IN THIS CHAPTER:
- Depression
- Low self-esteem
- Worried too much about people's opinions
- Bullied
- Bushy eyebrows

## BULLIED FOR HER BUSHY EYEBROWS

**Tania Speaks:** In elementary school, a lot of my peers had thinner brows. I always had bushy eyebrows that almost connected in the middle.

I always looked at myself in the mirror and thought I looked different from my peers. I didn't think it was a big problem until people started to say things about it. It made me self-conscious. I was tortured by my peers. They would say I had a unibrow, that my eyebrows were touching, that they were extremely bushy, and that I was ugly. Kids who I thought were my friends started to bully me for my eyebrows. I was pushed off the swings and shoved into lockers. It was traumatic.

At that time, the only person who I told about it was my mom. I did that because I saw her fixing her eyebrows. I figured she could take me to the salon and help me. When I went to her, she said I was too young to do anything to my eyebrows. All I wanted was to stop the bullying, so I decided to take it upon myself and shave off my eyebrows with the little razor that I saw my mom using. I was in the basement thinking I knew what I was doing, but I ended up cutting myself badly. I was bleeding, and I had to go to the hospital. My mom was furious. "I told you not to touch them!" she yelled. "Just leave them alone! Your eyebrows are beautiful. One day someone's going to love your eyebrows." As a kid, I didn't want to hear that. Of course, my mom was going to tell me my eyebrows are beautiful.

I went back to school a couple of days later. My eyebrow had healed a bit, but kids continued to bully me because now my eyebrows were lopsided. They didn't look the same, so it didn't solve the issue. I still got bullied after taking matters into my own hands.

## HOW THE BULLYING AFFECTED HER

**TS:** Bullying affected all areas of my life. I've always been a high achiever. I've always loved school and gotten straight A's. Once I got bullied, my self-esteem dropped, I wasn't confident in anything, and my grades dropped a bit. I didn't want to go to school. I would pretend to be sick and beg my mom not to send me to school. Sometimes when I pretended to be sick, she knew I was faking because she knew I really didn't want to go to school.

## GROWING HER EYEBROWS BACK

**TS:** After I graduated from elementary school, the bullying didn't stop. While in middle school, I knew I needed to do something to get my eyebrows back. I went to the stores with my mom, and she helped me navigate different beauty brands and what could work for my eyebrows. Unfortunately, nothing worked because I have sensitive skin. I got rashes, and my skin broke out from those products, which defeated the purpose of trying to fix my eyebrows. My mom told me that organic products would work better for my skin. I took it upon myself to do some research on Google and find some ingredients. I asked my mom to buy them, and I mixed them together in my living room. Once I started using the concoction on my eyebrows, they started to grow back.

## HER JOURNEY TOWARD STARTING HER OWN EYEBROW PRODUCT BUSINESS AT AGE FIFTEEN

**TS:** By the time I got to high school, kids started to notice a big change in my eyebrows. Other kids would ask me what I did to them. They said, "I remember what your eyebrows looked like in elementary school, and they're better now." I told them I had my own formula. They wanted to try it. I brought it to school and gave it away for free until I realized I could put a price on it. I would sell one for $3 and two for $5 from the girls' bathroom. The line would wrap around, and they would wait for me to put the product on their eyebrows. Then they would give me the money, I would give them the product, and I would be on to the next customer. I was doing it for fun at the time. I couldn't believe people loved my product.

Then my mom, who has a bachelor's degree in business, told me I should create a business out of it. All we had to do was register it. I didn't think any "real" customers would buy it, and I was scared. But I did my first event, and I sold all my products. That's when the journey of owning my own business began.

**SS:** Did you ever get in trouble for selling the product at school?

**TS:** Some of my teachers bought my product a little bit toward the end of the school year. I didn't get in trouble with them, and I'm not sure if they told the principal. They would have me bring the product to their classroom, but I don't know if they knew I was selling it in the bathroom too.

## BALANCING SCHOOL AND HER BUSINESS

**TS:** I would go to school, and then I would do events in the evening. As soon as school was over, I would pack up all my business stuff and go straight to the event. The event would end at around 10:00 p.m., and then I would get to bed at around midnight. By the time I had to wake up for school the next morning, I only got about five hours of sleep.

## STARTING THE BUSINESS INCREASED HER CONFIDENCE

**TS:** When I started my business, I built confidence. I was confident about being able to sell products, and I wanted to branch out into other products. I decided to graduate early, which meant I had to take college courses while

I was taking high school courses. I needed a great deal of confidence to juggle both. Gaining that confidence allowed me to graduate early and do other things that I probably wouldn't have done if I still had low self-esteem.

## ADVICE SHE WOULD GIVE HER YOUNGER SELF

**TS:** I would tell my younger self to remember that nothing lasts forever. I thought I was going to be bullied my entire life. I couldn't see past being ten, eleven, or twelve years old. I thought I was still going to be bullied as an adult. If I had known I was going to start a business, graduate early, and start college, I probably wouldn't have been as discouraged about getting bullied. I would have told myself that, "It's going to get better; you're not going to be bullied forever." I think that would have helped me the most.

## FIND A POSITIVE OUTLET

**TS:** Find an outlet, literally anything. My outlet was selling products. Even though the bullying subsided once I got to high school, it still impacted me. It was still a traumatic event in my life. Being able to sell my products and run my business helped me forget about the bullying. I tell kids who are getting bullied to find an outlet, whether it's cooking, baking, painting, or whatever; something to help them feel good about themselves.

Also, tell an adult if you are being bullied, even if you don't want to hear what they have to say. One day it's going to come back around, and you're going to appreciate the advice. I appreciate the advice that my mom gave me, and you will appreciate the advice from whomever it is that you tell.

## TOP TAKEAWAYS:

- *People will continue to bully no matter what, so be proud of who you are.*
- You are beautiful if you believe you are beautiful.
- Experiment to find out what works and what doesn't work in life.
- If you find solutions to your problems, other people can benefit from them as well.
- You can increase your confidence by finding what you love to do and are good at doing.
- Bullying won't last forever.
- If you are being bullied, find a creative outlet.
- If you are being bullied, tell an adult.

# 13
# HOW TO TAKE OFF YOUR MASK
## *NATHAN HARMON*

Nathan Harmon's parents got divorced when he was eleven years old. His mom got remarried and had more kids, Nathan wasn't too happy. He put a mask on to hide his true feelings. He started hanging out with the wrong crowd, who got him into drugs and alcohol. He wanted to commit suicide. He tried hanging himself. Then at age twenty-three, he got into a drunk driving accident that killed his friend. He was sentenced to fifteen years in prison, but he only served four years. After being released early, he made it a mission to make a difference. In a two-and-a-half-year span, he was the most-booked speaker for schools in the United States, being booked over 630 times. He still keeps in touch with the parents of the friend who died in the accident.

## CONNECT:
- Website: www.yourlifespeaks.org
- Instagram: Your_Life_Speaks
- YouTube: Your Life Speaks

## STRUGGLES INCLUDED IN THIS CHAPTER:
- Depression
- Involved in drugs/alcohol
- Toxic friends
- Death of a loved one
- Wanted to commit suicide
- Parents got divorced
- Put too much pressure on himself
- Hid his pain

- Eating disorder
- Served time in prison

## PUTTING A MASK ON

**Nathan Harmon:** I know what it's like to come from a broken family. My mom and dad got divorced when I was in the sixth grade. It really rocked me because my parents never fought in front of me. I was completely blindsided, and my dad was suddenly ripped out of my life. That was a big deal because he was my mentor, my hero. I always said he was my Superman. When the divorce happened, I naturally developed a habit that most of us do without even knowing it. I put a mask on.

My mom got remarried quickly, and then I had step brothers and sisters. I didn't sign up for that. It was a lot of not knowing how to deal with that at a young age. I was not trained on how to deal with the anger, the frustration, the bitterness, the hurt, and the pain. I didn't want to talk about it. It was like a volcano. The pressure built, and eventually, it started finding leaks. That was a destructive way for me to process their divorce.

I learned to put a mask on in my teen years by watching my peers and my parents. I learned how to fake happiness. On the surface it looked like I was good. Behind the mask were tears and pain. I was screaming, but I was silent. I had a voice when I was voiceless, and I didn't know as a young man that it's OK not to be OK. We're not meant to be an island, and we need each other. We're better together, but I didn't know that.

Pressure busts pipes. When emotional pressure builds, it's going to find way out. If we don't find healthy ways to talk about our emotional pain, the pressure will find its way out in a negative way, such as suicidal thoughts, self-harming, hurting people, bullying people, or drugs and alcohol.

## THE NEGATIVE EFFECTS OF PUTTING ON A MASK

**NH:** One of the first mistakes I made was I walked away from my friends. I had good friends at the time, but once I put on the mask, I started to isolate myself from other people. I'm a firm believer that who you surround yourself with is who you are. I found other friends where I felt the peer pressure to act, talk, and look a certain way. While trying to fit in with certain groups, I got involved with drugs and alcohol. Around age seventeen or eighteen, I thought about ending my life. I had a rope around my throat and was on the brink of hanging myself. I also got into self-harm. I can still see the scars on my hands today where I used to burn myself. I also battled an eating disorder. I was trying to find my value from everybody else. I woke up empty every day crying out for help. I was bullying myself. I was afraid to talk about it with anyone else.

## AN ACCIDENT THAT CHANGED HIS LIFE FOREVER

**NH:** When I was twenty-three, my friend, Priscilla Owens, came to pick me up as a designated driver, and then she gave me the keys to her car. I was driving drunk, and we got into a bad accident. The next night, July 18, she died.

Law enforcement members used to come into our school to talk about the dangers of drinking and driving, as did our teachers. I never expected it could happen to me. I was broken because I knew that not only had I affected myself; I had destroyed another family. Priscilla's family wanted me to call them three days after the wreck, but I didn't know what to say. However, three days after the wreck, they forgave me. They said, "We knew Priscilla was sober when she left. She's pretty strong willed. We don't know why she gave you those keys, and we don't think one dumb choice should destroy two family's lives. We want to forgive you, but we're asking you to try to make the world a better place. Don't let her die for nothing." That changed me. I still had to go to prison due to the accident though. I received a fifteen-year sentence.

## MAKING A CHANGE IN PRISON

**NH:** Thankfully, I didn't have to do the full fifteen years. I was released eleven years early. The reason for that, I believe, is I took ownership of my situation. I took ownership of my past, and I stopped blaming others. A mistake that a lot of us make is we allow things that we have no control over to control us. We forget that we can control how we respond. I took off the mask, which was the first step.

That mental shift came within thirty days of the accident. The warrant for my arrest finally came as they processed all that happened, and I turned myself in. It was then when I had to stop running from everything. Time is a powerful tool. When I was young, my dad used to tell me, "If there's breath in your lungs, there's hope in your heart." Priscilla's family had forgiven me in a radical way, and now my situation was bigger than me. I had a purpose. They wanted to see me make a difference.

Faith grew on me. I had an encounter with God. I wrote the words "Change the World" and slapped them on my cell wall. I decided I could wake up every day and make choices that built rather than destroyed, bringing my dreams of changing the world closer to me.

**SS:** What were some of your habits in prison that helped you stay positive?

**NH:** I'm a journalist, and I love to write. I did a lot of processing that way. I started adding exercise. I'm a big runner. I think it's when I get some of my best clarity is when I'm kicking those endorphins around. I also started finding good mentors who could guide me.

## HIS MENTOR

**NH:** I met a guy in prison who poured into me. He said he didn't want to see me make the same mistakes that he had made. He was always challenging me, saying, "Nathan, why don't you not want to change?"

"Oh, because of my friends," I'd say.

"Do they care about you?" he'd ask. "How many of them have come and visited you?"

"None," I said.

"How many have written to you?"

"None."

"So, why are you letting people live rent-free in your brain?" he asked. "Why are you letting people who don't care about you and who were helping you be destructive hijack your destiny?"

As soon as he said that, it was a "light bulb" moment that created a huge shift in my thinking.

## THE TOOLS AND RESOURCES THAT HE USED TO GET OUT EARLY

**NH:** I participated in a program in prison called Therapeutic Community, a cognitive thinking program aimed at changing the way prisoners thought. It was big on helping participants find their purpose. I also spent a lot of time in meditation, which I think is a powerful tool.

Indiana started a program to send inmates across the state and communicate their message to schools to make a difference. It was a pilot program to help inmates make good choices and work hard. I was chosen for it due to the work that I had done for two years while incarcerated. The governor of Indiana heard about my work, and I got a letter from the governor's office saying I was more effective out there than I was in prison. I walked out of that place eleven years early at age twenty-seven.

## NATHAN'S POST-PRISON JOURNEY

**NH:** I punched fear in the face. A lot of people in my hometown said I was a failure, and it was only a matter of time before I went back to prison. They said my dream of wanting to be an inspirational speaker was stupid and that I wasn't qualified, that I didn't have the ability to communicate and persuade an audience.

I decided not to listen to any of my critics. I reached out to schools, asking them to let me speak. I recorded a promotional video of me speaking in prison. I had spoken to over 7,000 people over 2 years while still incarcerated. I sent it to one hundred schools. One school brought me in. One turned into ten, then thirty, and then seventy, and then it was a snowball effect. I was good at it. Now I've received thousands of messages from kids who haven't committed suicide because of my talk and people who are on the verge, who are not healthy, but who are getting help. Kids who weren't going to graduate are now graduating. Talk about the power of words. I give ninety-minute talks, and everyone is fully engaged for those ninety minutes.

## TACKLE CHALLENGES HEAD ON

**NH:** Don't just talk to others about your challenges; go right to the source. It's not about being perfect; it's about progress. Understand the importance of getting the most out of every moment and the importance of other people. We need each other. The more we use each other, share with each other, and become part of a team, the better we are together. I've learned that the more we communicate and take off our masks, the more we realize other people are just like us. We start to realize that we're all beautifully broken in some way, and we all have problems.

## ADVICE TO HIS YOUNGER SELF

**NH:** Don't believe the lie that is keeping you safe. It's the very thing holding you hostage. Find the courage to admit the truth. It won't be as bad as you think. You're not alone. Sometimes your defense mechanism can be the greatest challenge to overcome. Take off your mask, and talk about your problem. It's going to be OK, even though you don't feel it will be.

**SS:** What's a specific way that someone can take off their mask?

**NH:** Find a caring adult who you trust. Finding that person can be a challenge, but once you do, it will help.

## TOP TAKEAWAYS:

- Eliminate your toxic friends. They will bring your ambition down and won't be there when you need them the most.

- Reading, meditation, journaling, and talking to a mentor can change your life.
- Make the best out of every situation, even if it's a negative one.
- Tackle your challenges head on.
- *Take off your mask, and stop hiding your problems.*
- Find a trustworthy and caring adult to open up to.
- Take ownership of all your problems.
- Your current situation will not last forever.

# 14
# HOW TO KEEP GOING EVEN WHEN YOU CONTINUOUSLY FAIL

## *HALA TAHA*

As a teenager, Hala would always try out for things but never make it. This included the volleyball team, the cheerleading squad, talent shows, advanced classes, and student council president. She felt like a failure and thought something was wrong with her. In college she realized nothing was wrong with her; she just hadn't been in the right environment. She went on to join a sorority, snag an internship at New York's top radio station, create a popular blog, get a 4.0 GPA in her MBA program, run a successful podcast called *Young and Profiting*, and create an influence of over 45,000 followers on LinkedIn.

## CONNECT:

- LinkedIn: linkedin.com/in/htaha

## STRUGGLES INCLUDED IN THIS CHAPTER:

- - Low self-esteem
- - Not good in school and felt dumb
- - Feared being a disappointment
- - No one supported her
- - Lacked good mentors/support system
- - In a toxic environment
- - Felt like a failure

## DON'T LET PAST SITUATIONS DICTATE YOUR FUTURE

**Hala Taha:** I would say that I was an average teenager—average grades, average level of popularity and social life. I would keep trying to do things, but they wouldn't really pan out. I tried out for the cheerleading team in high school. I didn't make it even though I was athletic. I played soccer all my life, but I didn't make the team. I tried out for the volleyball team, but I was a bit too short. I used to be in plays, but I was never the lead, even though I probably had the best voice in school. In high school, nobody could see me, and I felt invisible.

When I was in seventh grade, I was in the remedial math class. Because of being in that class, I felt dumb. It was like when the rich get richer, and the poor get poorer. They kept giving the same kids the same opportunities, but I was excluded from them. Thankfully, I was good at singing, and I used to get solos during every concert. Singing was the one area in my teenage career that I excelled at, and my choir teacher supported me.

Maybe I wasn't exerting enough positivity or there was something about my aura where I was never selected for the things that I was trying to do. That could have been my fault, or it could have been a product of my environment.

When I was in high school, 9/11 happened. I'm Palestinian, and I suddenly became way less popular than I was and lost a lot of friends after those planes hit. I think that might have been one reason why I was not chosen for a lot of roles, like being the lead in a play or participating in our talent show. Think about it: I had a solo every concert, so why wouldn't they think I was good enough to sing in the talent show? The difference was the gatekeepers. I don't think they wanted an Arab teenager to be in that position. I used to feel devastated every time I failed. I was immature, and I would get upset about it.

Things changed after high school. I went to the New Jersey Institute of Tecāology, where I joined a sorority and was put into a group of women who had similar interests. That helped me develop confidence. In college, I was given chances, and I met those opportunities successfully. I excelled. I was very popular, the lead in all the plays, and vice president of my sorority. Suddenly, I was one of the prettiest girls in school and got a lot of attention. Overnight, I was good at everything I tried.

Luckily, I kept trying. I didn't stop when I didn't make the cheerleading team. That didn't stop me from trying out for volleyball. It's always good to get back on the horse, no matter what happens. If I let high school dictate my life, I would be a complete loser right now, and I'm not a loser. Don't let past situations dictate your future.

## THE LAW OF ATTRACTION

**HT:** When I was in college, I got into the law of attraction. Jerry and Esther Hicks are authors who write about it. It helped me understand that you can attract whatever you believe you can bring about in your life. I started getting into visualization, affirmations, and being positive. It helped me attract new, positive things in my life and was a major switch.

When I started college, I was given an opportunity to be more social and excel in different situations. Then I started being more confident and more intentional. In my junior year of college, I got an internship at Hot 97. I was Angie Martinez's assistant. I ended up dropping out of school for a little bit to do the internship. That's when my life really started to differentiate from other people my age. The law of attraction helped get me there.

## CHANGING HER ENVIRONMENT

**HT:** I don't think I changed; my environment changed. I was put in a new environment, I was given a chance to start over, and I was able to shine. I made a better first impression. I think that made the difference. People saw me for who I was, not for the fact that I was Arabic. In middle and high school, I was considered the "ugly duckling," or people didn't notice that I was pretty. Then I got to college, and I was the one of the most sought-after girls in school. College was also more diverse, so maybe people there were more accepting of a kind of beauty that was different than the tall, blond-haired, blue-eyed type.

## "HOT 97" DAYS

**HT:** I started out in the production department and did well there. Then Angie Martinez, who is the number-one radio personality with the number-one show in New York City, recruited me to be her assistant. That was my second internship. Then she wanted me to be there more often, so I ended up dropping out of school for about one and a half years to take advantage of that opportunity. It was such a great experience. I met every famous person you could imagine. I used to make my money going out to parties with the DJs, co-hosting showcases with them, and selling tickets to artists who wanted to be involved in talent showcases. I got into the music industry and started my public persona, gaining a lot of momentum on Twitter. I had connections with several artists, and I started blogging for one of the DJs, DJ Enuff, who had a pretty popular blog site. I also used to do video blogs, where I would interview artists after they went on Angie's show. After the show, I did a quick interview with them and then posted it on DJ Enuff's blog. That was my first time doing any type of media where I was the focus. One thing led to another, and I ended up wanting to go back to school, so I stopped working at Hot 97.

## STRAWBERRYBLUNT.COM DAYS

**HT:** During my senior year of college, I started a blog called strawberryblunt.com, which was the story of hip-hop. It was also a way to empower women in the music industry. I recruited twelve girls to start through Twitter and Craigslist. I picked the girls who had industry jobs and worked at major places. Everybody had their own angle, whether they wanted to write about music, fashion, or do interviews. I learned how to create websites in two weeks by myself and then launched a WordPress site. I set it up and then taught everybody how to blog. We started this website, and within the first month, we were the 30,000th most popular website in the world out of millions and millions of websites. We got noticed immediately.

In addition to the blog, we ended up having four different Internet radio shows (back then there was no such thing as podcasts). We used to invite upcoming artists, such as Fabulous and Soulja Boy. We also interviewed celebrities, and we hosted parties and concerts to make money. That's what I was doing right out of college.

When I was about twenty-seven, I shut down the blog site. MTV had told us twice that we were going to get our own reality show, but it didn't happen. Feeling like we needed to focus on our careers, I went and got my MBA, during which I earned a 4.0 GPA, which was a big deal considering I didn't feel smart as a teenager.

## EVERYTHING HAPPENS FOR A GOOD REASON

**HT:** Sometimes I wished I had kept going with Strawberry Blunt. I kept picturing the image of a cartoon where a guy was mining for gold, and there was a little bit of dirt between him and the gold. That's where I probably was at, but I couldn't see it at the time, which kind of stinks. People still ask me what happened to my blog. Experiences are everything, and without that experience, I wouldn't have this podcast now, because Strawberry Blunt is where I honed my interviewing skills. That's also where I learned how to do digital marketing, which was why I was able to get a corporate job and a career. I taught myself how to do video editing, audio editing, graphic design, and web design, and I had way more skills than a lot of other people because of that experience. Even though it failed, it was very successful. It's a matter of perspective. I also met a lot of my lifelong friends on that journey and have memories that so many people probably will never have. Getting filmed by MTV, throwing concerts, interacting with celebrities, and having a dance show that was filmed were all amazing experiences. We shut it down, but I learned a lot and gained many skills, experiences, and memories.

## POST MBA

**HT:** I worked at Hewlett Packard Enterprise for five years. During my last year there, I decided I was going to start a podcast. I missed radio, and I wanted to merge my passions of business and broadcasting to start something new. I also wanted to help people in the process. I started the *Young and Profiting* podcast about a year ago. I can't tell you much else other than the fact that I knew how to do everything already. I knew how to audio edit, I knew marketing, and I knew how to interview people. Immediately, I got two big authors to come on my first episode. Things really started to take off. I have a team now of over ten people who work for my podcast. I love my podcast, and I'm so thankful for all of my past experiences. I get to do something that I think is truly meaningful. It's no longer about celebrity gossip. It's important educational content. It's personally fulfilling, and I love what I'm doing.

Then I got into LinkedIn, which is a social media platform that I decided was my best chance at getting in touch with my target audience. I started with 1,000 followers over a year ago. I was familiar with LinkedIn due to running company pages for different companies over the years. Now I have over 45,000 followers on LinkedIn.

## ADVICE IF YOU FEEL LIKE A FAILURE

**HT:** My advice is to stay positive and work on yourself. Try to get outsiders to tell you what you can improve on. If I were afraid to receive negative feedback and to work on myself, I wouldn't be where I am today. On the other side, while there is always room to improve yourself, sometimes it's your environment that needs to change. There will be more opportunities. Keep trying, and keep pushing through.

## WHAT TO DO IF YOUR PARENTS DON'T SUPPORT YOUR DREAMS

**HT:** Follow your passion. When you follow your passion, work comes effortlessly, and you end up taking more action. The other side of the coin is that you need to sustain yourself. You need to find a balance between sustaining yourself and finding a passion. I have a podcast, but I also have a full-time job at a great company called Disney Streaming Services. I have an amazing career that I spend 50 percent of my time on. Then my podcast gets 25 percent of my time, and other things get 25 percent. You need to have a balance. You can't expect your parents to support you forever. You also don't want to be broke, so you need to be responsible. Find a job that you love that helps you grow your skills and uses your passion. If you're working a full-time job, try getting a side hustle. Dip your toes into what you want to do. Make sure that you have a good balance and that you're also gaining skills that will be able to provide for you financially in the future.

## TOP TAKEAWAYS:

- *Every failure is a learning experience and an opportunity for you to keep trying.*
- Don't let past situations dictate your future.
- Use the law of attraction to achieve your goals.
- Sometimes you need to change your environment.
- Surround yourself with people who see the good in you.
- Gaining experience is key. The skills you gain can be applied to new experiences in the future.
- Stay positive, and work on yourself.
- Don't be afraid to receive negative feedback.
- Follow your passion, even as a side hustle or a hobby.
- If you are following your passion, make sure you are also able to sustain yourself and have income from a job.

# 15
# HOW TO DEAL WITH SOCIAL EXCLUSION
## *SATVIK SETHI*

The top three problems that Satvik faced in middle school in India were social exclusion, social anxiety, and bullying. Sometimes when he had to perform to a big crowd, he would have severe anxiety that manifested itself in different ways. While going through mental health challenges in school, he realized many of his peers were experiencing the same thing. Kids started to approach him in middle school to vent about their problems. He wanted to promote mental health awareness on a global scale, which is how Runaway App came about.

## CONNECT:
- Instagram: @SatvikSethi
- Company Instagram: @Runaway.App

## STRUGGLES INCLUDED IN THIS CHAPTER:
- Social anxiety
- Social exclusion
- Depression
- Low self-esteem
- Hated being alone
- Worried too much about people's opinions
- In a toxic environment

## FACING SOCIAL EXCLUSION
**Satvik Sethi:** Middle school is a time in your life when you're faced with many different challenges. You're going through puberty, you're trying to understand how the world works, you're faced with new social situations, and

you're suddenly in this place you've never been before. There's bound to be challenges. It's also a time when a lot of kids are finding their friend groups.

I had a friend group going into eighth grade, but then I started getting uninvited to some of the events that we would normally go to together. It took a toll on my mental health. At that time, I didn't understand that mental health was a thing. I became sad. Before I would be walking around the halls, going to class, and the other kids would be dapping me up and calling my name. I felt special. That all changed when my friend group started excluding me from their plans. Suddenly, I was one of the kids who was eating my lunch alone during recess, not talking to anyone. Slowly, however, I found a small group of friends.

I've realized that for me, it's more important to have a few good friends who I can share my problems with rather than being known by a huge group of people. Now I prefer the real connections way more.

## FRIENDS STARTED TO COME TO HIM WITH MENTAL HEALTH CHALLENGES

**SS:** I started becoming someone who my friends could talk to. That's where my mental health journey started. I was exposed to how bad mental health problems can be and the impact that such challenges can have on people. I wanted to help people get better, and I wanted to make sure that no one went through the same phase of life that I went through.

That goes back to how I was raised. Everyone at home was open with each other about the problems they faced. We were taught not to be judgmental. That's exactly what I tried to do with my friends. I didn't see someone with a mental health problem; I saw a friend who was struggling, and I wanted to help them. I would sit down, listen to them, and let them talk. I would let them know that things would get better and that whatever they were facing was only temporary.

Later, I realized I was using a powerful tool that many mental health professionals use, called active listening. This is where you let a person talk to you, you don't give any advice, you console the person, and you say that things are going to be fine. I was doing it in middle school. I thought it was super cool because I was able to help many people through that.

Everyone was facing issues that rose from social situations. It was easy to tell them that I knew how they felt. I would also be open about my struggles with my friends and let them know that they were not alone in the struggles that they were facing. That's how Runaway App got started before I even made it a name or a business.

## HIS SOCIAL ANXIETY

**SS:** Some of my social anxiety stemmed from the exclusion that I was facing. I started to think people were always mocking me or talking about me when I walked down the hallways.

I'm a musician, and I used to perform in high school. I've performed on stage many times in front of many people. Before stepping on the stage, whether it's for music or speaking, I'm always shaking. I'm so nervous and anxious about how it's going to go. The moment before I go on, I've thrown up and cried, but I still do it. I go on stage, I do my thing, and once I'm on stage, everything's great. When someone looks at me on stage, they won't know that I'm someone who is living with social anxiety.

I've been in many situations where I've had to be in front of people, and I still have a fear of being judged by people when I'm talking, and I'm always thinking that people are making fun of me.

Over the years, I've gotten better at controlling it. I think we should be supportive if our friends have it. I've seen a lot of people tell their friends that there's nothing to be nervous about. If your friends are nervous, let them be nervous. Tell them, "If you need anything, I'm here for you. Here's a glass of water." Instead of telling people that they don't have the problem, when obviously, they do, just be present, support them, and let them know that you're there for them.

## CHANGING ENVIRONMENTS CAN HAVE A POSITIVE IMPACT

**SS:** I changed schools from middle school to high school because I realized that the students at my middle school were not the kind of crowd I could see myself growing up with. The first step was me having an open conversation with my parents about what I was going through and how I needed to be in an environment that was better suited for my mental health. That led me to changing schools.

Once I was in high school, it was an opportunity for me to rebuild my identity. I had two years ahead of me in high school, and I worked extremely hard during that time. I got involved as much as I could and tried to make a positive mark. That's ultimately what led to me going to New York for college. It was a result of my hard work during high school.

## HIS ONE SUICIDAL THOUGHT

**SS:** I had a suicidal thought when things got a little too much. Social exclusion was happening a lot, bullying was on the rise, people were telling me their mental health struggles, and it was more than I could handle.

I was also seeing many actors and actresses committing suicide as a way of handling their challenges, and in a way, mainstream media and pop culture normalized the idea that if you were struggling, suicide was a reasonable way out.

I realized quickly how stupid that was. The first thing most people who are considering suicide think about is their family and what will happen to them. That itself was a terrible thought. I realized quickly that my problems weren't the end of the world. Six years down the line, I can't remember why I had suicide ideation or why I thought what I was facing was the end of my world.

Now, when I'm faced with a serious issue, I always ask myself, "Ten years from now, is this going to be something I remember?" If the answer is no, which it always is, then I move on. I say, "Today's a bad day, but tomorrow is going to be a good one."

If you are having suicidal thoughts, ask yourself what's bringing you that pain, and see if you can do something to prevent it. If it's your friends, try to distance yourself from them. If it's a social situation, take some baby steps to improve it. Can you have an open dialogue with your parents or a trusted adult about it?

You need to understand what's causing that pain and then try to work around it. Things will get better. I remember a famous quote: "This forest is really scary, but if you stop, you're going to be stuck in that scary forest. The best thing is to keep walking until you get out. And you will ultimately get out."

## INSPIRATIONAL STORIES OF PEOPLE HE HAS HELPED

**SS:** One of my favorite stories to tell is when I used to go on Instagram and find people to talk to. I've spoken to people from a lot of different countries who were complete strangers. In the end, we would become good friends, because we could talk about mental health problems.

One of the girls was from Sweden. She was sixteen at the time, the same age as me. We started talking about her problems at school and with her family, but then we started talking about our cultures. She told me a lot of awesome things about Sweden, and I told her a lot of awesome things about India. Then we started discussing our dreams. She said she wanted to be a photographer. I told her that was cool, because I love photography. We started sending each other photos we've taken. She messaged me last year out of nowhere, saying, "Hey, I wanted to let you know that I got a job as a professional photographer, and I'm going to be doing travel photography with someone. I wanted to thank you for being there that one night because I might not have made it here today if it wasn't for you reaching out and being a friend to me."

If you're in a position where you can help someone and impact their life in a major way, where you can be the difference between them seeing tomorrow or not, help them in any way you can.

## ADVICE HE WOULD GIVE HIS YOUNGER SELF

**SS:** I don't have any tips for my younger self. I think the reason I am where I am today is because of my experiences. Many times I think when people are given that question, they try to protect their younger selves and try to tell them to take the safest route to get here. Honestly, I would take the same route I have traveled.

I would tell my younger self to take it as it comes, and go with the flow. I would say that everything gets better. When I was younger, there were times when things were terrible, and I thought nothing was ever going to get better. Over time, I realized that as bad as things seem in that moment, everything ultimately gets better. You can learn something from every situation, even bad experiences.

## HANDLING BULLIES

**SS:** If I saw someone getting bullied, I wouldn't care about the consequences; I'd stop it. I would go up and try to break up the fight. If someone was getting roasted by a group of people, I would break it up and say, "You guys do realize that it's five versus one, right?"

If you are being bullied, let the bully know that you will no longer put up with it. If that doesn't work, get someone to intervene. Talk to a teacher, your parents, or to anyone else who can intervene.

## TOP TAKEAWAYS:

- It's better to have a small group of close friends than a lot of friends who don't value you.
- Ask yourself, "Ten years from now, will I even remember this?" If the answer is no, which it always is, move on.
- Have an open conversation with your parents or a trusted adult about what you're going through.
- If someone opens up to you about their problems, you don't need to tell them that everything will be OK. Listen, and tell them that you are there for them if they ever need you.
- *Go with the flow. You can learn something from every experience, even the bad ones.*
- "This forest is really scary, but if you stop, you're going to be stuck

in that scary forest. The best thing is to keep walking until you get out. And you will ultimately get out."

- If you see someone being bullied, stand up for them.

# 16
# FROM ILLITERATE UNTIL AGE FOURTEEN TO HONOR ROLL STUDENT
## *LOU JONES*

Lou Jones is widely recognized as a leader on youth, young adults and academic success. Lou has motivated and inspired audiences of all ages for nearly two decades with his humorous stories, captivating life experiences, and relatable personality. His mission is to inspire people to live their lives to the fullest and maximize their potential. Lou understands hardships because academics never came easy to him. Until age fourteen, he had a secret that he kept from his classmates: he was illiterate. Despite those challenges, he was able to overcome that hurdle and become an honor roll student, excel in leadership positions, and win the Spirit of Detroit Award.

## CONNECT:
- Website: www.loujones.com
- Instagram: @LouJonesInspires
- TikTok: @LouJonesInspires

## STRUGGLES INCLUDED IN THIS CHAPTER:
- Divorced parents
- Low self-esteem
- Illiterate
- Bullying
- Was in a toxic environment
- Felt dumb in school

# ILLITERATE UNTIL AGE FOURTEEN

**Lou Jones:** I grew up in Detroit, went to Detroit public schools, and was raised in a single-parent household. It was my mother and me. She discovered that I was having reading problems in the second grade, so she transferred me to a private school and paid thousands of dollars to help me. This went on for years. I went to tutors on Saturdays, but nothing helped. I begged her to let me go back to public school. She let me go in the sixth grade, but at the same time, she had a plan for me. She found a private tutoring program where a lady came to the house twice a week and taught me how to read. That took about a year from the middle of sixth grade to the middle of seventh grade. Then eventually I was reading at a ninth-grade level, and she told me to apply myself. But after years of being tormented by other students, my self-esteem was so low that I didn't apply myself until that summer when I was going from seventh grade to eighth grade.

My mother sent me to a summer church camp, and that's where my life changed. It was a positive experience for me. I saw something different. I didn't hear constant cursing, and we didn't talk about which girl we could hook up with. It was focused on God, getting better grades, and going to college. It was a different conversation from what I was used to. The people at that camp had a purpose for their lives.

When I got home, I held on to some of those same friends from camp and had a different perspective on life. I started to believe in myself after having my confidence shattered due to not being able to read for all those years.

After that summer I started applying myself. I went from a D and C student to an A and B student. I went on to the eighth grade and graduated in the top 10 percent of my class. After I graduated from high school, I went on to college.

# ADOPTING TO YOUR LEARNING STYLE

**LJ:** The tutoring program I was enrolled in did a test and discovered that the way I learn is different from a lot of people. I learn through memorization. I may not be good with vowels or breaking words down, but if I hear someone say something, it clicks. When they discovered that I learned this way, that's how they taught me. My tutor helped me learn the basics, and then once I had a foundation, the rest is history. I excelled in school.

I also had to read. I had to make sure I did my homework assignments because I always wanted to get ahead. I didn't read as fast as everybody else. The more I read, the better my comprehension got, and the more I succeeded. I worked hard to apply myself. Once they discovered my learning style, I was able to overcome my learning challenges.

If people have called you dumb, and your grades have always been low, find your own learning style. You are not dumb; you just learn differently than most people. There is nothing wrong with that. Once you discover your learning style, you can excel in school like I did.

## CHANGING ENVIRONMENTS

**LJ:** It wasn't easy to do better because I also was running the streets drinking, smoking, and doing drugs with my friends. I knew if I wanted a better future, I had to put myself in a more positive environment.

One day, my friends and I were in the basement of my friend's house passing around a joint (marijuana). It was my turn to smoke, but I just passed it to the next person. I couldn't take that chance after that life-changing experience at the church camp.

My friends were shocked. "Are sure?" they asked. "You put in money for it. You can smoke."

"I'm sure," I replied. I saw the staircase that led to the door to leave the house. I knew I didn't belong there, so I stood up, told my friends that I was going to leave, and then went up the stairs and out that door. That was my last experience with drugs and hanging around the wrong crowd. Sometimes you have to make a decision to walk away from the negativity.

If you want to do better in school or accomplish any goal, your friend group is extremely important. They will either lift you up or bring you down, so choose wisely. I started hanging out with the crowd who wasn't doing drugs. Sometimes you have to take a stand for your life and decide who you want to hang out with. When you do that, it may be a season of loneliness where you're by yourself, but you must focus on self-development. Over time you'll start to connect with the right people. Also, get an accountability partner to help you stay focused. It will eventually work out in your favor.

## HAVING A PURPOSE

**LJ:** What helped me change my life and do better was having a purpose. Back then I wanted to become a schoolteacher because I had some great teachers who were an influence on my life. I could see myself educating, and that's what I wanted to study in college. However, I decided to follow my calling to become a youth pastor, which was still in the realm of education. I had a focus on where I wanted to go in life. That gave me drive as well. I encourage other people to find out what their *why* is. Find out what your purpose is on this planet. When you have a specific goal, life becomes easier, because you have direction. If you have a why and a purpose, you can find a way around your obstacles.

## DISCOVERING YOUR PURPOSE

**LJ:** I realized my purpose was always there. For example, when I was eight or nine years old, preaching to the ceiling fan or the door, I could see hundreds of people in front of me, and I'd be talking to them about the stories of David. When I was younger, I never recognized that as my calling. Only in college did I realize those times were my calling. I've always felt called to minister to people and inspire them, but I never knew it. My mother knew all those years ago what my calling was. She went to the pastor about it, but the pastor told her not to tell me about it but to let me grow, learn, and step into it myself. My pastor feared I may run from it if I felt pressured, so my mom never pressured me.

I called my mother when I was in my second year of college and said, "Mom, I think I need to leave college and go to Bible school." That was after she paid all this money to get me to college. I thought she was going to yell at me, but I was wrong.

"Oh, I'm glad you finally accepted that," she said. "Alright, when are you going to make the move?"

I left Michigan State after two years and then went to Bible school. After I graduated, I went into full-time ministry for a few years and then went back to college, earning my degree in pastoral leadership. I have now served as a youth pastor for eighteen years.

I developed a mission statement for my life, which is to inspire people to live their life to the fullest. Everything I do, all the jobs I work and how I impact people's lives, is connected to that mission statement.

Tony Robbins says, "Where your focus goes, your energy flows." If you don't know your purpose, take time to focus on your passions and your talents. Eventually, it will evolve into your purpose or meaning in life. Don't overthink it; your purpose can be something simple.

Pursuing your calling successfully takes time. It's not an overnight process, so be patient with yourself. Where your focus goes, your energy flows. That means you need to focus on one thing instead of trying to do a million things. Experimentation is important too. Through experimentation, you will learn what you like to do and what you are good at.

## TACKLING FEAR HEAD ON

**LJ:** Don't allow fear to take over. The word "fear" can be seen as an acronym for "false evidence appearing real." Failure happens all the time, but you won't even get to the failure part if you allow fear to take over because you won't attempt anything. You need failure in order to learn and progress in life.

When I'm hesitating to go after a task or a goal or I'm going through something difficult in life, I attack fear with full force, overcome that specific challenge, and accomplish that goal. That's how I have been able to accomplish the things I have accomplished in my life.

## FIND AN ACCOUNTABILITY PARTNER

**LJ:** Don't go it alone. Speak up, and advocate for yourself. Find someone you trust to keep you accountable. Whether it's a family member, a counselor, or a youth pastor, connect with someone to let them know what you're struggling with, so you can get the support and help that you need. I call it an accountability partner. My wife and I have a couple of accountability partners. The only way to have an accountability partner is to speak up and let people know what you're going through.

## TOP TAKEAWAYS:

- *Discover your learning style.*
- Sometimes you have to decide to walk away from the negativity.
- Your friend group will either lift you up or bring you down, so choose wisely.
- Discover your why.
- You may have already discovered your purpose; you just need to dig deep to see what it is.
- "Where your focus goes, your energy flows."
- If you don't know what your purpose is, start experimenting.
- Attack fear with full force.
- Speak up, and find an accountability partner.

# 17
# HOW TO FIND YOUR PASSION IN HIGH SCHOOL
## *CALAH OLSON*

Calah Olson had her fair share of struggles before founding her company. Eventually, she found a positive outlet, which was art. She turned her passion for art into a business. By age sixteen, she finished high school. By age eighteen, she finished college and started her own clothing brand. Read this chapter to find out how she went from a depressed teenager to turning her passion into a business by age eighteen.

## CONNECT:
- Website: www.outsidersclothing.shop
- Instagram: @CalahOlson

## STRUGGLES INCLUDED IN THIS CHAPTER:
- Anxiety
- Depression
- Considered herself an outsider
- Low self-esteem
- Parents divorced
- Wanted to commit suicide
- People pleaser
- Put too much pressure on herself
- Always stressed

## STARTING HER CLOTHING BRAND, THE OUTSIDERS CLOTHING COMPANY

**Calah Olson:** I started this brand as a passion project. I've always been passionate about art, and I've always expressed myself through clothing. I've also considered myself an outsider, someone who doesn't follow the norm. I took my personality and shoved it into this clothing brand. I turned it into an amazing thing. Our message is to be yourself, not go along with the societal norms, and do what makes you happy.

**SS:** What inspired you to start your clothing brand?

**CO:** I've always wanted to do something with my art, but I didn't know how. Everybody told me that I couldn't make money as an artist, which is not true. I just didn't know how to go about it. Then I realized I have a passion for clothing as well, so I combined clothing and art.

## BECOME FEARLESS

**CO:** I've been through two of my parents' divorces. I've struggled with anxiety, depression, and suicidal thoughts. I transferred into independent studies, which are online classes to finish school early. That was my turning point, where I was able to pull myself out of my mental health struggles and step away from the negative people. I stepped back, and I had a talk with myself. I said, "Dude, what are you doing? You need to find a way to pull yourself out of this. You need to find a way to be who you are without being super worried about what everybody else thinks." I looked at the bigger perspective, and I was able to fix it.

It's still a work in progress. Nobody's perfect. Everybody is going to have those feelings come up again at some point. I had to do everything that scares me, and now I live by that. I have the word "fear" tattooed across my wrist. Fear builds confidence. You learn to trust yourself, and facing your fears teaches you to be fearless.

## IF YOU DON'T HAVE GUIDANCE, THEN READ

**CO:** Read as much as you can. When I was seventeen, I had thirty bucks to my name, and I had no idea what to do. I started a YouTube channel and watched interviews about people who were doing the same thing that I was doing or wanted to do. I try to read at least two or three books a month to refresh my mind. Honestly, pick up a book. If there's something that you're passionate about, find a book in that field. Find somebody who's done what you want to do, and learn from them because they can teach you a lot.

## ANXIETY-RELIEF TECHNIQUES

**CO:** One of the worst points in my life was when a second divorce was happening in my family. My step dad left us in a matter of four hours.

He just told us he was leaving. I was a sophomore in high school, and I was confused. I felt like it was my fault. To cope, I jumped into my art.

Whatever you're passionate about, jump right into it, and go all in. It's a good outlet for anxiety. I would sit there and paint for eight hours, and I wouldn't even realize it. It was something that helped me.

## IF YOU'RE ANXIOUS, ZOOM OUT

**CO:** If there is a situation giving me a lot of anxiety, I think of it like Google Maps. You can pinch the whole location and zoom out to see the whole world. I think about my anxiety like that. Here's my tiny little issue, and here's the rest of the world. My tiny little issue isn't the end of the world. Sometimes you must zoom out and realize there's a bigger perspective and meaning as to why you're going through this.

## OVERCOMING SUICIDAL THOUGHTS

**CO:** I've never had a lot of friends. Even in high school, I was always the oddball out. My suicidal thoughts and depression came from that, feeling like I was unwanted.

At age fourteen or fifteen, I had suicidal thoughts and thoughts about self-harm. I became addicted to self-harm. I got to a point where I told myself, "I'm done with this. I can't live my life with this weight on my shoulders." I Googled "how to not be depressed." I read other people's stories, and I started recognizing what I'm grateful for and recognizing what's going good in my life instead of focusing on what's bad. It changed my perspective, and that helped me get out of it.

**SS:** What would you tell a fifteen-year-old who is doing self-harm?

**CO:** I would say that nothing is worth hurting yourself for. At the end of the day, you are what you've got, and you are on this planet for a reason. You are perfect exactly how you are. Life is hard sometimes. It's easy to fall into negative self-talk. You don't deserve that. Find a positive outlet that makes something beautiful instead of self-harm, which leaves scars.

## OVERCOMING CONFIDENCE ISSUES

**CO:** I'm a huge theater nerd. I've done two Broadway shows. My proudest moment was going into theater and finding that other part of myself. It shaped me for who I am now.

Acting teaches you a lot about your emotions. It's about learning how to take your emotions and put that into a character. When I felt anxious, I would tell myself, "OK, Calah, let's turn off the inside and play the character."

**SS:** What other avenues have helped you overcome confidence issues?

**CO:** I had a little, wild moment of my life where I dyed my hair crazy colors and dressed however I wanted. That taught me not to care about what anybody else says. It was about trying new things. I shaved half my head, I dyed my hair rainbow colors, and dressed weird for a couple of months. That built my confidence because I thought it looked cool. If nobody else thinks it looks cool, that's fine. I'm happy, and that's all that matters.

## FIND WHAT MAKES YOU HAPPY

**CO:** Find something that you love. Explore new things if you haven't found what you love, such as art, computers, video, film, or theater. Then go all in on it. For me it was painting a bunch of canvases. It will guide your emotions, which is powerful. Finding something you are passionate about sets a fire inside. Do what you love, and do it more often. Create a routine around it.

It may seem like it's out of reach, but it's right around the corner. Just keep reaching. Eventually, everything will fall into place.

I'm a firm believer in listening to your gut. If you have a gut feeling about liking something, go for it. No one's stopping you except you.

## TOP TAKEAWAYS:

- Turn your passion into a living.
- Everyone is a work in progress.
- Attack fear head on.
- Nothing is worth hurting yourself for.
- Reading will improve your life.
- *When you are facing an issue, zoom out of the problem to put it into perspective.*
- Don't worry about what other people think of you.
- Find what makes you happy.
- If you haven't found what you love, explore new things.

# 18

# FROM COLLEGE GRADUATE AT SIXTEEN TO ENTREPRENEUR WITH A PERSONAL BRAND

*AMARA LEGGETT*

Amara Leggett, a.k.a. A Young Legend, transformed from experiencing criticism in middle school to blossoming into a teenage author, speaker, and two-time business owner. By age sixteen, she completed an associate of science degree and a high school diploma. During that time she also launched her own business, A Young Legend, through which she shared her educational and business experiences by blogging. In addition to sharing her journey through dual enrollment, Amara has delivered a TEDx Talk called "How to Develop a Plan and Make the Impossible Possible," reaching over 10,000 viewers and counting. She also authored *The Strategic Mind of A Young Legend*, all before reaching adulthood. After walking across the stage to receive her college degree, she built an outstanding personal brand and executed a New York City corporate speaking engagement within the first year. Today she is the CEO of the Dual Enrollment Co., offering education consulting services for students and parents navigating dual enrollment. She expects to complete a bachelor's degree in computer science in 2020.

**CONNECT:**

- Websites: www.ayounglegend.com and www.dualenrollment.co

## STRUGGLES INCLUDED IN THIS CHAPTER:

- Bullying
- Difficulty developing meaningful, like-minded friendships
- Living a life without distractions (e.g., social media)

## HER BULLYING STORY

**Amara Leggett:** I was judged for not owning the right pair of shoes or the latest iPhone, but I turned that negative energy into hyper-focusing on my education and diving into the world of business.

People would criticize me for the silliest things. Reflecting back, now that I am able to obtain those material items, I still don't desire them. Of course, I didn't understand this in eighth grade, but my purpose then and now is to build a legacy. Beyond this battle with materialism, I chose not to follow the social media trend, noticing how people were being attacked on such platforms.

When I speak to youth, I mention how it's great to have nice shoes but not if you can't afford a closet to house them. It's paramount that you think about what's really important to you.

## DISCOVERING HER LOVE FOR BUSINESS

**AL:** I fell in love with the idea of business and building a legacy at age thirteen. I began to understand the business mindset and the need to build for the future. As others were spending money on shoes, standing in long lines waiting to buy the latest phones, or waiting desperately to receive the most recent iPhone updates, I preferred to focus on my love for school and was excited to launch an early career.

I became obsessed with learning business, so much so that I modeled my end-of-year presentation on how to start a business. I dedicated the next two years to searching for my next business idea, one that was within my budget and focused on an extremely underserved subject.

## THE PURSUIT OF DUAL ENROLLMENT

**AL:** Dual enrollment is a national program that allows students to be enrolled in two institutions simultaneously. The most common scenarios are to be enrolled in middle school and college or high school and college.

Dual enrollment already existed in my state under the name Postsecondary Enrollment Options (PSEO), but college courses were only available to eleventh and twelfth-grade students. In 2014, Ohio released the new and improved College Credit Plus to provide students as young as those in grade seven with a free college education by receiving dual credit. I entered high school with seven completed high school credits, leaving room in my schedule to try college courses during my freshman year. Each semester for the next two years, I increased the number of college classes by utilizing the maximum amount of dual credit allowed. I saved $20,000 by graduating from a local community college in December 2017.

When students first join dual enrollment, they will probably go to their school for most of the day until their scheduled college class occurs. Once they transition to full-time college, at that point they will receive majority dual credit until they graduate.

## GRADUATING EARLY FROM HIGH SCHOOL

**AL:** If you would like to go through the dual enrollment program, I suggest identifying your goals, such as graduating with a bachelor's degree by age eighteen, participating in college sports, or receiving a tecāical degree through a community college.

Financially, if you will need to rely on full financial aid to attend college, I highly recommend considering dual enrollment. Student debt can delay future endeavors, such as buying a house, investing, and saving early for retirement. One college credit taken or one dollar saved is better than nothing at all.

## TIME MANAGEMENT AS A STUDENT AND AS AN ENTREPRENEUR

**AL:** I currently manage an internship, attend school full-time, and run two businesses. Time management is key when balancing work that continues for long periods of time.

If I'm at school and have a bit of time to respond to emails and book appointments, I take it. After work, I may do a podcast interview or write a new blog post. Find what you love in everything you do to keep you motivated.

Make strategic goals. If you have made plans to dedicate five hours on Saturday to your business and spend the rest of the day with your family, block it off on your calendar, and maximize productivity in the time that you do have.

## BEST ADVICE

**AL:** The best piece of advice I received was "Imagine how you will feel after you've done that frightening thing. You're here for them." This was shared with me by Julie Wilkes before I went on stage to deliver my TEDx Talk.

That is a powerful piece of advice for any entrepreneur. Your purpose is to provide others with value. Any time I lack the motivation to do work in my businesses, I am reminded by an email or a direct message on social media from people who are checking to see if I am OK because they noticed I have not been active. If that isn't a sign, I don't know what is.

## BUILDING A NETWORK THAT MAKES MONEY

**AL:** My favorite activity is to attend networking events. One summer I attended three to five networking events a week for approximately five months. Between my LinkedIn strategy and my growing contact list, the influence of the people I was meeting continued to grow.

By nurturing relationships and showing up in my community, I began to monetize it with book sales and speaking engagements. Now I am recognized for the brand that I have built at such a young age. My brand has brought me several jobs and other opportunities.

## THREE STEPS TO A SUCCESSFUL PLAN

**AL:** First, look twenty years into the future, and then work backward from there. Set a goal so big that you can't achieve it until you've grown into the person who can.

Second, you don't have to be great to start, but you do have to start to be great.

Third, figure out the best way to achieve your dreams. When things get tough, rejection tests whether or not you are serious. Failure is nothing but a lesson to be learned.

## TOP TAKEAWAYS:

- Start your personal brand to attract the opportunities you want.
- Dual enrollment allows you to start and finish college early while saving money on college tuition.
- If you enjoy what you're doing, it will not feel like work.
- *Age is nothing but a number.*
- Don't underestimate the value of your network and how you can leverage it to build your net worth.
- Look twenty years into the future, and work backward from there.
- You don't have to be great to start, but you must start to be great.
- Rejection tests whether you're serious about your dreams.

# 19
# WHY YOU SHOULD STOP MAKING EXCUSES TO ACHIEVE YOUR DREAMS
## *TEMI JOHNSON*

Temi Johnson started inspiring his friends and family at nine years of age. He wants to speak on the big stage one day. It hasn't been easy for him. Temi lives in a developing country, Nigeria. At one point, his friends stopped talking to him and told him he was too young to be a motivational speaker. In the beginning, his dad didn't support him either. Discover the mindset this young man has and how he is achieving his dreams despite these challenges. He doesn't make any excuses, and neither should you!

## CONNECT:
- Instagram: @Tojtek_Media

## STRUGGLES INCLUDED IN THIS CHAPTER:
- Family put too much pressure on him
- He didn't like his friends
- The challenges of living in a developing country

### HOW HE STARTED INSPIRING PEOPLE
**Temi Joāson:** It started when I was in the fourth grade. I would inspire my friends and teach them a lot about life and entrepreneurship. We'd speak almost every day after school. I'd talk to them and help them. I'd teach them that their bad grades wouldn't determine where they went in life. I also taught them not to be lazy. I taught them that they couldn't be perfect all the time. I also taught them that failure is where you will find suc-

cess. Success doesn't come easily. It comes through tough times, through life's battles. Only by moving through failure will you find true success. Those are some of the messages I taught to my friends at school.

Some of them started their own businesses. Some of them moved on well in life, but after sixth grade, we parted ways. I would also inspire my family. I'd tell them what books to read and the messages in them.

In grade seven, I decided to share my message on Instagram. I posted my first motivational video. I wasn't getting likes, and I had less than two hundred followers, but I continued giving out content, and then my followers grew from zero to where it is today.

## HIS CRITICS

**TJ:** Everything good has its critics. Some of my friends would tell me that I couldn't do it and called me stupid. When I was in grade five, I don't know why, but everyone decided not to talk to me for a week. It didn't get to me because I had my family, and I occupied myself with the book I was reading. I listened to and ignored the hate at the same time.

## LESSONS HE LEARNED FROM BOOKS

**TJ:** One of the lessons I learned from books was that sometimes we set goals that are too small. I learned that success is your duty. It's not something you should be forced to get; it is something that you should feel obliged to get. Another thing I learned is to think big and that it doesn't matter what situation you are in. Your situation should never determine your future destination. Finally, I learned that everything that happens on the outside happens on the inside first.

## STRUGGLES IN A THIRD-WORLD COUNTRY

**TJ:** We face many challenging situations in my country. For example, we have terrorists, and the economy is bad. Lots of basic things are hard. I've learned that I shouldn't always look at the bad things that happen around me, I should look at the good things as well. A lot of people look down on me because I live in a developing country. You must push through those things.

**SS:** Even for this interview, we had a hard time connecting. You had power outages two days in a row. You kept on trying, and that didn't stop you. Other kids in developing countries want to make a difference, just like you. What would you tell them about how to start?

**TJ:** I'd tell them to just do it. It might seem hard at the beginning, and it will never be easy. If you are persistent, you'll find that things get easier as you continue your journey. You will also get a lot of support along the way.

## USING NEWTON'S THIRD LAW FOR YOUR LIFE

**TJ:** For every action, there's an equal and opposite reaction. I always say that if you don't take action, there will be no reaction that will boost you in whatever you're doing. The belief, the time, and the effort that you put into something will always create an equal and opposite reaction. The reaction will be success or failure depending on your action.

**SS:** Can you give an example from your own life?

**TJ:** When I started my podcast, I noticed that I always sent one email, and the person didn't reply. I realized that the more energy I put into it, the more energy I would get out of my podcast. I started sending twenty emails and got more replies.

## OVERCOMING THE PRESSURE FROM FAMILY

**TJ:** My mom always supports me in what I'm doing. My dad wants me to have the best grades. I do my best in school, and I get good grades, but he wants me to put all of my time and energy into education. He doesn't support my podcast. He wants me to get good grades, graduate, and get a job. I want to get good grades, but I don't want to go through the route everyone else takes because people who succeed take the road less traveled.

**SS:** A lot of kids don't have parental support. They have their side hustle and school. How do you get around that?

**TJ:** The best thing is not convincing them but showing them. My dad is noticing that I'm picking up. For example, Omar the Rockstar is a big entrepreneur. I worked so hard to contact him. One day I got on live on Instagram, and he gave me a challenge that if I uploaded for thirty days straight on YouTube, he'd give me a certain amount of money. My dad is seeing that I'm gaining traction because some big people are following me. He has seen me appearing on people's shows. He's starting to support me a little. I'm still not there yet, but I'm getting there.

## JUST DO IT

**TJ:** The best thing is to "just do it." Belief is the number one thing. Believe in whatever you're doing. Never struggle for good enough; struggle for greatness. Even if it means going to sleep two hours later than your normal time, do it. Even if it requires you to save up a lot of money, do it. Even if it means a sleepless night, do it. Do whatever you know you can do, and remember that success is never easy.

Whenever you experience failure, remember that failure is finding another way of getting there. There's something I shared on my Instagram page. I said, "Whenever things are not going right, remember before an arrow launches and goes far, it was first pulled back." You might be in the stage where your arrow is still pulling back before it's ready to be launched.

## TOP TAKEAWAYS:

- It's OK to start small.
- Listen to and ignore the hate at the same time.
- Think big.
- Success is your duty.
- When you're persistent, you'll find it easier to get through the journey.
- For every action, there's an equal and opposite reaction.
- *Don't convince your parents about your side hustle; show them.*
- Just do it.
- Struggle to be great, not good enough.
- Failure is finding another way of doing things.

# 20
# HOW TO KEEP GOING WHEN LIFE GETS TOUGH
## *CEDRIC SPAHR*

Cedric Spahr was born in Germany. He and his parents booked a flight to move to the United States, but his mom didn't board. That left his dad, an alcoholic, to raise Cedric on his own. Cedric was suicidal at six years old. Fast-forward to now. He is in college and built a TikTok brand that got over 250,000 followers in nine days. He uses it to provide mental health and relationship tips. His mission is to inspire others to overcome the kinds of struggles that he faced when he was younger.

**CONNECT:**
- TikTok: @PsychologyIsBae

**STRUGGLES INCLUDED IN THIS CHAPTER:**
- Anxiety
- Social anxiety
- Depression
- Parents' divorce
- Poverty
- Wanted to commit suicide
- Came from another country
- Felt inferior
- Skinniest kid in class
- Bullied
- Always stressed
- Parents never around

## FROM GERMANY TO THE UNITED STATES

**Cedric Spahr:** I was born in Germany, where my dad was stationed with the army for over a decade. He met my mom there, and then they had me. When he finished his contract in Germany, I was six years old. We planned on moving back to the United States. We packed our bags and went through the security check. When we went to board the plane, my dad walked on first, and I walked on behind him. When I turned around to see where my mom was, she was walking away. That's the last time that I saw her for a while. I was confused, I didn't understand what was going on. When I sat down, I asked my dad where my mom went. He told me that she probably wasn't coming with us. I was really confused.

She stayed in Germany, so it was just my dad and me. He became a heavy alcoholic, and we didn't have any money. In school I got bullied because I couldn't speak English, I didn't have money, and I was skinny.

On the first day of first grade, I had an accident on the floor because I didn't know how to ask to go to the bathroom. The kids who I went to school with had both parents, they had decent money, and I was the outcast. That followed all the way up through high school.

**SS:** What did you tell your dad?

**CS:** I told him that I was getting bullied, but he didn't care because he was always drunk. We never had a connection. I was by myself.

## YOU ARE ON EARTH FOR A REASON

**CS:** When we were still in Germany, my dad told me, "You were put on this earth for a reason. You might not know what that reason is right now, but you have a purpose." That stuck with me. Every time I had a suicidal thought, I told myself "This is temporary. We'll get through it day by day. I can't wait until I'm older." That's how I got through my problems. That and the help of my grandma, who would come to visit every once in a while.

**SS:** Did you eventually find a support system?

**CS:** I eventually made some friends toward the end of first grade. I'm still friends with one of them. He's my best friend, and he helped me out. I would go to his house a lot and ended up staying with him because my dad was always drunk. My friend and his parents were my support system. They made me feel like I had a purpose and that I was worth something, whereas my own family didn't. I also wrote and played a lot of music. That was my positive outlet.

## STARTING HIS TIKTOK AROUND MENTAL HEALTH

**CS:** I made my TikTok brand around mental health because I enjoy studying psychology. It helps me understand how our minds work. If you can find out what triggers you, you can use that to your advantage. Then you can learn more about yourself and how to handle situations differently. At the end of the day, we want to be loved and accepted for who we are. The reason behind the page was to be relatable and let people know they're not alone in their fight. Psychology is a big part of that, and that's why I started the page.

## FAVORITE TIP CEDRIC POSTED ON TIKTOK

**CS:** My biggest tip would be accepting people for who they are. We all have our own backgrounds, struggles, and insecurities. We should love each other for our uniqueness.

## A LIGHT AT THE END OF THE TUNNEL

**CS:** There's a light at the end of the tunnel. My youth pastor always told me that God gives his strongest soldiers the hardest battles. There's a reason you're going through it, and it's going to make you stronger. You're going to be able to look back and laugh at some things that have happened. Then you will be able to teach others. These struggles are going to make you a better person and make you grow up faster.

## YOU CAN GET THROUGH ANYTHING

**CS:** I had a huge mental shift during my freshman year in high school.

I used to play basketball in high school. This one kid and I were competing for the same position. His dad was the coach. The kid would push me, punch me, and bully me in the locker room, so that when we had practice, I wouldn't do well. I'd be benched.

I started taking karate. Martial arts involve a lot of emotional awareness, mental development, meditation, and peace. The instructor got my mind in the right place. He was a good father figure for a while. I did that for three years.

**SS:** What lessons did he teach you?

**CS:** He taught me that people with the biggest insecurities are the ones who make others feel bad. The ones who are jealous of you or envy you are the ones who try to hurt you the most. No matter what happens, and no matter what they say, they're not going to break your spirit.

You can get through anything. The human body and the human mind

125

can get through tough situations that make us stronger. That's the biggest lesson he taught me: Stay strong, and you can get through anything.

## OVERCOMING SUICIDAL THOUGHTS

**CS:** I believed that God existed. I prayed a lot and felt like I shouldn't commit suicide. I had to put my hope and my pain somewhere. I told one of my best friends about my thoughts. He told me not to do it, and I ran with that. I had a dream that I was going to do great things one day, though I wasn't sure what those things were. I felt like God answered my prayers by sending me the friend who I met in elementary school because he always wanted to hang out after school. I told him that I was depressed, but he always wanted to be around me anyway. Everyone should find a friend like that, someone who will always make you feel wanted.

## GET OUT OF YOUR SHELL

**CS:** College breaks you out of your shell for the most part because you're forced to be around people who you don't know.

If college is not an option for you, break out of your shell some other way. Surround yourself with people who you don't know. It's so much better when you're out of your shell. You make friendships that you would have never made otherwise and have some awesome conversations.

## DON'T BEAT YOURSELF UP

**CS:** If you're scared of failure, you have social anxiety, and you hate when you embarrass yourself, don't beat yourself up over it. It's a waste of time to beat yourself up over something that happened in the past. If it's in the past, you can't change it. The only thing you can change is how you think about it and how you react to it. Learn from it. Life goes on. The only thing that's consistent in life is change. Things aren't always going to be how they are right now. Life might suck right now, but it won't suck forever. There's a light at the end of the tunnel. There always is, and there always will be.

## TOP TAKEAWAYS:

- Accept people for who they are.
- *There's a light at the end of the tunnel.*
- Struggles make us grow up faster.
- The people with the biggest insecurities are the ones who try to make other people feel bad.
- Don't commit suicide.

- Pray.
- Get out of your shell.
- Don't beat yourself up.

# 21

# HEALTHY HABITS YOU CAN FORM TO OVERCOME ANXIETY AND DEPRESSION

*MARK METRY*

Mark Metry is a twenty-two-year-old entrepreneur. He was raised in a small town where he was different than the other kids and got bullied because of it. He thought making a lot of money in high school would help him overcome his anxiety and depression, but it didn't. At age eighteen, he used to go on long walks in rough neighborhoods, hoping something would happen to him.

One night while he was walking, he felt like someone hugged him. As a result of that experience, he decided he wanted to overcome anxiety, depression, and obesity.

Now his podcast, *Human 2.0*, is ranked in the top one hundred podcasts on Apple, he was featured in *Forbes*, he has built a LinkedIn brand of over 70,000 followers, he was selected to be on an Amazon Prime TV show, and he is the author of *Screw Being Shy*.

Most importantly, he's at peace with himself. How did he overcome his challenges to become successful? He formed healthy habits.

## CONNECT:
- Website: www.markmetry.com
- LinkedIn: linkedin.com/in/mark-metry
- Instagram: @MarkMetry

## STRUGGLES INCLUDED IN THIS CHAPTER:
- Anxiety

- Social Anxiety
- Depression
- Low self-esteem
- Wanted to commit suicide
- Felt inferior
- Not good in school and felt dumb
- Worried too much about people's opinions of him
- Health issues
- Wanted to find new friends
- Felt like a failure
- Always got distracted
- Obesity

## HIS BULLYING STORY

**Mark Metry:** Growing up, I experienced my fair share of bullying and racism. People would say horrible things to me, steal my belongings, and write things on them. I felt alienated.

I also had some health issues. I had asthma, appendicitis, problems with my skin related to my sleep, problems with my gut, irritable bowel syndrome, and I could never focus. I became a super-withdrawn person and went into survival mode. Any room I'd walk into, I told myself, "Put your head down. Nobody wants to talk to you. Sit in the back of the class."

Bullying made me closed off from the world. I developed severe social anxiety and could never talk to people. I couldn't even be my true self around people who I liked. We create these fears that end up impacting us for the rest of our lives until we figure it out and start to attack them head on.

**SS:** How did you try to overcome bullying at a young age?

**MM:** The way I coped with it was by playing video games and being on the Internet. I would also code websites and code apps when the first iPhone came out. I did a ton of different projects, and I was learning.

## MAKING MORE MONEY AT A YOUNG AGE DIDN'T MAKE HIM FEEL BETTER

**MM:** I started a YouTube channel that had over 35,000 subscribers. Then I discovered this game called Minecraft. I started the world's number-one Minecraft server with over a million people on our website and tens of thousands of premium members. It became a six-figure business when I was only fifteen and sixteen.

I always thought that once I made money, my life would change, and I would be happy. When I made that money, I quickly realized that wasn't the case at all. I was still a loser. I still didn't have any self-esteem or self-confidence. I had made money, but my life didn't get better. That really confused me.

## HUMAN 2.0

**MM:** I didn't know what the words "anxiety" or "mental health" meant. I didn't know that you could change negative things in life.

I went off to college, and I had two different ideas in my head. I had this survivor's identity: "I'm a loser. I suck. I can't talk to people. There's nothing good about me, except for maybe the money." Then I had this other idea in my head: "Dude, you've done so many cool things in your life that most people wouldn't ever do." Based on that, I asked myself, "I wonder who I could be?" I realized the loser thought was wrong. I told myself I could do better.

I tried to drown my old negative voice out with video games, binging Netflix, and then binge eating food. I was over 220 pounds.

At that point I was isolating myself. I went from class to home and watched Netflix. It got to a point where I didn't know what to do. I'd go outside, and I'd take long walks at 2:00 a.m. because I didn't know how to stop the pain and all the negativity that was going on in my head.

I was living in Boston at that time. Boston is a great city, but it neighbors another city called Dorchester, which is a not so great place. It has a lot of gang violence and shootings. I told myself, "I'm going to start walking outside and just hope somebody kills me. I hope somebody ends my life. I don't know what's going on; all I know is that I want this to stop."

One night I think I had a divine spiritual intervention. I was out on one of those walks, and the streets were completely silent. Suddenly, in that silence, for the first time, I heard the real voice, the real Mark, the real me.

I don't know what it said, but it gave me hope and made me curious. It was a massive turning point for me. I felt relaxed. The way I describe it to people is it felt like somebody hugged me.

I think people try to commit suicide because they feel hopeless. They think that tomorrow will be no better than today. If you believe that, life will be tough.

Feeling hopeless is actually a good thing. It's your brain and body trying to update. Just like software and apps on our phone, there's a version 1.0, and there's a version 2.0. That's what your brain is trying to figure out what to do. You need to find healthy coping mechanisms besides playing video games, doing drugs, and watching TV all the time.

## TRANSFORMATION THROUGH NEW HABITS

**MM:** I started to shed weight right away. The weight is what I could see in physical reality. It started one day when I tried to put on my pants, and they didn't fit; they were too tight.

I began to tackle that one thing. I went on the Internet and researched how to lose weight. I stumbled across real science that shows how you can lose weight based on what you eat. For the first time in my life I began to eat a natural diet of vegetables, fruits, nuts, seeds, and animal fats. That gave me so much energy. I felt like my brain turned on for the first time, and I lost all the weight.

I started running and hitting the gym. Then I started resting more, getting seven to eight hours of sleep per night. Once I started implementing everything daily, my physiology started to change, and I gained more energy.

Then I asked myself, "What else can I do?" I started to read a book for the first time in my life. That was when I was around eighteen or nineteen years old. Then I started applying mindfulness tecāiques and journaling.

## HOW YOU CAN TRANSFORM INTO YOUR 2.0

**MM:** Your human 2.0 is the second version of yourself. For me it was when I started to lose weight. For you it can be volunteering at a homeless shelter or traveling to an extreme area. Don't think about yourself; go see the struggles in humanity. If you can't go volunteer at a homeless shelter, volunteer at a retirement home, where you'll see eighty-year-olds who have dementia and don't know their family's names. You'll start asking yourself, "What am I really afraid of? Why should I care about what this person thinks? When I'm on my deathbed, will this really matter?"

I'm a big proponent of self-care, doing things for yourself. But if you spend too much time focusing on yourself, you're always going to find problems. Honestly, sometimes it's best not to think about yourself a lot and try to help other people instead. In that, you'll discover who you are.

Gandhi has a great quote about this. It says, "Lose yourself in the service of others." When you begin to see that, you begin to realize that they're going to end up giving you power. You start the cycle of trying to do better because you want to do better for those other people.

I also think there's a deeper part of it. Whether you believe in God or are spiritual in some way, you have a relationship that's much deeper than every single person.

## HEALING HIS HEALTH PROBLEMS

**MM:** I was never diagnosed with a learning disability, but I felt like it had one. When I stepped into class, I couldn't focus or remember anything. When a teacher called me out, it wasn't because I was busy. I just didn't know how to think about it.

I had a lot of health issues, including asthma and irritable bowel syndrome. I started to live a healthier lifestyle, and then I went back to my doctors. They ran tests, and they told me that everything I had was gone. I don't take any kind of medicine; it healed holistically on its own.

If you look at the gut microbiome, we have millions of bacteria, fungi, mold, and yeasts living inside of us. They have developed through a symbiotic relationship for millions of years. If you look at a human cell, you are looking at an animal cell. Mitochondria is an ancient bacteria that formed a symbiosis with the human cell. We not only have these bacteria in our stomach and our intestines that help us digest our food, we also have them in every single cell. What does mitochondria control? Energy. Mitochondria is the powerhouse of the cell.

Your body can fall into a state of dysbiosis, which means your gut microbiome is unbalanced, and it's not working correctly. This can be caused by a variety of reasons: trauma, stress, eating the wrong kinds of foods, not sleeping, or not moving your body the way that we were created to move. It can cause stomach issues. The biggest gateway drug to anxiety is simple sugars. Artificial chemicals and artificial ingredients can also destroy your microbiome.

You can get your gut tested. A friend of mine started this company where he licensed tecāology from the US government that is the world's only functional gut microbiome test, called Viome. It will tell you what kind of foods you are allergic to. Anxiety and depression can be a symptom of you eating the wrong kinds of food.

The number-one thing that you have leverage over in your life is the food you eat. Eat healthier, and watch what happens. Your energy level will go up. Find a diet that works for you, not one based on what you heard works for someone else.

## LITTLE BY LITTLE

**MM:** Life is a game. In a game, you don't play to get past level one or level two. You play to get past all the levels and win. In life, the game never ends. Once you understand that, you stop looking for these short-sighted ways to think about life because you'll never accomplish anything that way.

Ask yourself the following questions: What can I do a little bit every day to try to get a bit better? Who can I talk to? How can I learn this? What can I do to get more curious about this? If I'm going to sleep, how can I make sure I sleep to the best of my ability? I'm going to sleep seven and eight hours. If I'm going to eat or drink, I'm going to make sure everything that goes into my mouth is something that makes me strong, not the reverse.

Make sure you move too. We weren't designed to sit inside all day on our laptops. Moving on a regular basis is part of life.

Your breath is what stays with you from the moment you're born until the moment you die. When you breathe, focus on your breath, and control it. Many of us don't even think about our breath. Breathing can be conscious. As soon as you remember that you have a breath and start focusing on it, you'll be calmer. Many breathing exercises and tecāiques can help you with this.

If you're socially anxious, do exposure therapy. Work your way up to talking to people. Start by going on the street and asking a stranger for directions or ask for the time. You can begin to do these things to slowly be able to talk to people.

## TOP TAKEAWAYS:

- More money will not make you happier.
- Feeling hopeless is actually a good thing. It is your brain and body trying to update.
- Find healthy coping mechanisms to get over your struggle.
- Regular exercise can change your physiology.
- *When you lose yourself through the service of others, you gain power and a deeper meaning for your life.*
- Develop a sense of spirituality.
- Get your gut tested to see which foods you are allergic to.
- Take little steps to improve your life.
- Focus on your breathing and control it.

# 22
# HOW TO OVERCOME SELF-HARM AND DEPRESSION
## *NYAH JONES*

Nyah Jones is a TikTok Influencer with over 800,000 followers who shares tips on how to overcome mental health struggles. She wants to share positivity because she struggled with anxiety, depression, and self-harm throughout high school. She ended up in the hospital with conversion disorder, which forced her to recognize that she couldn't beat this on her own. She eventually went to therapy, where she started the healing process.

## CONNECT:
- TikTok: @NyahJones_
- Instagram: @NyahJones_
- Twitter: @NyahJoness

## STRUGGLES INCLUDED IN THIS CHAPTER:
- Anxiety
- Depression
- Wanted to commit suicide
- Hid her emotions
- Always stressed
- Self-harm
- Hospitalized for conversion disorder

## ADMITTED TO THE HOSPITAL FOR CONVERSION DISORDER

**Nyah Jones:** Conversion disorder is when your mental health starts to affect your physical health. It can affect you in different ways. Sometimes, it can take your sight or your hearing. My anxiety got so bad, and I wasn't doing anything to cope with it. I was bottling it up, and I wasn't talking to anyone about it. I woke up one morning and felt weak in my legs. My mom was really scared. We went to the doctor, and they couldn't find anything wrong with me, so we decided to go home and wait it out. It kept getting worse to the point where I couldn't walk. We went to the emergency room four times in one week because I was pretty much paralyzed from the waist down. I didn't have much feeling, and I didn't have reflexes, but every time we went to the emergency room, they couldn't find anything wrong with me. With conversion disorder, you have symptoms, but all your tests come back negative, like there's nothing physically wrong with you.

After my fourth trip to the ER, they decided to admit me to the hospital. They said it was conversion disorder because none of the tests were coming back positive. I went through hours of physical and occupational therapy every day. I was against talk therapy at first, but I forced my way through a few sessions. They released me in a week. I got my strength back in my legs. Everyone heals at a different time.

## OPENING UP WILL MAKE YOU STRONGER

**NJ:** I have never been one to show my emotions, I've always been the one with a smile on my face, a happy kid. I never cried. I bottled everything up so tight.

My mom pushed me to deal with it. I was diagnosed with anxiety because I was having panic attacks, which were difficult, but I got through them. One day I was at the doctor's office. She was going over symptoms of depression when my mom asked, "Do you think you could have depression?"

"No way," I replied. "I'm always happy."

My mom talked to me about it in the car later and said it runs in our family and that it goes hand in hand with anxiety. It took me forever to admit that I might have depression too, but I eventually accepted it. I broke down, and my mom signed me up for therapy.

It was rough at first. I didn't want to go because I don't like talking about my feelings. I was forced into a couple of sessions. My mom had to trick me into going to my first session. I thought we were going to the grocery store. When we pulled up at the therapist's office, I was not happy. It's good that I went though because that's when I started facing my challenges.

The moment you open up and admit how you're feeling, it gets better. If I never broke down to my mom, I would still be crying by myself in my room. You're not a burden for talking about how you feel and getting help

136

for it. It's OK to put yourself first. I think you're stronger for opening up about something. Fight it, and work to heal yourself. Taking the initiative to get better is the bravest thing you can do.

## OVERCOMING SELF-HARM

**NJ:** I used the blade from a pencil sharpener to cut myself. I started before I was in the hospital. I kept it to one spot, very hidden, so no one could tell, and I would do it in the shower, which was easy. I kept it a secret for a long time.

My parents started asking me about my mental health, but I would dismiss it. One night my mom asked me if I was self-harming, and I couldn't answer because I was crying too hard. After that, she assumed I was. She would check on me every now and then. I would feel ashamed if I had fresh cuts.

My parents did everything to help me overcome it. My mom did all kinds of research on alternative methods to self-harm, and I started using some of them. Eventually, I felt the need to do it less. It felt impossible to stop, but then I started doing some of the alternative methods, and eventually, I weaned off it.

**SS:** What caused you to do it?

**NJ:** I think I felt numb. People think depression is all sadness, but I would lie on my bedroom floor staring at the ceiling for hours, and I couldn't feel anything. Feeling the blade on my skin and seeing the blood flow was an easy way to feel pain. At least I could feel something.

The best alternative is to talk to someone, which is way harder than it sounds. If you have one person you can go to instead of picking up the blade, it makes a world of a difference. There are also alternative methods. You can rub an ice cube on the spot where you are cutting or color that spot with a pen. I wrote out my feelings to make me feel better. Every now and then when my feelings are spiraling down, I write in my journal and look back at it and appreciate how far I've come. I write when I'm sad, so I can appreciate it when I'm happy.

I would also look up quotes on Pinterest and write them down because it got my thoughts focused on other things.

## HER GOALS WITH HER TIKTOK ACCOUNT

**NJ:** My old TikTok videos are cringeworthy. I started doing the trends, and it felt good when someone followed me. I posted more and more. I got featured a couple of times when the app was called musical.ly, and I started to grow my base. When I transitioned into TikTok and got verified, I realized I had 100,000 people following me. I decided I could make videos for people who are struggling with mental health. I wanted to make them feel like they were not alone. I started advocating for mental health after I was getting over my struggles. I would post videos saying, "If I can get through it, then you can get through it. You're not the only one who feels this way. There's still hope to be found."

I want to transfer my following on TikTok onto other social media apps to have more presence. If my messages can reach one person who needs them, I feel accomplished. I recommend sharing your story because you never know whose life it can impact.

## FACING MENTAL HEALTH CHALLENGES WITH UNSUP-PORTIVE PARENTS

**NJ:** If you go to school, a guidance counselor is someone to talk to. You can also talk to your best friend, your best friend's parents, or any adult who you trust, as long as you're getting your feelings out. If you bottle them up, it's just going to get worse.

I even talk to my cat sometimes. Also, find some positive outlet. Painting and journaling are positive outlets for me. I also look at poetry books to lift my mood or watch my favorite cartoon shows.

## WHAT TO DO IF SOMEONE OPENS UP TO YOU

**NJ:** If someone trusts you enough to open up to you about their problems, don't dismiss them. Don't say, "Oh, it's OK. Other people have it worse." If you don't know what to say, just be there, and listen to them. Checking on people makes so much more of a difference than you can imagine because you never know what people are going through. Everyone's fighting their own invisible battles. If you're a jerk to everyone, you could be pushing someone closer to the edge without realizing it.

## TOP TAKEAWAYS:
- Opening up makes you stronger.
- A couple of alternatives to self-harming are rubbing ice on the spot where you normally harm yourself or coloring it with a pen.
- Journaling is a good way to see how far you've come.
- Go to your guidance counselor if you don't have supportive parents.
- Find a positive outlet.
- Looking up positive quotes can help you feel better.
- *Even if your message can impact one person, you should feel accomplished.*

- Don't dismiss someone who trusts you enough to open up to you.
- Don't tell someone who's telling you about their problems, "Oh it's OK. Other people have it worse."
- Be nice to everyone. If you're a jerk, you could be pushing someone closer to the edge without realizing it.

# 23
# HOW TO DEAL WITH CHANGING SCHOOLS AND HOUSEHOLDS

## *ANTHONY BERTONCIN*

Anthony Bertoncin is a TikTok Influencer with over one million followers and the host of the *Fitness Enlightenment* podcast. His parents got divorced when he was a toddler, and he was constantly switching between households, which also forced him to change schools. He never found any friends who had the same interests as him, and he got bullied for being skinny. Now his primary mission is to inspire people.

## CONNECT:
- TikTok: @Bertoncin
- Instagram: @AnthonyBertoncin

## STRUGGLES INCLUDED IN THIS CHAPTER:
- Low self-esteem
- Bullied
- Problems developing meaningful and like-minded friendships
- Parents got divorced
- Constantly switching schools and states
- Skinniest kid in class
- Hated being alone
- Worried too much about people's opinions

## SCHOOL TO SCHOOL, HOUSEHOLD TO HOUSEHOLD

**Anthony Bertoncin:** My parents got divorced when I was about three years old. That's not the most ideal situation. Growing up, I had two

Christmases, two birthdays, and a bunch of different holidays at different households. On top of that, my parents often switched houses. I think I moved twelve or thirteen times before high school, switching houses and switching states between Kansas and Missouri. With the moves came switching schools. I struggled to maintain the same friend groups.

I felt lonely a lot of the time. I got into videography, photography, and entrepreneurship. Every time I switched schools, I'd try to find people who had similar interests, but I didn't find many people who were into chasing their dreams and entrepreneurship.

## HARD FOR PEOPLE TO ACCEPT HIM

**AB:** Finding people to relate to was hard. In high school, bullying became a factor, mainly because I was skinnier than everyone else. I wanted to play football and get into different friend groups. People always asked me, "What are you interested in doing in the future? What are your hobbies?"

"I want to travel for a living making videos," I'd say. "I want to drive fast cars, be able to provide for my family, buy my mom a house in Italy." They would look at me funny. We are taught to believe we should go to school, go to college, and get a job. It was hard for other people to accept my vision.

## FINDING FRIEND GROUPS WITH THE SAME VISION

**AB:** When I was eighteen, I found a group of friends who had entrepreneurial dreams. I also found out about a news and media company and started talking to them over Instagram. Direct messaging is how we met originally, mainly because I was doing personal training with someone from the team. That person was doing a lot of my workout plans.

**SS:** What would you tell people who are stuck with friends and classmates in high school who don't support what they're doing?

**AB:** Pursue your passions. I know a lot of people (me, specifically) who changed passions a lot. I wanted to be in the NBA and the NFL. For those of you in middle school and high school, do what makes you happy outside of school, and use whatever free time you have to pursue that passion. If you can't find friends in your hometown, clubs, or school, I recommend social media. When I began college, I couldn't find anybody I could relate to. Nobody was into the same stuff as me. So, I started making friends online from all over the place. I was Facetiming all my entrepreneur, videographer, and photographer friends when I was working at home. If you can't find friends in your city, find a supportive community online. Facebook groups, Instagram groups, and DMing people is the best way. Provide free value to people. That's what I did, and that's how I got in with a lot of my entrepreneurial friends. If you DM somebody popular, most of the time they won't respond. But if you provide something of value for free, it's a good way to get in contact with the people who you want to be around.

## ADVICE IF YOU'RE BEING BULLIED

**AB:** I always tell my followers and people in my livestreams that communication is key if you are being bullied. People often tell me, "My bully is going to threaten me or hurt me if I tell somebody what's happening." But you must tell people, so they can protect you from that. Tell your friends, tell your teachers, tell your parents, and tell your friends' parents. If people don't know about it, it's not going to stop. It won't stop until you take action to make it stop. I know what it's like, and it's not fun.

## LEARNING SELF-DISCIPLINE

**AB:** The biggest lesson I've learned with fitness is self-discipline. In my second or third year of working out, I started a program called summer shredding. I put my body to the test for ninety days. I committed to working out every day, dieting, and doing a physique show. It was the first time I dedicated myself like that. For ninety days I hung up fitness posters. I wanted to make it on one of the calendars. I committed ninety days to getting super shredded, big, and dieting. I was constantly telling myself I could commit myself for ninety days. Now I use that in different aspects of my life, like if I want to grow this business, if I want to network with people, or if I want to grow my audience on social media. I can do it if I take the time and make it happen.

**SS:** How can someone in high school use discipline?

**AB:** It's good to establish discipline early. Set up routines, especially if you're playing sports. I know a lot of people who had to go to practice, go home, get homework done, eat healthy, and do other things. Learning discipline at a young age is super beneficial because you'll use it throughout your life. As a sixteen-year-old, figure out what you're passionate about, and chase your dreams. You may not have stuff figured out at age sixteen, and that's OK. Pursue whatever interests you. Put your hands in a bunch of different things to see what intrigues you. When you're young, you have a lot of time to experiment. Establishing discipline will benefit you in the long run when pursuing your passion.

## YOUR VALUES AND MORALS MUST ALIGN

**AB:** Many people don't even know what their morals and values are

143

because they don't take the time to analyze them, write them down, and keep track of them. I was one of those people. "If you change your morals, you change your values, you change your life." That's from Tony Robbins' book, *Awaken the Giant Within*. Earlier this year I let go of my morals and values. They got completely out of line. With all the people I was around, money was a major priority for me. I had so many friends my age and younger who were making six or seven figures. I felt like I was behind because I wasn't at that point yet. I was comparing myself to something that I didn't deserve to be at yet. I was impatient.

I was doing everything for the money. I got involved with things that weren't me, including cannabis and CBD. I was shooting videos and photos that I normally wouldn't shoot. I became somebody else. That all ended when I got drugged by a bunch of people who I trusted. I was almost hospitalized that night. It was the first time I genuinely thought I may die. That reestablished me and helped me find God again. I realigned my morals and values. That's when I realized that money was not my priority. Everything I do now is to provide value to others, myself, and my family. Take time, Google, and watch YouTube videos on how to write out your morals and values. If you change your morals, your values will change, and so will your life.

Right now, my religion, family, and my passion are my top three values.

## WHAT CAN YOU DO IF YOU'RE GOING HOUSE TO HOUSE, SCHOOL TO SCHOOL?

**AB:** Communicate. If you're angry or frustrated, communicate to the person who made you feel that way. A lot of kids witness their parents getting divorced. When those children grow up, they might divorce their partner. So many people are going through the same situation as you, if not a thousand times worse. Maybe your dad passed away. Maybe your dad is in the military and got shipped to Afghanistan. Maybe your parents got divorced, and you haven't seen your dad for six years. There are so many situations that can be ten times worse. Communicate with a parent, a counselor, friends, or talk to people at your school. I guarantee that someone else is going through a similar situation. Talk to that person, talk about your feelings, get advice from them, and get advice from other people. Tons of resources are available. Afterwards, it's going to pay off, not only for that situation but for the rest of your life.

## TOP TAKEAWAYS:

- Focus on your passion.
- Find friends who share your passion. If you can't find them at

school, try social media.
- *Tell your friends and family members if you are being bullied.*
- Discipline is a good thing to learn early on.
- If you have a goal, visualization reminders are powerful.
- Your morals and values must align.
- Write down your morals and values.
- Communicate everything.
- Schools have a lot of good resources if you want to talk.

# 24
# HOW TO FIND YOUR SELF-WORTH AND TALK POSITIVELY TO YOURSELF

*JENNA SMITH*

Jenna Smith is a TikTok influencer who gained over 160,000 followers in nine months after she fell into a depression. Her parents got divorced when she was fourteen years old. Jenna sought validation by dating at a young age. She started dating boys who abused her emotionally. Jenna stayed in these relationships because she thought she didn't deserve anything better. She self-harmed for years, was diagnosed with PTSD and depression, and she had panic attacks. Eventually, she found the courage to set herself free and started positive self-talk.

## CONNECT:
- Instagram: @I.Used.To.Be.Afraid
- TikTok: @User.Is.Unknown

## STRUGGLES INCLUDED IN THIS CHAPTER:
- Anxiety
- Low self-esteem
- Parents got divorced
- Self-harm
- PTSD
- Wanted to commit suicide
- People pleaser
- Afraid she would never find love

- Felt inferior
- Hated being alone
- Sexual abuse and controlling boyfriends

## HOW JENNA DEALT WITH HER PARENTS' DIVORCE

**Jenna Smith:** I started dating at around age eleven. As my parents were getting a divorce, I felt a void in me that I needed to fill. I turned outwards. I was looking for the same love that I was not receiving, mostly from my father.

It affected me deeply. I didn't talk about it much because it was a taboo. We weren't supposed to talk about family issues. I kept it inside. It affected my self-confidence, and it affected the way I felt and received love. It felt like someone had thrown a picture of me on the ground, and the glass shattered.

I had self-harming behaviors. I would cut myself, and I had some suicidal tendencies. After one of my suicide attempts, my mom decided to put me into counseling. That helped because I was no longer just keeping it in.

## STOPPING HER SELF-HARMING BEHAVIOR

**JS:** My counselor helped me a lot, but I still continued to cut myself until I was an adult. What finally got me to stop was realizing the example I was creating for my kids. My kids were infants at the time. I realized if I took out my pain by physically harming myself, my kids would think that was how they should express their emotions and heal from their pain. I did not want my kids to learn that. I began to find healthier options. For me, the main solution was meditation. I would take a moment to take deep breaths to bring myself back into the present moment. I also got into painting. Instead of using my hands for self-harm, I used my hands to be creative.

**SS:** Do you have specific meditation practices?

**JS:** I pull up a picture on my phone or computer, turn on some soft music, take deep breaths, and count to ten. I try to focus on that image and pretend I'm there. For moments where life was dark, that was an escape for me. I started focusing my energy on relaxing every part of my body.

I'm a highly anxious person, and my mind is constantly running one hundred miles an hour. Meditation, even if it's only five minutes a day, helps me tell my brain that my thoughts are not in control of me. I am in control of my thoughts.

## OVERCOMING EMOTIONAL ABUSE FROM POSITIVE SELF-TALK

**JS:** At a young age, I started seeking love. I wanted to fill the hole that I felt inside. After my parents divorced, I got into a serious relationship that lasted for three years. While in that relationship, I was always afraid that he would leave me. I did anything he requested. It was a type of peer pressure. I did it at all costs. I did not want to be abandoned. I didn't want to feel what I had felt as I went through my parents' divorce. My only identity was having my boyfriend around. He would mistreat me all the time. I hated myself for not putting any value on myself, but I didn't know how to stop or how to get out of it. I wish I had told myself, "Your worth is already inside of you. You don't need anyone outside of you to tell you how important you are or how amazing you are." It's essential for you to repeat positive self-affirmations even if you don't believe them yet. It's true; your worth is inside of you. If you go along with what all your friends or your boyfriend or girlfriend are trying to tell you, you will lose your mind. Don't do anything that you don't feel is being true to yourself. If someone else judges you for that, you don't need that person in your life.

**SS:** How did you get out of that toxic relationship?

**JS:** One day when I was seventeen years old, I woke up and told myself, "I don't want to live this way anymore." I started to change. It was little by little. I started to change how I thought. I started to do positive self-talk. Instead of constantly saying negative things like, "You're not good enough. Nobody loves you. If you don't do what he says, he's going to leave," I started saying, "I don't want to be treated like this anymore. Let him leave. I'm a good enough person who will find love someday, but I can't force that." At first I didn't believe any of it. I didn't believe any of the things that I told myself. I almost had to force feed myself those positive thoughts. As I thought more positively, my life changed completely. I am now in a very healthy relationship. We celebrated our ten-year anniversary.

If you can love yourself first and have confidence in yourself, then go seek a partner. You will be in a more stable and happier relationship than going into one trying to gain that love for yourself.

Positive self-talk allowed me to find a healthy marriage and relationship once I was ready. It allowed me to love myself for who I am, for my weaknesses, for my strengths, and for the mental illnesses that I have.

**SS:** How can someone turn negative self-talk into positive self-talk?

**JS:** Set aside a time to do it each day. For me, it was when I woke up in the morning or as I was going to bed. Instead of scrolling through your phone, take a minute, and think of three things that you love about yourself. If you can't think of anything, think of who you want to become. Describe those characteristics. As you do that, your thoughts will become your words, your words will become your actions, and your actions will become your character. In the beginning, force it, and make it a habit. Eventually, it will become your second voice. The negative self-talk will disappear, and that positive, confident voice will take its place.

## THE GROUNDING TECHNIQUE

**JS:** It took years and a lot of work to overcome my anxiety and PTSD. I would have severe panic attacks. Whether it was a hand motion, a certain smell, or even a sound, it would set me off, and I would panic. It got so bad that if I were in a large group of people, my vision would go blurry. I would get extremely nauseous, and I would freeze. It was embarrassing to have panic attacks in public. It got to the point where I stopped leaving my house because it was too embarrassing, and I thought others were watching me. I realized most people would not be judging me. Most of the time, people are not watching you; people are minding their own business. Whatever you're feeling, allow yourself to ride through the emotions, and get the help that you need. Don't stay silent about it. Counseling was one thing that helped me, especially with my panic attacks and PTSD.

The best tecāique that helped me is the grounding tecāique. I would take a deep breath and list everything I could see. "I see a window. I see the couch. I see the curtains." Then I would go through what I could hear. "I hear the TV. I hear my phone ringing." Then I would list what I smelled. "I smell my candle. I smell cinnamon." As I did that, my brain could no longer focus on reliving past or future events. It would force my brain to come back to the present moment. It got me out of those panic attacks.

## HEALING IS NOT LINEAR

**JS:** Healing is not linear. You must ride the waves and embrace it each time you have a dark day. If you're constantly trying to look for brighter times, you will slowly go up. There will be dips though. I was doing amazing in my healing. I had overcome a lot of the things that held me back from interacting with people. Then my nephew, who was nineteen years old, committed suicide. It was a huge shock for me. He was very depressed, and we tried to get him to go to counseling, but he didn't want to talk about his issues. After that, I felt like I was starting all over at square one.

Life events will try to knock us down, but just because bad things are happening around us does not mean we have to go back into negative behavior. You must separate the issues. You have to say, "This bad thing happened in my life, but this bad thing is not me. I can continue to be a positive force in the world. I can continue to love myself, while grieving sad things that happen around me." That's helped me to continue in my healing path, but I still had days where I laid in bed and cried. Life is never going to be happy all the time. Even if you overcome your depression and talk positively about yourself, you're going to lose loved ones, and you're going to go through heartbreaking events. But you can't internalize it to where you start self-harming again or take on the guilt.

People who are the happiest in life are the people who can say, "I am not the abuse that happened to me. I am not my parents' divorce. I am not the suicide of my friend" or whatever problem they are going through. That is not your identity. Your identity is that you are an amazing person. Your heart is beautiful.

## CREATING HER INFLUENCE ON TIKTOK

**JS:** I started on TikTok when I was going through one of my depressive modes, in April 2019. It's so funny because I'm not an extrovert. I am someone who used to have anxiety when going out with friends. That month, I lost my second loved one within two years. It took a toll on me. I decided that I needed something in life that was happy, something that wasn't so dark. I needed something that was ridiculous, humorous, and fun. I started TikTok because it looked ridiculous.

I chose the name User.Is.Unknown because I didn't want anyone to find it. I thought I was going to go on there, be ridiculous, and have fun. I wanted it to be a creative outlet for when I was feeling sad. Within nine months I gained 160,000 followers.

People need someone who isn't concerned about other people's opinions. That is something that I've had to practice. That was not me as a teen. I cared about what everyone said about me, and I internalized it. Finally, I realized I couldn't listen to anything anyone had to say about me. I had to decide who I was, decide whether I loved myself or not (the answer is yes; you should love yourself). I said, "If I love myself, what others think about me isn't important."

## TOP TAKEAWAYS:
- Meditate as many times as you need to.
- Don't do something for someone because you are afraid they will leave or neglect your love.

- Learn to love yourself first before you try to love someone else.
- *If you feel anxious or feel a panic attack coming, use grounding tecāiques to shift yourself back into the present.*
- Set aside time each day for positive self-talk.
- Healing is not linear.
- You are not defined by the challenges that you are going through.
- Love yourself, and don't care what anyone else thinks about you.

# 25
# HOW TO FIND YOUR OWN VOICE AS AN INTROVERT

*ANDRE HAYKAL JR.*

Andre Haykal Jr. is a teen entrepreneur. He is the host of the top one hundred podcast *Real Talk University* and the author of *What They Won't Teach You*. Andre has always been an introvert and was reserved about his goals because he was afraid of what his friends thought about him. When he turned eighteen, he started finding his own voice and sharing it with the world. He has inspired many people across the globe.

## CONNECT:
- Instagram: @AndreHaykalJr
- Book: *What They Won't Teach You*

## STRUGGLES INCLUDED IN THIS CHAPTER:
- People pleaser
- Put a lot of pressure on himself
- Speaking and writing insecurities
- Problems developing meaningful and like-minded friendships

## ENTREPRENEURIAL VENTURES IN HIGH SCHOOL

**Andre Haykal Jr.:** My first business was in tenth grade. It was an online business where I resold sneakers. I always had a big interest in and a love for Jordan and LeBron sneakers. In tenth grade, I was not able to afford more than one pair of these shoes. Then I found a way to sell them for double the price I bought them at. I started to do this and slowly built up capital. That allowed me to buy more and more. Eventually, I turned it into an online business where I did it for other people. That was my first business.

I always knew I wanted to do something bigger than a simple online business, but that venture taught me economics, customer service, and how to deal with failure. No one else I knew was going through the same challenges as me. It was kind of tough, but I learned a lot from doing that. It also allowed me to have an income that I wouldn't have had otherwise. I didn't do an after-school job, and I didn't have to get a summer job because I was making more than enough money with my shoe business.

## HE WASN'T COMFORTABLE SHARING HIS GOALS

**AHJ:** I was not getting invited to parties. I was not in the same friend groups that other kids were in, and I was not a popular kid. In high school, I pursued entrepreneurship on my own. I never told anyone about it. No one knew what I was doing or what I was into. It was my own thing. I had friends but not on the level of sharing what my passions were because no one else in the group was aligned with them. It was not a part of their lives. I wish I could have shared my voice and shared my passion with others around me. I didn't do that until I graduated.

## HOW ANDRE SURROUNDED HIMSELF WITH LIKE-MINDED PEOPLE

**AHJ:** I knew that to continue to succeed in entrepreneurship, I had to surround myself with people who thought like I did. I decided to put myself out there and connect with other entrepreneurial people. That was tough for me because I never felt comfortable doing that. Throughout the summer I found some groups to join. I also found some good friends and mentors and learned a lot from them. I met a friend in college who shared many of the same interests. I had never talked to many people who were entrepreneurial and the same age as me. As we shared our interests, we realized that nobody else had them. We started a podcast where we would interview successful entrepreneurs and share those stories in the hopes of inspiring people. We wanted students to realize they weren't limited to finishing their degree and getting a job. We've done interviews every week since last year, and we've grown our network of like-minded people to an extent that I never could have imagined.

## OVERCOMING SPEAKING AND WRITING INSECURITIES

**AHJ:** Starting my podcast and writing my book was the toughest thing to do because my two biggest insecurities were writing and speaking. I'm not confident in my English abilities. I was a good student, and I had a high GPA and did well in class, except for English. I hated putting myself out there, but I knew I needed to do it. Some people learn from listening to podcasts, some people learn from attending events, and other people learn from reading books. I knew that if I cared about making an impact, I had to hold myself accountable to write a book and start a podcast. It was a lot easier than I thought it would be, and it is one of the funnest things that I've ever done.

**SS:** How did you get over your insecurities? How can an introvert who feels the same get over that hump?

**AHJ:** It comes down to action. You can sit and think about all the excuses, or you can draw up all the possibilities that could come from what you're about to do. If you act, your fear will go away. Ask yourself, "How can I make this to the best of my ability?" Once you find something that you're passionate about, something that will keep you up at night and help you overcome your anxiety, take immediate action. As soon as you take action, everything else will go away. You'll realize there's never a perfect plan. You must get started; otherwise you never will.

## REDEFINE THE WORD "FAILURE"

**AHJ:** We naturally put a lot of pressure on ourselves. It's easy to beat yourself up after a failure. I reflected on my past failures. I had a list of every venture I had tried and the word "fail" next to it. To me, they were not failures. One, I made money from them, more money than I would have made if I had taken a simple after-school job. Two, I learned a ton of different entrepreneurship lessons, such as customer service, sales, building a team, firing people, and app development. Third, I met people who I would never have connected with if I didn't put myself out there.

Iterate. You're not going to hit a home run on your first swing. It takes time after time after time to learn the lessons that you need to set up whatever your future success is going to be. I wouldn't be where I am today if it wasn't for those iterations. I'm grateful for each one of them. I wouldn't be who I am without my failures, and I would never go back. I have no regrets.

## DON'T START OUT TRYING TO BUILD THE NEXT UBER OR APPLE

**AHJ:** In high school, you're so limited in regard to the time you have to work on something like this. You're so young. The best thing you can do is focus on what you can learn, which will set you up for a larger amount of success when the right time comes. I started off doing that. Buy and sell cards, buy and sell shoes, do something to make money, but at the same time, know that you are learning. You are learning economics, learning supply and demand, learning customer service, sales, and learning how to do things over the Internet that most high school kids don't know. You're putting yourself out there and getting yourself an experience that will allow you to bring in an income that most high school students don't see.

There are tons of possible side hustles. You can learn how to build websites, or you can learn how to manage people's social media. If you want to build the next Uber or be the next Steve Jobs, build the skills necessary to reach that point. These big companies weren't the first thing that these entrepreneurs built. They had so many other projects before that. Team up with a few of your friends, and start a clothing business. By the time you graduate from high school or college, you'll have enough money, knowledge, a network that you can tap into, and some experience that you can fall back on to begin the journey of building your own Apple or Uber.

## THE ICEBERG ILLUSION

**AHJ:** On social media, all you see is the tip of the iceberg: the success, the money, the fame. No one ever sees the bottom of the iceberg, which is four times the size of the top: the hours spent working, the sleepless nights, the time, the money, the investment. That's the truth. There's nothing truer to success than that analogy.

## SALES TOOK HIM OUTSIDE HIS COMFORT ZONE

**AHJ:** Working in sales was huge for me. As an introvert coming out of high school, not many people have that ability or that skill set. I took a job at the end of my senior year in high school at a local sales organization, which involved cold calling every day. That experience was awesome because it took me outside of my comfort zone. Many people can benefit from that. Getting a sales job will help you grow and lead to more opportunities. Everyone should learn how to sell.

## WORST PIECE OF ADVICE: PLAY IT SAFE

**AHJ:** As a society, we tell everyone to play it safe. The idea behind playing it safe makes no sense, especially at our age. We're so young. I'm nineteen years old, and if my entrepreneurial ventures don't work out in the next six years, at the very least, I have a college degree, and I have a family that loves me. I also have a network of people who have built up over their six years from doing what I've been doing. I could go get a job and live a normal life like other people do. We have so many years to take risks and try things out that other people are unwilling to try. The Internet makes it much easier to take a risk. There's no reason not to take a huge risk in high school or college. Most of us don't have house payments, car payments, or kids to take care of, so there's nothing holding us back. What you will regret is not taking a risk.

## FOCUS ON THE INPUTS, NOT THE OUTPUTS

**AHJ:** I have goals, but I'm not the kind of person who sets concrete goals. The way I look at goals is different than a lot of people. Many people focus on the outputs, like $100,000 next year, a house, or a family. I focus on the inputs. I realized early on that I can't control certain outcomes, but what I can control is the inputs. Say I want to make $100,000 next year, and I calculate that might require one hundred cold calls a day. Then my goal is to make one hundred cold calls a day. If I get $100,000, great. If not, it doesn't matter because I still met my goal. I don't get caught up in the results.

That was one of my biggest weaknesses. I set huge goals, and I was doing so much work and making so much progress, but I still fell short of those goals. It killed my momentum and my confidence. Have the confidence that the results will come when they're supposed to come. It might not be when you expect them, but they will come as long as you manage your inputs.

## THE SUCCESS TRIANGLE

**AHJ:** I've come up with what I call the "success triangle." It involves three things: consistency, continuous learning, and patience. Once you get started with something, stay consistent. As you're staying consistent, remain open to learning. Continuous learning is super important. The last step is patience: patience with the results, not the input. A lot of people get that last point wrong. Some people think they will be successful in ten years and don't have to put in as much work. That's not what I mean by patience. Patience is waiting for the results after you work hard. Consistency, continuous learning, and patience are the three points of the success triangle. If you combine these three with what you're doing and do something that you feel good about, you'll be in good shape.

## TOP TAKEAWAYS:

- Don't be afraid to share your passion.
- If you really care about sharing your message, you will forget about your insecurities.
- Surround yourself with like-minded people.

- Even if your venture doesn't work out, you did not fail; you learned, made some money, and grew your network.
- Start small side hustles to learn the skills you need to execute your big idea.
- *Get into sales, so you can get outside your comfort zone and grow.*
- Take risks now, so you won't have any regrets later.
- When creating goals, focus on inputs, not outputs.
- When pursuing a goal, stay consistent, learn continuously, and have patience.

# 26
# HOW TO START A
# BUSINESS AT
# AGE FIFTEEN
## *MARKO STAVROU*

Marko Stavrou is a fifteen-year-old entrepreneur who lives in South Africa. He is the host of *Young Entrepreneurs Network*. He used to be insecure about being a young entrepreneur. His classmates would make fun of him for reading, listening to podcasts, and creating videos. No longer a people pleaser, he interacts with successful entrepreneurs around the world and is building a global brand.

## CONNECT:
- Instagram: @Marko.Stavrou

## STRUGGLES INCLUDED IN THIS CHAPTER:
- Worried too much about people's opinions
- People pleaser
- Victim of peer pressure

## DON'T LET OTHER PEOPLE'S JUDGMENT STOP YOU

**Marko Stavrou:** I got into entrepreneurship at age thirteen when I started selling sneakers. As the journey continued, I started getting my name out there online. People were judgmental of my success and of what I was doing, either because they were jealous or because they didn't like that I was different. I was in a school where things were a certain way, and those who were different were judged. The other kids laughed at me when I was reading a book in class or listening to podcasts. When I did a video, they would say I was wasting my time.

It's all part of the journey, but it got into my head. It was very hard to ignore. Sometimes I didn't post videos because the other kids would make judgmental comments on my posts and on my podcast. People's judgements limited me from connecting with people. After finding my purpose, I decided that people's opinions and judgments would not define me or my future. I realized I am responsible for my future. If I let other people take that away from me or disturb my path, I would be doing a disservice to myself and my family. I wanted to achieve a goal, and I wasn't going to let someone else say whether I could or couldn't achieve it. For the friends who judge me, I say, "I will love you unconditionally. I'll support you, but I'm going to move to another circle." I changed the people I was around.

## THE TRANSITION TO STOP CARING ABOUT WHAT OTHER PEOPLE THOUGHT

**MS:** I stopped caring what others thought when I found my purpose and calling. My purpose is to help teens live a life of fulfillment and to create thriving businesses.

Other kids would say I was missing out on my childhood, that I should be partying. They would question why I was writing a book during the holidays. My response was, "No, you're missing out on your childhood because you could be hanging out with millionaires or billionaires. You could be reading, growing yourself, and going to events. You could be impacting other people by having a podcast or posting on social media."

My motivation came from my purpose and from impacting lives. I imagined someone sitting next to me and saying I had changed their life. I have this podcast that's thriving; it's doing so well. Focus on the impact you can be making, and you will no longer care what others are saying.

## BECOMING LESS OF A PEOPLE PLEASER

**MS:** We fear people's opinions about what we wear, what we say, how we sound, and what we look like. To stop caring about what people thought of me, I put my shirt and my pants on backwards. I would go to a shopping center or to events wearing stuff backwards. Sometimes I wore the wrong shoes, clothes that didn't match, or put my shirt on backwards. People would look at me funny, tell me my shirt was on backwards, and my family would even ask me if I was OK. If you do this, after a while, you will realize that people don't really care what you do. They're going to ignore you. You are worrying what people think for no reason. The same thing applies to focusing on the work that you want to do. Focus on your message and your mission. Do something that you're passionate about. Continue down your path, and people will eventually follow.

## WHAT IF YOU DON'T KNOW ANYTHING ABOUT STARTING A BUSINESS?

**MS:** If you've never been involved with business, or you don't know if you like business, the first thing you need to do is make yourself aware of the different aspects of business: marketing, sales, drop shipping, podcasting, and so on. Once you are aware of what's out there, you can find out what you like, don't like, and what you're good at.

I started my podcast for a couple of reasons. First, to develop my speaking skills. I want to speak on stage because I think it's a great way to help change people's lives. Second, I'm able to connect with whoever I want. I've connected with a lot of people by direct messaging them on Instagram and inviting them to come on my podcast. Now we can build that relationship.

If you still don't know what you want to do, write down ten passions that you have. Then search industries in that field that you love. For example, if your interest is talking, there's speaking, podcasting, news, and radio. Take action, and experiment with those passions. There are different types of entrepreneurs. To get started, work for different types of companies. Spend a few months learning different skills, and connect with the CEO. That will expedite your learning. It will also help you decide what type of company you want to start.

## "I DON'T HAVE THE TIME"

**MS:** Often, the biggest excuse with people is "I don't have time." I read twenty books and listen to sixty-five podcasts each month. I leave home at 6:00 a.m. and come back at 6:00 p.m. I still have two hours of homework after that.

When the teacher is out, instead of going on your phone, read a book, or listen to a podcast for ten minutes. There's so much time, whether it's a break, waiting for someone to pick you up, or after doing homework. Don't procrastinate or do distracting activities. I decided to listen to a podcast every single day and be disciplined to use my time wisely.

A lot of people talk about people who get lucky going viral. My favorite quote is "It takes a long time to reach overnight success." It takes a lot of discipline and sacrifice to become an overnight success. You must be willing to do what other people are not doing. Yes, people get lucky with viral videos, but what you don't see is them putting out hundreds of videos before that.

## THREE STEPS TO SUCCESS

**MS:** First, change the people that you surround yourself with and what you feed your brain, and your soul. I was never going to interview people who are multi-millionaires by thinking in a certain way. Don't watch TV or any negativity. I only listen to and take advice from people who are providing solutions and changing people's lives. Listen to the right people, and follow the right people on social media. I only follow five of my friends on social media. I've unfollowed all the others, and I follow the people who are going to help me get to the right place. Who are you listening to? Who are you taking advice from? "Show me your friends, and I'll tell you your future." It's a great quote that works.

Second, get a mentor. The only way to get an awesome mentor who has made millions of dollars, impacted millions, and/or written many books is to bribe them with your time. One thing that they cannot buy is time. If you provide them value, like being their personal assistant, writing their emails, or doing their Facebook ads, they will be more willing to mentor you. The best thing you can do is learn a skill to provide to them, whether it is Facebook ads, drop shipping, marketing, email marketing, or podcasting. Be open with them. The more open you are on where you want to go, the more likely it is that they will help you reach your goals.

Third, break down what you want. Many people don't know where to start. First, search on the Internet, and ask yourself, "What do I need to do to start a company?" Then start figuring out those concepts because that's going to help you create whatever you want. Use your passions to create a business. When things get tough, you need to be able to tell yourself, "I love doing this, and I'm going to push through." Don't hop on a trend because everyone else is doing it. That's the quickest way to lose motivation when times get tough.

## TOP TAKEAWAYS:

- Don't let other people's opinions of you stop you from pursuing entrepreneurship or your passion.
- When you find your purpose, you won't focus on what other people think of you.
- If you're really concerned about someone else's opinion, wear mismatched and backward clothes. At first people will be concerned, but after a while, people will stop to worry. The same goes for when you pursue your passion.
- If you don't know how to get started in business, learn the different aspects of it.

- Write down ten of your passions, and search industries in that field to specify what type of business you want to get into.
- Everyone has the time to develop themselves. Use your down time to read and listen to podcasts.
- *Change the people you surround yourself with and what you feed your brain and your soul.*
- Find a mentor.
- Break your goals down.

# 27
# HOW TO PRACTICE SELF-LOVE IN HIGH SCHOOL
*GUTI*

Guti is a TikTok Influencer with 900,000 followers. He posts daily videos that tell stories that contain hidden inspirational messages. His family moved from Venezuela to Canada when he was eight years old. He had a hard time fitting in at first because of the cultural differences. Soon enough, he started fitting in because he adapted to their culture. Eventually, he realized that trying to fit in was a long road to unhappiness, and he started becoming his true self. Guti believes everyone will be happier if they are themselves and practice self-love. By practicing self-love, you can overcome any challenge.

## CONNECT:
- TikTok: @UrBoyGutii
- Instagram: @UrBoyGuti

## STRUGGLES INCLUDED IN THIS CHAPTER:
- Low self-esteem
- Death of a loved one
- Insecure about not having a girlfriend
- Came from another country
- People pleaser
- Bullying
- Felt inferior
- Feared being a disappointment
- Worried too much about people's opinions
- Victim of peer pressure

## TRYING TO FIT IN WHEN MOVING FROM VENEZUELA TO CANADA

**Guti:** When I moved from Venezuela to Canada, I was eight years old. I didn't know English, and I was living in Montreal, so I had to learn French before I learned English. I couldn't speak to anybody. One good thing is that my parents moved into a safe neighborhood. It was a secure city where I didn't have to worry about having bad influences around me. Still, it was hard for me to adapt to the culture in Montreal, specifically as a Latino. We didn't fit in from the start. We had to find our way into the culture. I started speaking French after four or five months, and then after a year I was confident with the language. I tried to hide my Spanish accent because back then it wasn't cool. I did everything possible not to get noticed as an immigrant.

My name is Javier, but I tried to switch it to Xavier, so people wouldn't label me as an immigrant. I feared the judgment of people around me because I was different. People in Montreal looked a certain and acted a certain way, and I wanted to fit in.

## GOING BACK TO HIS ROOTS

**G:** When I got into high school, my mentality changed. My mom saw me trying to fit in with the locals, and she got upset with me. She didn't want me to lose my roots. The summer after my freshman year in high school, she sent me back to Venezuela. That is when I realized who I am as a person. It was a pivotal moment in my life. It still defines who I am today because I got to understand my culture. I learned the way people speak to each other and the confidence that comes from there. So many beautiful things come from my country. I have a strong attachment to it.

I brought my culture back during my second year of high school, and I was a totally different person. I wasn't trying to fit in or hide my accent. I wasn't trying to be quiet. I was trying to be myself as much as I could. In the second year of high school, I was more myself. I also hung out with people who had the same values as me.

## THE PRESSURE TO HAVE A GIRLFRIEND

**G:** In high school, people tend to start dating. I felt pressured to date a girl because it was something cool, not because I wanted to. It got me into a lot of trouble, especially with my first girlfriend. If you're not ready to be in a committed relationship, and you are only with the other person to look cool and please the people around you, you're not benefiting yourself or that person. You are playing with somebody else's life because that person is not going to feel happy with you, and he or she will start having doubts about himself or herself and not feel fulfilled.

I stayed with my first girlfriend for three years. I was in my fifth year of high school, and I realized I had spent all my high school years with her. I asked myself, "Why am I still with this girl? I don't even see a future with her." I didn't want to be in a committed relationship, so I broke up with her. Afterwards, she was depressed and told me that she couldn't believe she would not be spending her life with me.

I spent four hours on the phone with her and tried to convince her that her life wasn't just about me. I told her that she had people around her who were ready to share their lives with her and give her the love that I might not have been able to give her. After that relationship, I've been careful about who I get into a relationship with because people's feelings matter.

## BE YOURSELF; NOT EVERYONE WILL LIKE YOU

**G:** Something I learned through the years is that there is no reason for you to please people who don't put food on the table for you. Be yourself. You were put on earth for a reason, and you are unique. Often, I see people act or dress like others to fit in. The truth is, you don't need to be accepted by everyone. You have your own identity and your own life. If you are yourself, the right people will come into your life. Don't try to be somebody else because you'll attract people who won't fit your personality and who will prevent you from growing.

At a certain age, I discovered that I must make myself happy first and then spread the happiness around me. I have the people who I need right now. I know who my true friends and my family are. These people can see where I am and help me grow.

## QUALITY NOT QUANTITY

**G:** People judge success or happiness according to numbers. In elementary school, someone asked, "How many friends do you have?" and someone said, "I have fifteen friends." Others would feel bad because they only had five friends. It's the same thing when we go on social media. My TikTok account has a different vibe than most other TikTok accounts. It's educational and a bit entertaining. It has a message. A lot of accounts have many more followers than I have, but they get fewer likes. In real life, it doesn't matter. The real game is about the connection, the bond, and the relationship that you build with people. I have so many followers who talk to me and come to me for advice daily. That's the real game.

That's how life is. The better your relationship is with a human being, the more value that gives you as a person. It's not about how many people follow you or how many friends you have; it's about how many people care for you and are there for you when you need them. I've had the same six friends since I was fourteen years old.

## EXPANDING YOUR CIRCLE OUTSIDE OF HIGH SCHOOL

**G:** Don't base your life on those four years. If you play Call of Duty, there's bunch of groups online where you can find friends who share the same interests as you. You can go on TikTok and start commenting on pages that you find interesting. There are so many ways today to expand your circle. You don't have to keep it in high school. When you have a lot of friends in high school, it doesn't mean anything after.

Life is not about what happens in high school. If someone accomplishes something in high school, it doesn't mean they'll accomplish anything later in life. Because you are a nerd in high school doesn't mean you'll be one later. I have friends who hated high school and didn't fit in. They got into college, and it was a completely different story. They were so much more respected. I would simply say, find your interests. With social media, you can find people who have the same interests as you. Be patient. Life is short but so long at the same time. Once you make it through high school, you'll see the potential that you have. Don't base it off high school.

## OVERCOMING HIS GRANDFATHER'S PASSING

**G:** My grandfather took care of me when my family had nothing and raised me like I was his own child. Losing him was like losing a limb. The only way I knew how to cope with it was to make him proud. His last words to me were in Spanish, translated as "I like you, I love you, I adore you." That's why I preach about self-love. Telling myself that or imagining my grandpa telling me that completely resets my energy.

My grandfather always seemed to be happy. He had his crew come over after 6:00 p.m. or 7:00 p.m., after they were all done work. They would watch baseball, drink a bit of whiskey, and relax. They would have good times together. He would always come home and say, "I love you," to my grandma at least once a day. He had an energy that was contagious. I told myself I wanted to be the best at what I do.

One thing my mom has told me is, "You never cope with someone's death. You just learn how to live without that person." I set a goal to do the work that would make him proud. I overcame my grandfather's passing by digging deep into the work I was doing. I wanted to make him proud. His passing was the loudest cry of my life. I was yelling.

## PRACTICING SELF-LOVE WHEN LIFE GETS TOUGH

**G:** Growing up as a teenager who was an immigrant, I had a lot of problems with my parents, and it wasn't always happy at home. I was playing sports with older people because I was six feet one inch at age fourteen. I was always getting bullied because I wasn't as good as them. I never understood why people bullied. No one should ever do that. I would cope with it by listening to positive music. Every time I found a song by anyone who was positive, I would repeatedly listen to it, which made me feel a hundred times better.

Do more than one thing that you love. I also love basketball, and I would play basketball every single night. It made me feel better, and that's how I dealt with my problems in high school.

I would surround myself with my friends. I would try to spend as much time with people who I loved and who I knew would make me feel good.

## TOP TAKEAWAYS:

- Don't forget your roots.
- Surround yourself with people who you can be yourself with.
- Don't get into a relationship just to be cool. You will be playing with the other person's life, and there will be consequences.
- *It's not about how many friends or followers you have; it's about the connection that you have with them.*
- Expand your circle outside of high school based on your interests.
- You never cope with someone's death; you just learn to live without that person.
- If you are having a rough time, do some activities that make you feel good.
- Listen to positivity, and surround yourself with people who make you feel good.

# 28
# INSIGHTS INTO SOMEONE'S LIFE WITH BIPOLAR DISORDER AND DEPRESSION
### *NATASHA TRACY*

Natasha Tracy is an award-winning writer, speaker, and influencer with over 34,000 Twitter followers. She is also a consultant who offers her insight into living with bipolar disorder after more than a decade of mental illness research. She had a rough childhood. Starting at age twelve, she fell into a severe depression and had low self-esteem. She became self-harming and wanted to die.

## CONNECT:
- Website: www.natashatracy.com
- Twitter: @Natasha_Tracy

## STRUGGLES INCLUDED IN THIS CHAPTER:
- Depression
- Bipolar disorder
- Self-harm
- Low self-esteem
- Parents got divorced
- Wanted to commit suicide
- Felt inferior
- Put a lot of pressure on herself

## WHAT IS BIPOLAR DISORDER?

**Natasha Tracy:** Most people walk around with a fully functioning brain, but my brain has some issues. We see changes in a bipolar brain on a scan. Some parts of my brain are shrunken compared to other people's brains. Bipolar disorder is about having very high moods and very low moods. Those high moods are known as hypomanias or manias, depending on their severity, and the low moods are known as depressions. To be diagnosed with bipolar disorder, you must have exhibited both kinds of moods. We also tend to have a mood called a mixed mood. In a mixed mood, both the high and the low symptoms can be present at the same time. For a high mood, you tend to see a lot of energy and a lack of self-regulation.

For example, during a manic spree, a person with bipolar disorder might go out and spend $10,000 on handbags that he or she can't afford. When that person is depressed, it's the opposite. He or she has very low energy and may not want to get out of bed. The person is likely sleeping a whole lot of hours, although sometimes people don't sleep at all during the depression phase. It can be very debilitating. Statistically, people with bipolar disorder experience more lows than highs, more major depressions than manias or hypomanias.

**SS:** What are some misconceptions about bipolar disorder?

**NT:** I think the biggest misconception about people with bipolar disorder is that we're violent. That is not necessarily the case at all. People with bipolar disorder who receive treatment are no more violent than anyone else. A person with bipolar disorder who also has a substance abuse disorder has an increased likelihood of violence. But the average person with bipolar disorder who's being treated has an average level of aggressiveness, just like anyone else does.

## NATASHA'S STORY

**NT:** When I was twelve years old, my life became difficult. My parents were getting a divorce, and my father was an alcoholic. He was mostly an absent father. Later, I learned that he had been diagnosed with bipolar disorder as well. I didn't know that at the time. At that point, I became seriously depressed and even suicidal. The first time that I harmed myself, I was twelve. I did it because I was so depressed. I felt worthless and that there was no way to get out of that. I felt I deserved to self-harm. That led to many years of self-harm.

172

## EARLY SYMPTOMS OF BIPOLAR DISORDER

**NT:** The symptoms I remember early on were mood swings. When I'd have a friend over when I was ten years old, I would become incredibly energetic, run around, and not stop talking. Then I wouldn't want the person to leave. I was desperate for them to stay. I would have this exciting experience while they were there, but when they left, I felt abysmal. Now I realize that this type of mood fluctuation is typical in bipolar disorder. I experienced symptoms of depression when my friend left. The high energy when they were there resulted in low energy when the friend left. I also remember feeling so lonely, lost, and worthless, like a piece of trash. For a nine-year-old child, that isn't normal.

I was an intelligent kid, and initially, I did well in school. As I became a teenager, my grades slipped because of my depression symptoms. I was extremely sad and tired. I would skip school because I hated it. I hated everything. I wouldn't go to class and sometimes wouldn't complete assignments. I was lucky in that I had enough innate knowledge that I could get through the classes and get grades that were high enough for me to get into college.

## ENOUGH WITH THE SELF-HARM

**NT:** I finally started taking responsibility for my mental health when I was nineteen or twenty. I started seeing a psychiatrist. I also started seeing a counselor who was well versed in bipolar disorder and depression. When those things came together, and I could finally start taking responsibility for my mental health as an adult, that was my turning point. I told myself, "OK, I need to stop these negative behaviors and try to replace them with positive coping activities."

## BEST COPING MECHANISMS

**NT:** One of the things that I do a lot of in my day-to-day life is implement cognitive behavioral therapy (CBT). A skill that I use all the time is to apply logic rather than emotions to a situation. My emotions can be really messed up because of my bipolar disorder, but I can still use logic to make good decisions. For example, something as simple as missing the bus when heading to school. That's not a big deal. When I was depressed though, I would beat myself up about it. I would feel like the world was terrible and that it was all my fault. Now I use better coping tools. I look at such situations in a logical light and say, "Look, this is a small thing. It's a small part of my day. It's a tiny part of my week. I can get through this. I can take the next step. I can take the next bus. I can walk. I can do whatever I need to do and get through the situation. This isn't my fault, and I'm not a bad person." That type of self-talk is important for me to get through the events that would normally send me into an emotional spiral. I can stop that from happening now.

## WHAT WOULD NATASHA TELL HER YOUNGER SELF?

**NT:** The first thing that I would tell my younger self is that what she is going through is not her fault, that she is not a screw-up, and she is not crazy. I would give her a hug. I felt so bad about myself. I felt so bad about what I was going through and how I felt about it. I felt like I wasn't even a person. I felt like I was a creature who didn't behave or think like other people. I would say to her, "You are like everyone else. You're just dealing with a brain disorder that other people don't have." I would tell her that it will get better. At that time, I didn't think it ever would, but it did. It gets better with time, effort, and help.

## GET PROFESSIONAL HELP

**NT:** The most important thing that someone who is battling bipolar disorder can do is get professional help from those who have experience helping young people. If you, as a fifteen-year-old, see a psychiatrist who doesn't normally see fifteen-year-olds, the help is not going to be nearly as good as someone who normally works with teenagers. If you have a child who's ten years old, and he or she is experiencing massive mood shifts, find out what's going on. You need to talk to someone who's familiar with that age group and can help with that. Dealing with bipolar disorder and depression is hard, and it can be scary, but you can't handle it on your own. You are strong and powerful, but the problem is the disease. You need to get people in your corner who can help you to fight back.

A high school counselor is a good place to start. For example, if you are fifteen, that might be your only access to mental health care. If that's your only access, use it. Ideally, go from a school counselor to someone who's more qualified to deal with mental health issues. In my experience, school counselors are not properly trained to handle brain disorders. For that you need medical care. Hopefully, your school counselor can recommend someone in the community who can help you with your bipolar disorder.

## HOW TO HANDLE BIPOLAR SYMPTOMS

**NT:** First, I consistently seek help from a psychiatrist and take my medication. Those are the most important things that I can do each day. Once I do that, there are many other things to do as well. For example, bipolar disorder has a lot to do with your circadian rhythms. You should maintain a strict schedule that you can control, because your body is not going to create one for you naturally. I go to bed at the same time every night, and I wake up at the same time every morning, no matter what. Weekend, weekday, holiday, it doesn't matter, because regular sleep is important for my brain and my wellness.

If I'm doing everything I can—exercising, eating right, maintaining a schedule, and taking my medication—sometimes symptoms still pop up. When that happens, I reach out to my psychiatrist, so he knows what's going on. I also tell the people around me, the people who support me, my loved ones, because they can help me get through the rough patches as well. I have some trusted people in my life who love me, and I can tell them, "I'm struggling right now, and I need your help. I need you to come visit me. I need to have a phone conversation, or I need to have a text conversation." I do whatever I need to do to get through that moment, so I can get to the next moment where things are going to be more bearable.

## ANYONE CAN OVERCOME AND LIVE WITH BIPOLAR DISORDER

**NT:** Anyone can overcome and live with bipolar disorder. The way you live with bipolar disorder might not be the way I live with bipolar disorder. You will find your own version of normal and your own way of living with this disorder. If you have bipolar disorder, you can still live a life like everyone else. You can have a family. You can have a job and buy a house and a car. Everything can be pretty normal. Others who have bipolar disorder may not feel like they are able to live their best life. They may not be able to work because of the illness and may even be on disability. That doesn't mean it's not your best life, and it doesn't mean you're not fighting and winning against this disorder. People with bipolar disorder have wonderful lives, they have loved ones, they have reasons to be here, and they are helping people.

## TOP TAKEAWAYS:

- Take care of your mental health first by taking responsibility for it.
- Use cognitive behavioral therapy when going through emotional turmoil.
- You are not a mess-up, and things will eventually get better.
- *A high school counselor is a good place to start looking for help.*
- Get professional help with someone who specializes in what you are going through.

- People who have bipolar disorder are just like everyone else.
- If you have bipolar disorder, create and maintain a routine.
- Develop a strong support system.
- If you have bipolar disorder, find your own version of normal and your own way of living.

# 29
# HOW TO OVERCOME AN EATING DISORDER
## *FRANCESCA ROSE*

Francesca Rose is recovering from anorexia, orthorexia, and an exercise addiction. She went to a clinic at the end of 2009 and has been on the road to recovery ever since, utilizing different healing strategies. Currently, she is an author, blogger, and influencer who inspires people to recover from eating disorders and helps them have a healthier relationship with food.

## CONNECT:

- Website: www.francescaeatsroses.com
- Instagram: @FrancescaEatsRoses

## STRUGGLES INCLUDED IN THIS CHAPTER:

- Anxiety
- Depression
- Low self-esteem
- People pleaser
- Fear of rejection
- Put a lot of pressure on herself
- Worried too much about people's opinions
- Eating disorders
- Exercise addiction

## WHAT ARE ANOREXIA, ORTHOREXIA, AND EXERCISE ADDICTION?

**Francesca Rose:** Anorexia is an eating disorder where a person heavily restricts his or her food intake, usually to lose weight. It is sometimes noticeable from an outsider's perspective and sometimes not. External factors include loss of a menstrual cycle, losing a lot of weight, hair falling out, and being very moody, depressed, and anxious. Internally, people with anorexia are preoccupied with food. That's what people don't see.

Orthorexia is similar, but it is a preoccupation with clean eating and the desire to eat pure food. People who suffer from this only want a certain type of water and are very careful about how they prepare food. It often results in people not being sociable with friends or family because they don't want anybody else to prepare their food. They must know what's going into everything.

Exercise addiction is what the name implies. It is an obsession with exercising, which is often used to numb bad feelings and as a form of punishment to make up for any foods that were eaten. If someone suffering from this doesn't complete the exercise or exercises of the day, the person experiences a lot of anxiety, restlessness, and guilt. That perfectly describes me.

## MISCONCEPTIONS ABOUT EATING DISORDERS

**FR:** Someone who may not look like they have an eating disorder may very well have an eating disorder. There's no specific body type. For a long time, I believed that if someone had an eating disorder, they'd have it for a long time. That belief kept me sick and possibly also made me complacent with my recovery. On the outside it looks like you're doing all the right things to be on the right track of recovery. On the inside, there's still a lot of preoccupation with food, guilt, shame and anxiety. The idea that you can't get better is a myth. You can get better. I've seen it in me and in people who I follow on social media.

## HOW FRANCESCA'S EATING DISORDERS FORMED

**FR:** From a young age, I had an awareness of what was healthy and what was not. My eating disorder started in mid-2007, going into 2008. My thought patterns around food started to become more obsessive. In my final year of high school, 2008–2009, people noticed. At the end of the school year, I went to a clinic for treatment for a few weeks, and that was the start of my long journey. While I was still in school, I was seeing a dietitian and going to a therapist. I still felt like I was going through recovery.

I had a big fear of rejection as well as a fear of becoming a woman and what it meant to fully step into myself. By controlling the shape of my body pre-puberty, I was trying to control scary changes that were happening to my body. I was afraid that if I let everything go, my whole world would spin

178

out of control. I also had a perfectionist inside of me who wanted to be the best. I had this sick and twisted mentality that by being the thinnest person in the room, still being able to get good grades at school, and being able to do a number of extracurricular activities, I was a superhuman. It was a dark, egocentric approach to life, which wasn't helping me at all. I started becoming numb and not feeling happy emotions. Life became kind of gray and sad. I wanted to hold onto being a small person and having this eating disorder, which gave me an identity.

## NEGATIVE BEHAVIORS THAT SHE WAS FORMING

**FR:** I started changing how much I ate. I didn't want anybody to prepare my food. That meant I didn't go out to eat with friends or go to birthday parties. I became quite reclusive and isolated. I also became sneaky around what I ate, and would lie about it. I would also lie about how much exercise I did and when I was doing it.

## FRANCESCA'S TURNING POINT

**FR:** My recovery process is an ongoing thing. Many people came into my life at the perfect time. As much as I resisted the clinic, and as difficult as it was, it saved my life in many respects. I did some solo traveling to the States, Central America, and Europe. I got a wonderful, fresh perspective on life again and reclaimed my power and independence. Around that time, I also decided to go off contraceptive pills, which created a fake menstrual cycle. I was still getting a period when I was underweight. From the outside, it looked like everything was fine because my period was coming every month. When I went off the pill, I knew I would have to gain weight if I wanted to establish a healthy, regular cycle. While I was traveling, I threw my pills in the trash, and I knew I wouldn't be able to get any while traveling. I was volunteering at a yoga retreat in the middle of nowhere in Spain. It was an empowering trip. That was the start of something good.

As I got older, through the help of others, I slowly started to realize my own self-worth and my inn greatness.

## YOUR BODY DOES NOT DEFINE WHO YOU ARE

**FR:** Probably the trickiest thing is trying to remember that my body doesn't define who I am. Ultimately, an eating disorder is not a direct link to food. It's an unhealthy coping mechanism that I've chosen to keep me safe. I think the biggest challenge of my recovery is learning to trust my greatness, not to care too much what other people think, and not to be too concerned about being perfect all the time or being the best in the room. It's about ego.

**SS:** It's a journey within yourself.

**FR:** One hundred percent. Well said. You must be comfortable with vulnerabilities to shine. That's how we all connect. If we can all share our vulnerabilities with one another, we will connect. At the end of the day, we want to be seen and appreciated by others. An eating disorder creates this big wall where we can hide from our true self. I was afraid of my emotions and thought my vulnerabilities were signs of weakness.

## BEST HEALING STRATEGIES

**FR:** Therapy is great if you can access it, and there are some great affordable ways to go about it. If you can, get access to a counselor or a dietician who practices in intuitive eating or the HAES model, which stands for Health at Every Size. That's the best route to go. Meditation, being in nature, dancing, reciting mantras, yoga, community, friends, and journaling are all great ways to heal. You must have an internal desire to get better. You can go to all the therapy the dietitian appointments, and you can say the right things, but it won't help unless you want to get better. You must make peace with those sneaky, manipulative things that people who struggle with these issues do to themselves. It's a commitment at every meal to choose recovery. Every day you must ask yourself, "Do I say 'yes' to recovery? Do I say 'maybe'? Do I say 'no'?" Say "yes," and keep on going.

## DEALING WITH BODY IMAGE STRUGGLES

**FR:** It's not easy. We've been told that there's a certain body type that we must achieve. If you look a certain way, you are considered more attractive, more successful, more productive, more efficient, and even more intelligent. It's amazing how some body types come with these associations whereas people who are larger are discriminated against or stereotyped. You must say "no" to those societal pressures, peer pressure, media pressure, and parental pressure. It's not easy. I have compassion for everybody (including myself) who struggles with their body image. It's not easy to get over the messages that we are bombarded with constantly. Don't compare yourself to someone who is on a different journey than you.

## IT'S GOING TO BE OK

**FR:** I'm imagining myself at fifteen or sixteen years old. I want to give her a big hug and tell her that, "You may not believe me, but it's going to be OK. I know it doesn't feel like it. I know it feels like nothing's OK, but it will be."

When someone is mean to you, it usually means they are going through something difficult themselves. They're using you to deflect their pain. People act mean without realizing it. In those situations, speak out, and be honest. Speak to somebody who you feel safe with. When I got bullied, I kept it in and didn't tell anyone. It was hard. And then with my eating disorder, I didn't say anything, and that was difficult too.

Don't compare your recovery to anybody else's. Everyone's recovery looks a bit different.

## ADVICE FOR THOSE WHO HAVE LOVED ONES WITH EATING DISORDERS

**FR:** Approach the person in a safe place. Don't do it at the dinner table or in an attacking voice. And don't comment on body size or shape. Something as simple as "Wow, you're looking really skinny" can provide a lot of ammunition for somebody to continue what they're doing.

Well-meaning people may say, "You're looking good. You're looking healthy," and that can be misconstrued as, "I'm fat. I'm bad. I'm ugly." This can send somebody into a spiral. I would never go up to a person and comment on his or her body shape or size. What I would say is, "I would love to see your light again. I would love to see the joy in your eyes again. What can I do to help?" Maybe go out in nature, and then open that conversation. "What do you need to do to find joy again?" Then do those things with that person to regain that spark. When you have an eating disorder, the wonderful things that you might have used to do, like creative and social activities, fade away. Bring that back to find perspective in life again. I also suggest if the person is open to it, ask if they can get professional care. Most people are more open to hearing from a neutral party than from a family member or a friend.

## TOP TAKEAWAYS:

- Don't believe anyone who says you can't permanently overcome an eating disorder.
- Your body does not define who you are.
- You must be comfortable with being vulnerable with yourself.
- See a therapist or a dietician who practices intuitive eating or the HAES model.
- Meditate, be in nature, dance, recite mantras, do yoga, spend time

with friends, and journal.

- You must have the internal desire to get better.
- *Say no to societal pressures on how you are supposed to look.*
- Speak out if you are being bullied.
- Never comment on someone's body size.
- Don't compare yourself to someone else's journey.

# 30
# WHY YOU SHOULD STOP FIGHTING IN SILENCE
## *BRYANT REED*

Bryant Reed is the author of *Tested Never Defeated*, the owner of TND Fitness, a youth speaker, and is currently training for a one-hundred-mile run. When he was younger, he suffered from Croā's Disease in silence, going to the bathroom fifteen times a day. Bryant couldn't take it anymore, so he got into sniffing chemicals and tried committing suicide. He went on to join the Army, and later he became homeless. He continued to suffer in silence until he finally grew tired of it and decided to change.

## CONNECT:
- Website: www.tndfitnesscoaching.com and www.coachbryantreed.com
- Book: *Tested Never Defeated*

## STRUGGLES INCLUDED IN THIS CHAPTER:
- Depression
- Kept his problems silent
- Wanted to commit suicide
- Struggled with money
- Worried too much about people's opinions of him
- Croā's disease
- Huffing chemicals

## STRUGGLING IN SILENCE

**Bryant Reed:** In your teen years, you go through a period where you don't know who you are, what your value is, or where you fit in. Those were some of the issues that I went through. I also developed Croā's disease. During freshman year in high school, my stomach was pretty much in shambles, and I had to use the bathroom sixteen times a day. That put me in awkward situations where I'd be in class, and I wouldn't necessarily make it to the bathroom in time. I was that kid on the bus or playing sports who was using the bathroom constantly. I would also be taking a test, and instead of raising my hand to ask if I could use the bathroom, I would run out of the classroom to use the bathroom. People didn't know what was going on because I didn't tell them. I was hiding it.

To cope, I ended up huffing chemicals. I would go into the locker room or sit on my couch, and I'd inhale different chemicals to ease my pain. I was constantly in pain, whether physical or emotional.

## HE WAS SUICIDAL

**BR:** During my sophomore year, I decided I didn't want to struggle with this anymore. I was dealing with Croā's disease and depression. I told myself that I was going to end my life. I went into the bathroom and put chemicals in the sink. I put chemicals in the bathtub. I put chemicals literally everywhere. I stuffed a towel under the door, and then I lay back and huffed the chemicals with the intent of suffocating myself. The only thing I remember after that was waking up in my bed with all the chemicals in the trash can and me feeling completely fine. At that moment, I went to the mirror and said, "This is it. You are no longer going to try this again. You are going to overcome whatever you're going through." I didn't know how, but I knew I was going to figure it out.

## ASK FOR HELP

**BR:** I didn't ask for help because I thought people would think something was wrong with me. I thought everybody had a perfect life because they had a smile and perfect parents. I thought they wouldn't understand my struggles. Nobody wants to feel like there's something wrong with them. That's how I felt.

**SS:** What would you have done differently if you could go back?

**BR:** If I could go back and do it again, I would communicate from day one. I would break down in my parents' arms and tell them everything. "I'm struggling with trying to figure out who I am. I don't know who I am, and it's driving me crazy. I'm struggling with this addiction to huffing chemicals. Help me." Those are the two biggest words that I would probably use, "Help me." My parents would have helped me, and I would not have had to carry that burden on my own.

184

## HIS STRUGGLE AFTER THE ARMY

**BR:** When I was in the army, I had the option to deploy again. I went on so many deployments that it wore me out. I couldn't do it anymore.

When I got out of the military, I struggled even more. In the military, I was getting a steady paycheck, and my bills were taken care of. When I got out, I couldn't find a stable job. I dabbled in different jobs. I worked at GNC and earned close to minimum wage. I was struggling to get by. I had a son who I was trying to take care of. I was also in a relationship. Then everything went south. My job was doing poorly, and my girlfriend and I split up. I was still trying to provide for my son, but I ended up getting evicted from my apartment and sleeping in the store, where I was the manager. There were nights when I slept in my car and other nights when I slept in the Walmart parking lot, trying to figure things out. I would open and close shifts while trying to scrounge up enough money to pay my bills. I was living in Washington State at the time, where it was freezing at night. I didn't have enough money to do anything besides eat at McDonalds and then maybe pay some bills. I was behind on my car payments. I should have asked for help, but once again, I suffered in silence. My parents had no clue because they were in North Carolina. They had no idea that their son was sleeping on a cardboard box on the floor of a GNC shivering at night because he had nowhere else to go.

## FINALLY ASKING FOR HELP

**BR:** I was close to rock bottom. One day I didn't have any money, and I knew I had a bill coming up, so I took all the money from the cash register. I planned to put the money back the next day. That same day, my regional sales director popped in for a visit. His first job was usually to count the register. For some reason that day, he did not count the register. He trusted me as the manager because he had known me for a long time. He asked if everything was good with the register, and I said, "Yeah, it's good." He did all the double checks, we talked for a while, and then he left. At that moment, I told myself, "Bryant, you are going to end up in jail. You are going to tarnish your entire life by not asking for help. This is it." A month later, I saved all my money, packed my car up with my little tote that contained what few clothes I had, and I drove from Washington State all the way to North Carolina in two and half days. I went back to my family, told them what I was going through, and asked for help. After that, I started putting the pieces of my life back together.

## TRAIN YOUR MIND

**BR:** Training for long races gave me perspective. When things get tough, are you going to keep going? Are you who you say that you are? As I preach motivational stuff on social media, how am I going to continue to prove to myself and prove to everyone that I do the hard things that are necessary? I do the hard things because I think your grit, your willpower, is like a muscle. I'm training for that moment where things are going under. I ask myself, "Am I going to quit? If my business doesn't hit my goals, am I going to give up? If something happens with a family member, I need to help the family keep it together." I'm training for this race for that reason. Lots of people don't know how to do hard things. They love this comfort level, and then when bad things happen, they're not prepared for it. You won't be prepared for any of the things that life throws at you unless you train your mind. I found my way to train my mind, and you must do the same. Whether you pick a particular race, play a particular game, or open a business, find a way to train your mind.

## BE YOURSELF

**BR:** Now is not the time to figure out who you are; just experience life. If you dress a little differently or if you listen to different music, and others like something else, just be yourself. Do what you do. Don't try to fit in with everybody else. Everybody else will do their thing. As an adult, none of that matters. One day you will wake up, and you tell yourself, "I will dress how I want to dress. I will talk how I want to talk. I will be who I want to be for myself." You're going to win. Eventually, you're going to figure out who you are. For now, be who you feel comfortable being.

## YOU'RE GIVEN THAT TRAUMA FOR A REASON

**BR:** One kid who I coached had just lost his mom. I told him not to try to feel like a tough person and hold it all in. I said, "Dude, cry if you need to, punch a hole in the wall if you need to. Get your emotions out. Be tough, be strong for your family, but it's OK. You're sixteen, and this is heavy. You lost your mother. That is tough." I also told him, there's going to be a point where he heals and has the opportunity to help someone else who is going through a similar trauma. You may be in trauma and not realize that you may have been given that trauma to help somebody else who's going to help somebody else who's going to help somebody else, because we're all in this together. You will go through trauma at some point in your life. It is your duty to heal, so you can help others who have gone through the same thing.

186

## CHANGE YOUR WORLD

**BR:** I always hear people say "I'm going to change the world. I'm going to make an impact." If you're going to change the world, start by changing your world. Start with the small things. If you see a piece of trash, change the world by picking it up. If somebody in your circle is struggling, help them out. You're changing the world by helping somebody else. Don't think about the big picture. I know with social media you may compare yourself with someone who has a lot of followers and think they are making a larger impact. You can't compare yourself to others. If you want to change the world, start by changing your world, and then everything else will fall into place. That's what I've done and what I believe.

## TOP TAKEAWAYS:

- Communicate to an adult about what you are going through. You are not in this alone.
- No one's life is perfect. Don't be ashamed to share your struggles with others.
- Asking for help does not make you look weak.
- Decide to change your life.
- You won't be prepared for any of the things that life throws at you unless you train for the hard things.
- Be yourself.
- If you have gone through trauma, and you have healed yourself, it's time to heal other people.
- *If you want to change the world, start by changing your world.*

# 31
# THE POWER OF FORGIVENESS
*MARC MERO*

Marc Mero was a WCW/WWE champion and is now an international motivational speaker for youth. He grew up wanting to be a professional athlete, but Marc started hanging around the wrong crowd and got addicted to drugs. Between his drug addiction and his fame as a WCW/WWE champ, he neglected his mom, even though she cared so much for him. When she died while he was on a wrestling tour in Japan, it took him a long time to forgive himself for being a jerk to her.

He hit rock bottom and wanted to commit suicide several times before finding his passion for youth. His sister died at age twenty-one, his brother and his mom died two weeks apart, and his dad died from cancer. He learned to forgive himself for the bad times, and now he impacts millions of lives around the world.

## CONNECT:
- Website: www.thinkpoz.org
- Facebook: Facebook.com/MarcMeroPage
- Instagram and Twitter: @MarcMero
- YouTube: Youtube.com/TheMarcMero

## STRUGGLES INCLUDED IN THIS CHAPTER:
- Depression
- Death of loved ones
- Couldn't accomplish his original goals
- Wanted to commit to suicide
- Put a lot of pressure on himself

- Drug addiction
- Was in a toxic environment

## THE POWER OF WRITING DOWN YOUR GOALS

**Marc Mero:** It all started by having a dream, a goal. Ever since I was little, I have written down my goals. At ten years old I wrote down that someday I'd be a professional athlete. I wrote that I was going to win rookie of the year because I had heard about a hockey player who won rookie of the year. In 1991, I won the Pro Wrestling Illustrated Rookie of the Year award for wrestling. The goals I wrote down became a reality. I believe anything can become a reality if you write down your goal and work hard toward it.

## DECIDE TO GO AFTER YOUR DREAMS

**MM:** I was thirty years old. I had a bunch of buddies over to my apartment, and one of my friends was flipping through the TV channels. He landed on professional wrestling. I said, "Stop there. Let's watch this." As I was watching it, I got an overwhelming feeling. I call it an "aha moment." I said, "Oh, my gosh. I can do that." My buddies busted out laughing. They said, "Marc, look at the size of those guys. Those guys will pick you up over their head and throw you right out of the ring."

I said, "Man, I'm telling you, I could do that."

One of my other buddies said, "Marc, you're thirty years old. What are you going to do, start a pro career now?"

I responded with two words: "I believe."

I found out there was a wrestling school in Tampa, FL. I was living in Venice, Florida, which is just over an hour away. The wrestling school was led by famous wrestlers at that time. While training, I drove with a bunch of guys up to Atlanta, which is about an eight-hour drive. We were hoping to get picked as one of the guys who gets beat up on television for under $150 bucks and then drive eight hours home. Sure enough, they picked me. My first bout was a tag-team match. Dusty Rhodes who was a big-time wrestler at the time pulled me aside afterwards to go to the office. He told me I looked like Little Richard, the singer. That's how the Joāny B. Badd persona started, and that was the start of my wrestling career.

## MANY YEARS OF DRUG ADDICTION

**MM:** I decided to become a professional boxer early on. I had my first professional match scheduled in New York. Two weeks before my fight, I shattered my nose in an accident, so I needed reconstructive surgery, and I had to take time off. The doctors told me it would be about almost a year before I could come back and start having full contact. In that time off, I started hanging out with the wrong people. I remember thinking, my whole life, all I did was train. Between football, hockey, and boxing, I never took time off. For the first time, I couldn't train, so I wanted to go have fun, thinking I'd come back in a year. One year turned into two years, two years turned to four years, and four years turned into ten years of drug addiction. That's where my life really spun out of control. It wasn't until I was thirty years old that I went into wrestling, and that dream was rekindled simply by a belief inside.

## WE BECOME WHO WE SURROUND OURSELVES WITH

**MM:** I tell students all the time, "Your friends are like elevators. They're either going to take you up, or they're going to take you down. Show me your friends, and I'll show you your future." We become who we surround ourselves with. Think about the people who you're around. How do they treat others? How do they treat their parents? Do they have respect for people? Are they kind to others? I found my happiness by helping people. My compassion and my empathy for other people was incredible. There's no greater joy than helping another person. That's what really turned my life around.

## DON'T LIVE IN TIME; LIVE IN MOMENTS

**MM:** I no longer live in time; I live in moments. I cherish every moment. It's not what's in your pocket that matters; it's what's in your heart. Life passes so quickly. I had millions of dollars at one time, and I lost it all. Then I reinvented myself. Just because you're having a bad day or some bad years, it doesn't mean it's the end of your story. You're the author of your story, and you can write a new page. You may have had some bad chapters, just like me, but it doesn't mean that's the end of your story.

When we get older, we become complacent. One day turns into the next, and we settle for the status quo. We say things like, "Those were the days." When you believe that "those were the days," you're basically saying your best days are behind you. I want to believe that the rest of my life will be the best of my life. My best years are still ahead of me. I get up every morning with a positive attitude. Happiness is a choice. I don't care what anyone says because it's not about our circumstances; it's how we respond to them that makes all the difference. I found a new way to respond to adverse situations.

I live with an attitude of gratitude. I'm so grateful for things like my health. In thirteen years, I've never missed a speaking event. I cherish that. People don't realize how important health is until they don't have it, until they're very sick or can't do something that they love doing.

If I have twenty years left on this planet, I'm going to be blessed. I want to live every moment like I choose. We've got some new tours coming up around the world. My heart goes out to people who are younger who feel their lives are already over. You must find a reason to get up. It's not the end of the story. Don't believe that.

## FORGIVE YOURSELF

**MM:** Having forgiveness in my heart has also helped me. Sometimes we become so bitter or resentful from hate. Forgiveness releases you from a prison that you put yourself in, an emotional prison. One of the hardest people to forgive is yourself. Stop beating yourself up over something that happened months or years ago. You're not going to change it by beating yourself up. Forgive yourself. You made a mistake, now move on. If you hurt other people along the way, apologize to them. Say, "I'm sorry I messed up." They may not accept your apology, but at least you gave it your best.

I had to forgive myself because I beat myself up for too long. I still make mistakes; nobody's perfect. When someone tries to put me on a pedestal thinking that I'm this perfect guy, I tell them I'm not perfect. I make mistakes too. When I make a mistake, I ask for forgiveness, and I try to learn from that experience. I make sure it doesn't lead to another mistake. It becomes a learning experience in my life.

## GO AFTER YOUR GOALS, AND DON'T WORRY ABOUT JUDGEMENT

**MM:** Don't compare yourself to other people. You're not defined by other people, their opinions, or what they have done. Work on yourself. We often spend so much time on things that don't matter. If you put that much effort into building your career, researching, going after your dreams, and writing down things that you want to do, you will go further in life.

Harvard University did a ten-year study on students who write down their dreams and goals and those who don't. The amazing thing about this study was that most of the students who wrote down their dreams and goals saw them become a reality. Also, after ten years, those students were making ten times more money than the other Harvard graduates who didn't write down their goals or who didn't have goals at all.

Act toward your dreams, so they can become a reality. Don't spend your life worried about how many followers and likes you have. Don't worry about what your followers say about you. Everybody has an opinion. Until they have walked in your shoes and lived your life, they can't judge you. If we spent as much time loving people as we do judging them, this world would be a better place.

## TRANSITIONING FROM WRESTLING TO SPEAKING TO YOUTH

**MM:** After wrestling, I made some bad choices again and hit rock bottom. My life spun out of control. I got a job as a personal trainer at Gold's Gym in Orlando, FL. My clients got great results, and I ended up saving enough money that I could start my own gym. I got a call from Melbourne High School. The coach wanted me to come and speak to the football team. I thought that was cool. I love sports, and I used to play football. I felt so empowered by the difference that I was making in the students' lives. They were engaged in my presentation. They must have told someone else, because another school called me to come and speak. That was cool. I started doing more presentations. My presentations were good before, but now they are great. When I started to speak from my heart, everything changed. It's been an amazing journey.

I had a video that went viral about me speaking about my mom. I was speaking to schools in Atlanta at the time. My friend, former wrestler Diamond Dallas Page, had his film crew there to film my presentation. A couple of days later, he shared a clip of my speech. A week later, it had 100,000 views, and then it got millions. Between all the shares between the two companies, we calculated that over half a billion people saw that video. My phone really started to ring after that. In the first month that the video came out, we had 3,000 requests for me to speak to schools all over the world. I find great joy in speaking to kids.

Find your calling in life. When you find your passion, you will never have to work a day in your life. I haven't been working for thirteen years.

## AN IMPORTANT LESSON THAT HIS MOM TAUGHT HIM

**MM:** One thing my mom taught me is you can make more money, but you can't make more time. All she ever wanted to do was talk to me, but I never had time for her. I was bored talking to my mom, or I didn't have time for her. I didn't realize how much a mother or a parent can love a child. We often don't think about what they go through. They can feel lonely as a single mom or dad. The time we have with them is so precious—maybe not for you but for them.

I beat myself up so much when my mom died. I could not forgive myself. "Why was I such a jerk?" I asked myself. "She loved me so much." She was always at my sporting events cheering me on, but after the game, I blew her off and went with my friends. I'd give her attitude. I would hate it if someone treated me the way I treated her. After my mom died, I learned about love and how important it is. I didn't want to take it for granted anymore.

It's so important to reach out to people. Maybe you have a friend or a family member who you used to do everything with, but you had a falling out for some reason. As I got older, one thing I learned is sometimes it doesn't matter who's right or wrong. We all make mistakes, and we all need forgiveness. Be careful who you let fall out of your life. Repair broken relationships. Talk to them, or at least try to. You never know when someone's last day is. Tomorrow is not promised to anybody.

## ON THE VERGE OF SUICIDE

**MM:** I went through a dark period of life. I had depression, anxiety, and fear of losing everything. My mother and my little brother died two weeks apart. My sister died at age twenty-one from cancer. My dad died of lung cancer while I was holding him in my arms in the hospital. He was looking right at me. I have lost so many friends. This past year, 2019, I lost six of my close friends and family members. It's been a tough year. I'm not suicidal anymore, but in 2003 I wanted to end it all. I thank God every day that I didn't make that decision. I never would have known all the beautiful things that were coming my way. I tell people, there are some storms you can walk through, some storms you must run through, and some storms during which we must hang on with everything we have. Don't let go, and don't give up, because I promise you that after every storm, the sun will eventually shine brighter than you could ever imagine. Don't give up.

I have joy in life because I was in that dark place, at rock bottom, but I got through it. Every day, you walk a little more, you run a little more, and you get yourself in a place where, suddenly, you meet someone, and your life is changed forever. I have met some of the most incredible people, and I never would have known them if I had ended my life. I never would have known the joy of finding my passion.

194

## TOP TAKEAWAYS:

- Write down your goals.
- Decide to go after your goals.
- We become who we surround ourselves with.
- Don't live in time; live in moments.
- *It's not what's in your pocket that matters; it's what's in your heart.*
- Your best years are still ahead of you.
- Have forgiveness in your heart.
- Don't worry about judgement; everyone has an opinion.
- Don't take your loved ones for granted.

# 32
# WHY YOUR DREAMS ARE NOT TOO SMALL
### JONTE "NOT SO SMALL" HALL

Jonte "Not So Small" Hall is the "first shortest" Harlem Globetrotter. He was raised in Baltimore around drugs, and other people invited him to do drugs and sell them. But he kept his eye on the prize: basketball. He knew that one day he would go pro. After some setbacks, like taking care of his mom, who was suffering from multiple sclerosis, a lot of "no's" and naysayers saying he couldn't do it because he was too small, he finally earned a spot with the Harlem Globetrotters.

## CONNECT:
- Instagram: @JonteNotSoSmall

## STRUGGLES INCLUDED IN THIS CHAPTER:
- One of the smallest kids in class
- People doubted him
- Bullying
- His mom was sick

## AVOIDING DRUG LIFE
**Jonte Hall:** I had strong parents. They were strong willed and kept my brother and I grounded. My mom said, "If you want to go out in the streets, don't look back." Every parent has rules, and if you don't obey them, you have to go. At an early age, I saw a lot of violence, but my heart was set on becoming something great. I got my first basketball at age six. That kept me grounded and focused. Right then and there, I knew I wanted to play basketball. Regardless of what I was seeing, that gave me the confidence to pursue basketball and not get caught up in the streets.

## FOUND A WAY TO PLAY BASKETBALL

**JH:** After receiving my first basketball at age six, I started playing organized basketball at age nine. Back then there weren't a lot of basketball courts in the part of Baltimore where I grew up at. So, we'd get a milk crate and a saw. We'd cut the bottom out and hang it on a pole or nail it to a tree. I got my practice there, from sunup to sundown. I still don't know how I did that in 98-degree weather.

Whatever goals you may have, you may not have all the resources to pursue them, but when there's a will, there's a way.

## WHAT TO DO IF YOU DON'T HAVE A POSITIVE INFLUENCE IN YOUR LIFE

**JH:** It's tough when you don't have positive influences in your life. When you don't have that, you must dig deep. Know who you are as a person, and follow your heart. Don't get discouraged about your environment or your upbringing. If you want to be a lawyer, an athlete, or a medical professional, dig deep. You must have faith that you can get out of your situation.

## YOU'RE NEVER TOO SMALL TO DO ANYTHING

**JH:** When I do speaking engagements, I don't want people to think I'm just a basketball player. I always push the idea that you're never too small to do anything. I always emphasize, "Pick something that you love, that you're great at, or that you have some type of potential in. Focus on whatever that is." Try to focus on just that one thing, so you won't get overwhelmed. If that one thing doesn't work out, find another passion to pursue. That's what I preach when I go into schools. You must believe that you can accomplish your goals.

Growing up, I was put down and bullied verbally. People said I was too small. For my height to be in the history books with an iconic, world-famous team is amazing. I went from being cursed for being short to being praised in the history books as part of a world-famous team. Anything is possible. If I could do it standing at five feet two inches, anybody can do it. I like this quote: "As long as your heart stands tall, you're not so small."

## OVERCOMING NAYSAYERS

**JH:** We must dig deep and become comfortable with ourselves—with being short, tall, small, or overweight. That's how I overcame a lot of the naysayers. I knew I had a mission. I knew I wanted to help my mom get healthy. I wanted to get out of the projects. Growing up, I knew I wasn't going to let anybody stop me. That was how I dealt with the naysayers. I said, "Jonte, you can't get caught up in what they're saying. You must prove them wrong." That motivated me. When I can prove somebody wrong, I get excited about that. "I'm short, so what?" That made me spend extra hours in the gym to work on things to be great at.

I'm still going through that on my journey of becoming a speaker and stepping away from being a Globetrotter. After being to fifty-seven countries and all fifty states, my heart was telling me to make a positive influence. I was willing to risk it all and go for it. I still deal with naysayers who say, "Why did you do that? You aren't going to be no successful speaker. You're from the projects." I'm still proving people wrong. There are going to be naysayers in your life, so tune them out.

## ONE MORE SHOT

**JH:** In my first year of high school, I was about four feet eleven inches with shoes on. I was tiny. During high school, I played junior varsity and had a solid first year. I got moved up to varsity in grade ten. That year I realized I wasn't going to grow much, so I wrote to colleges to tell them to come see me play. Of course, none of them responded. I wrote to colleges throughout my entire high school career. I'd exaggerate my height a bit and say I was five foot five inches. Nobody responded.

After I graduated, I played basketball for a community college. I didn't play much. That was a learning experience. I was going through the naysayers. I kept working, and I took somebody's starting job during the middle of the year. Then I had to drop out of college to take care of my mother. My mom has MS (multiple sclerosis). I said, "Mom, I'm going to take care of you." I dropped out of college and had to work a nine-to-five job. I did janitorial work, and I did it with pride. I knew in the back of my mind that I was going to make it.

You're going to get bumped off course. It may be out of your control, but you must dig deep. You must tell yourself that eventually you will accomplish your goals. Stay focused and pray, and it will happen.

I saved my money and then went to a tryout in North Carolina. I wanted to see where I was as far as basketball. I tried out for the NBA Development League. Think of the NBA as varsity and the NBA Development League as junior varsity. That was my first tryout. I didn't make it; my height played a major role. But I got an opportunity to see where I was at as far as my skill level. Out of 200 guys, I was among the last 25 to be there as well as the smallest one there.

199

I came back home feeling good about myself. I was in the gym all the time. I kept trying out, but there was a time where I was about to give up. I was that close to giving up. I had a lot of people telling me that I wasn't going to make it. At that time I was twenty-three or twenty-four years old, and it was getting to me. I still wanted to play. I wasn't even in my prime yet. I gave basketball one more opportunity. I emailed the Washington Generals, the Globetrotter's opponents, and they gave me an opportunity. It wasn't a lot of money, but I got the exposure. I did that for a year and a half. The Globetrotters loved me so much that they gave me a tryout, and I made history. That's how my story started.

That's all it takes. It only takes one person to change your life, somebody to notice you. It takes one more shot

Stay persistent, stay dedicated, stay grounded, and don't get out of character. When you get out of character, you lose your faith and your confidence. When that happens, it's easy to get sidetracked.

## YOU NEVER KNOW WHO LOOKS UP TO YOU

**JH:** One of my best memories happened in 2018. A young lady made me feel like I was Michael Jordan. I found out she was a huge "Too Tall" fan, my Globetrotter name. My coach said, "Too Tall, you have a number-one fan in the audience." I thought he was joking around, but then I saw her, and she was so emotional. She was shaking. She yelled, "Oh my gosh! Oh my gosh! I'm such a huge fan." She was crying. I gave her my headband and my wristband, and that right there was the highlight of my career. You never know whose life you are impacting.

## TOP TAKEAWAYS:

- Where there's a will, there's a way.
- When you don't have positive influences in your life, dig deep inside.
- Focus on only one passion at a time.
- Become comfortable with yourself.
- Don't get caught up with what other people say about you.
- Give yourself one more shot.
- Stay persistent, stay dedicated, stay grounded, and don't get out of character.
- You're never too small for your goals and dreams.
- *You never know who is looking up to you.*

# 33
# HOW TO OVERCOME YOUR FEAR OF PUBLIC SPEAKING
## *GRANT BALDWIN*

Grant Baldwin is a speaker, podcaster, author, entrepreneur, and an all-around regular guy trying to make a little dent in the world. He has always gravitated toward public speaking and was a youth pastor after college. After he found out he was becoming a father, Grant took a hard look at what he wanted to do. He pursued his passion for public speaking and has given thousands of presentations around the United States to schools and corporations. He married his high school sweetheart and has three beautiful daughters.

He talks about how any high school student can overcome the fear of public speaking and possibly make a career out of it. He also talks about when his parents got a divorce and how he married his high school sweetheart.

## CONNECT:
- Website: www.grantbaldwin.com
- Instagram: @GBaldwin
- Podcast: The Speaker Lab

## STRUGGLES INCLUDED IN THIS CHAPTER:
- Divorced parents
- Felt alone

## HOW GRANT'S EARLY YEARS SHAPED HIS PRESENT

**Grant Baldwin:** As a teen, I was really involved in my church. I had a lot of great friends there. My youth pastor had a big impact in my life. He was a phenomenal speaker. That influenced me in regard to what I ended up doing later. I went to Bible college, worked in different churches as a youth pastor, and had a lot of opportunities to speak. The work was really rewarding. My teen years were formidable, but the best part of high school was meeting my sweetheart. We're still together today. We've been together for twenty-three years and married for eighteen. We have three beautiful daughters. That was the best thing that came out of my teenage years.

## HIS PASSION FOR SPEAKING IN HIGH SCHOOL AND COLLEGE

**GB:** I took a public speaking class in high school. I also did a bit at church, where I occasionally taught a Sunday school class. I didn't do a ton of it, but it was one of those things that resonated with me, and I wanted to do more of it. I felt like I was decent at it, and I wanted to pursue it. I wasn't quite sure how I would though.

In college, I worked for a guy who was a full-time speaker. I got to help him with the business side, including travel, contracts, and logistics. I enjoyed that and got to see behind the curtains of being a speaker. That was the path I was on as a youth pastor at a local church. If you have something you are passionate about, and it comes easily to you, like speaking was for me, then pursue it.

## LESSONS THAT HIS YOUTH PASTOR TAUGHT HIM

**GB:** My youth pastor taught me a lot about faith, serving, leadership, and helping others. He was a great leader and a great mentor. He believed in me and gave me opportunities to lead. He helped me see my potential and gave me a lot of confidence. I highly recommend that you find a mentor who can guide you like my youth pastor guided me.

## HIS PARENTS' DIVORCE AND HOW OTHERS CAN COPE

**GB:** My parents got divorced during the summer between eighth grade and my freshman year of high school. I certainly had low points. It had a big effect on me. At that time, none of my friends' parents were divorced. I felt like I was alone, like I was on an island. I didn't feel like I had anyone to talk to, and I was embarrassed about it. It was difficult, but later I realized it was a good opportunity for me to be able to help other students. When I spoke about my parents' divorce as a teenager, students would say, "Hey, I just found out my parents are getting a divorce" or "My dad just left." At the time, I didn't like the situation, but now I have a great relationship with both of my parents. You do your best with what you've got. It's been cool to see how I've been able to use that to help influence students who are going through something similar.

It's like the seasons. There are four seasons, winter, spring, summer, and fall. Some of them are better than others. I enjoy spring and fall. Winter can be miserable depending on what part of the world you are in, but it's not permanent. Spring comes, and it'll be better than winter.

I think of it a lot in that way. When bad things happen that are outside of your control, it sucks in that moment, but it will help build gratitude for what you have. Even though my parents got divorced, I was grateful I had great relationships with both of my parents. That means a lot to me. I don't know that I would go back and do anything differently or change much about it. At that moment, you need to adjust and figure it out. It becomes your new normal.

## MAKE SURE TO ENJOY WHAT YOU'RE DOING

**GB:** Bringing a child into the world causes you to question everything. When my wife was five months pregnant with our first child, it caused me to think through what I really wanted to do. One of the things I enjoyed was speaking, and as a youth pastor, I had a lot of opportunities to do that. There were also parts of the job that I didn't enjoy. It was stressful at times. When she was pregnant, I asked myself, "Is this what I want to do with the rest of my life? If it isn't, what would I rather be doing?"

Some of the best advice I got was at a conference I attended. The speaker at one workshop said, "The career that you're doing, if you don't enjoy at least eighty percent of it, you need to do something else." I remember thinking, *That's crazy. I didn't know there are people who enjoy eighty percent of their work. Is that even possible?* It resonated with me because at the time I wasn't enjoying anywhere near 80 percent of what I was doing. I decided I wanted to do something else, though I wasn't entirely sure what that would be. It was a kick in the pants and a motivation for me. I knew I was going to figure it out and do something different.

## HOW TO OVERCOME THE FEAR OF PUBLIC SPEAKING

**GB:** Giving a speech can be intimidating, daunting, and stressful. I enjoy speaking, but my wife hates the idea of public speaking. It stressed her out when she had to give a speech in class. For me, I had nerves and butterflies, but I still enjoyed it. The best thing anyone can do when preparing for a talk is to practice and prepare. It's like a test. If you had to go into class right now to take a test, and you hadn't studied, you'd feel stressed. If you study, you may still feel some of those butterflies, but you will feel more confident. Giving speeches is the same way. The more that you practice, the more comfortable and confident you will be going into the presentation. Practicing is the only way to improve your public speaking skills.

## TIPS FOR TEENS TRYING TO BUILD A SPEAKING CAREER

**GB:** One of the best things you can do to become a better speaker and get more comfortable as a speaker is to look for as many opportunities to speak as possible. Speak in clubs at school, in class, in leadership opportunities, and outside of school. The more you speak, the more comfortable and confident you will get. It's no different than anything else. The way to become a better writer is by writing. The way to become a better musician is by playing music. The way to become better at playing a sport is by playing the sport. If I wanted to get better at shooting free throws, I could read about shooting free throws, I could watch YouTube videos about shooting free throws, or I could practice shooting free throws. The same thing is true with speaking. The way to get better as a speaker is by speaking. If you are good, speaking will lead to more speaking. There's a correlation between speaking a lot and confidence. Public speaking is outside of many people's comfort zone. The more you do something uncomfortable, the more confident you will become.

## A BLIP ON THE RADAR LATER

**GB:** When you're going through troubles, you feel like what's happening in that moment is your entire world. The reality is, if you fast-forward in time, it becomes a blip on the radar. My parents got divorced twenty-three years ago. At that moment, life sucked. I look back now and realize that in the grand scheme of things, it made me a stronger person and helped me grow as an individual. It helped my wife and I in our own marriage because we went through it together. We know what it's like to be a kid whose parents split up. We don't want to do that to our kids.

Take a long-term perspective. Today might suck, but it will get better. You may have flunked a test, broken up with your boyfriend or girlfriend, or gotten in a fight with your mom or dad. It's not always going to be like that. If you take a long-term perspective, you'll realize that everyone has bad days, so there's no need to beat yourself up constantly over such days.

## TOP TAKEAWAYS:

- If you are passionate about something, and it comes easily to you, pursue it.
- Find a mentor who can guide you.
- Having your parents get divorced can be miserable, but think of it as a season. Those feelings are not permanent.
- During tough moments, it helps to build gratitude for what you have.
- If you don't enjoy at least 80 percent of what you're doing, do something else.
- Prepare for a presentation like how you would for a test.
- If you want to become a speaker, take every opportunity to speak.
- *Speaking helps you gain confidence because it takes you outside your comfort zone.*
- What is happening to you now will be a blip on the radar later.

# 34
# LIFE LESSONS FROM A FORMER PROFESSIONAL BOXER
## *EDWARD ASHLEY LATIMORE JR.*

Edward Ashley Latimore Jr. wrote his destiny. He was raised in the projects around fighting, crime, and drugs, and he didn't have much money. It took him a while to figure out how he was going to make a living. He went to college at age eighteen, dropped out, picked up professional boxing, then joined the National Guard, so he could return to college to get a physics degree while growing the successful brand that he has today, with over 100,000 Twitter followers. Now he provides authentic life lessons to people around the world.

## CONNECT:
- Website: www.edlatimore.com
- Twitter: @EdLatimore

## STRUGGLES INCLUDED IN THIS CHAPTER:
- Raised in low-income housing
- Didn't have much money
- Was in a dangerous environment
- Didn't know what he wanted to do with his life
- Alcohol addiction

## HIS TEENAGE YEARS

**Edward Latimore:** My family was poor, and I grew up in a public housing project, raised by a single mom. I learned quickly to take care of myself due to the neighborhood I was brought up in. I was brought up with crime and fights happening around me. People there either become friendly or antagonistic. I was fortunate that my mom put me in a good high school. It took a while to get accustomed to it because I had different experiences than a lot of the kids there. I remember talking to one of the kids and he told me he'd never been in a fistfight before, and it was a foreign concept to him. Where I was raised, fights took place all the time.

Even with everything going on, I knew college was a way out for me. I went to a decent high school, but I still lived in the hood. I wanted to be surrounded by different people who had higher goals and ambitions. It was important for me to get out of the environment I was in.

Achieving my level of success, I was an anomaly in my family. If you want to achieve success, there is power in how you were brought up, but that isn't everything. Everyone has advantages and disadvantages. In the end it boils down to taking it upon yourself to figure out how you are going to be successful and then working hard at it.

## PUT YOURSELF IN A BETTER ENVIRONMENT

**EL:** There are so many ways to put yourself in a more positive environment. The average person is not going to write their golden ticket through sports or some type of performance, which is why it is extremely important to experiment and leave all options on the table. You never know which one you will be good at, but the quickest way to take those options off the table is to get arrested or have a kid. It's not impossible to achieve success if that happens, but it will push your timeline back. Fortunately for me, I never ran into any of those issues.

## MAKING A KEYSTONE DECISION

**EL:** A keystone decision is when you make one decision that impacts your future decisions and can change your life. It has a compounding effect. It eliminates a lot of bad decisions that you could have made. I think about my decision to stop drinking. By making that one decision, I eliminated a bunch of other bad decisions that I could have made that would have stemmed from alcohol.

## PREPARING FOR COLLEGE

**EL:** When I first went to college, I didn't know why I was there. There was no reason for me to continue. I wasn't mature enough for college. I got sucked into the party culture and drank a lot of alcohol. I wasn't there for the right reasons.

My recommendation is not to go to college when you're eighteen years old. There's research out there that says the human brain doesn't stop developing until age twenty-five. The last part of the brain to develop is the prefrontal cortex, which is the front of the brain and is the part that is responsible for your decision-making ability.

You will likely change your mind regarding what you want to do. You should go get some life experience and try to be somebody before you go to college. College is not an end all, be all. At age eighteen, I wished I would have traveled and learned new skills. You're never too old to go back to college, and when you do go back, it will be more effective than going to college at an early age, not knowing why you're there. When I went back to college the second time, I was laser focused.

## LIFE LESSONS FROM BOXING

**EL:** I went into boxing because I didn't know what to do after dropping out of college. When I got into boxing, my mindset switched from fixed to growth. I became convinced that I could learn anything. I learned that if I put my mind into it and worked, I could overcome any difficulty. I also learned how to sell myself, convincing people to invest in me and drive an hour to see me fight. I learned how to get people to like me.

## STARTING A BRAND

**EL:** I started my personal brand with no money or resources. I had no idea it would go so far. The best way to grow your brand is not to focus on your brand so much but to do something that will give you some experience, and then talk about that on social media. What made me successful was what I went through in life and sharing it with the world to impact lives. I was always trying to find a way out and a way to grow. We are in a great era of social media for us to be able to do that.

## HOW TO STOP CARING ABOUT OTHER PEOPLE'S OPINIONS OF YOU

**EL:** You have to live *your* life, not someone else's. I don't worry about what my friends or family think because I have to live my life and make sure I'm OK. Think of yourself as a leader. When you do that, you make decisions like a leader. When you're a leader, you don't worry about the popular opinion; you have to make decisions based on what's best. You must also decide what's best for you. I have to live with everything I have done, the consequences and the benefits. You are no different.

## GET IN SHAPE

**EL:** The best action step you can take to have a better life is to get in shape. Physical training is more about what it does to your mind than what it does to your body. If you can discipline yourself to eat right and exercise hard, you have demonstrated that you are in control. What gets people in trouble is they give in to temptation. If you can show you have discipline in regard to your physical health, you can have the discipline to overcome other challenges in your life and not give in to the temptations that get people in trouble. Also, when you look better, you feel better, and when you feel better, you perform better and become more confident. Make your body and your physical health a priority.

## TOP TAKEAWAYS:

- In the end, it boils down to taking it upon yourself to figure out how to be successful and work hard.
- If you want to achieve your goals, put yourself in a more positive environment.
- Keep all of your career options on the table.
- The quickest way to push your timeline back or take options off the table is to get arrested or have a kid at an early age.
- By making one positive decision, you can eliminate many future bad decisions that could have stemmed from it.
- Don't go to college right out of high school. Get some experiences first, and then go to college.
- *The best way to grow your personal brand is to do something that gives you experience and then talk about it.*
- The best way to stop caring what people think of you is to think of yourself as a leader.
- The best action step you can take to have a better life is to get in shape.

# 35
# WHAT TO DO IF YOU'RE SEXUALLY ASSAULTED
## *MAKAILA NICHOLS*

Makaila Nichols is the bestselling author of *Blatantly Honest*. She is a nationally recognized speaker on bullying, body image, and other social topics. Makaila has built a brand from her *Blatantly Honest* series and now has a charitable foundation to help children across the country. In her spare time, she has developed a podcast series called *Blatantly Honest with Makaila Nichols*. Her career started at age fourteen when she was recruited to be a model. That's when her eating disorders started forming. In high school, she was bullied, and she felt anxiety and depression because of it and was sexually assaulted while being slut shamed for it, something that she had no control over. Makaila's story explains how she overcame these challenges and what you can do if you are facing similar problems.

## CONNECT:
- Website: www.makailanichols.com; www.blatantlyhonest.org
- Instagram: @MakailaNichols

## STRUGGLES INCLUDED IN THIS CHAPTER:
- Anxiety
- Depression
- Insecurity
- Peer pressure
- Bullied
- Eating disorder
- Sexually assault

# GETTING STARTED WITH MODELING

**Makaila Nichols:** I was walking through a mall and noticed a guy was watching me. I wondered why he was following me and what he was doing. Eventually, he came over and said, "Hey, I'm a model scout. Have you ever thought about modeling?" I told him it was not my thing and that I was very much a tomboy. But later I reconsidered it and I ended up modeling. I went to a scouting convention. I talked to various people, and different agencies offered me contracts. I signed with an agency when I was fourteen years old, and I was one of the youngest girls on their roster. It was very exciting.

**SS:** How did modeling feed into some of your insecurities?

**MN:** Models are held up to many expectations. If you look in magazines, you see these picture-perfect women and men. It was always a tiny girl. When I was playing sports, I was the tomboy and very active. I would put on a lot of muscle, which was a no-no in that industry. They said I needed to lose weight. They told me to lose twenty pounds, even though I was already tall and skinny. I suffered from eating disorders because I wanted to be something that I wasn't.

# OVERCOMING AN EATING DISORDER

**MN:** It was hard. I suffered from anorexia and bulimia. Bulimia is when you eat and then throw up to get rid of it. Anorexia is the thought of not wanting to eat. I didn't realize how much of a problem it was because I thought I was doing the right thing. My parents said, "Hey, Makaila, you're looking a little yellow. We can see all your bones." They took me to a nutritionist, and they told me what I was doing was not healthy. My parents helped me get through my eating disorder.

If you want to overcome an eating disorder, the first step is to be honest with yourself. Tell yourself you have a problem. Also, stop comparing yourself to people in magazines and on TV. Not everyone is supposed to look that way. You must address the problem you have with yourself. Help is available, and you need to take advantage of it.

# GETTING BULLIED

**MN:** It started off when I was younger because I lived a privileged lifestyle, and I got to experience things that my peers didn't. They became jealous of that. They kept thinking I thought I was better than them. People would throw food at me, exclude me, and slam me into lockers. I would sit with people at lunch, and they would move. Even my teachers picked on me. We went on a trip, and we were supposed to eat pizza. I decided not to eat pizza because I was having a hard time losing weight. Two of my teachers pulled me out of the room and told me that I was disgusting and looked gross.

I also had two friends who I thought were my best friends, but they turned their backs on me. I didn't even see it coming. They started to go after me. I experienced a lot of cyberbullying.

Bullying started in elementary school. There was no way I could prevent it. I told myself, I am who I am. If you don't like that, then, oh well.

Bullying is a traumatic experience for everyone involved. Bullies are bullies for a reason. Many times, they are going through their own battles. The first step to prevent bullying is realizing there is a possibility that you might be a bully. You may say mean things to people and not realize it. The words we say matter. If you're being bullied, you need to vocalize it to that person and tell them it bothers you.

## GETTING SEXUALLY ASSAULTED

**MN:** I used to be the girl who was hanging out with all the guys. No one looked at me twice. I was tall and not really developed. I was one of the guys. When I started modeling, all that changed. Other boys found me cute. One popular guy, the captain of the football team, and I were hanging out. We were friends, and we'd hang out every day. Then suddenly, he started taking jabs at me. He started smacking me on the butt, and it escalated quickly. He tried to kiss me and do other stuff. I asked him what he was doing and told him that we were just friends. One day, he just went for it and sexually assaulted me.

I was traumatized by the experience, and I didn't realize what it was. I didn't realize it was assault. I didn't realize that I didn't have a choice in that situation. For a year I kept it to myself because I was already being bullied. I already felt alone, and I didn't want people to come after me for another reason. I let the abuse happen many times. I let it happen to me for so long, and I was scared of speaking up. One day my parents get called into the principal's office. I vividly remember walking in, seeing my parents and the guidance counselor, and I almost threw up. In that moment, I knew that they knew everything.

**SS:** What can someone do if they are in that situation?

**MN:** When confronted by danger, people tend to respond in one of three ways: flight, fight, or freeze. I froze. If you find yourself freezing, there's nothing wrong with you. It's a natural human response. You can't be afraid of the judgment you'll face by coming forward. You need to accept that this isn't right, and your biggest advocate is you. That's so hard to feel especially when you're a victim of sexual assault,

213

rape, or abuse. Come forward. If not for you, do it for someone else who might become a victim of that person.

I kept it in for so long that people were blaming me. They called me words like "hoe" and said, "She wanted this." Those words do a lot of damage. Consent can change at any time. That's something people need to keep in mind. If you change your mind, and the other person continues, that's assault and rape. The victim cannot be blamed.

**SS:** You had amazing parents. I'm sure some other parents aren't as supportive. If someone doesn't have supportive parents, where can they go?

**MN:** Go to people who genuinely care about you, like your friends. I tell myself every day that people genuinely care. It might seem weird, but you can also talk to a stranger. If you're ever on a plane, start talking to the person next to you, sometimes just venting to that person can help. You can also find a doctor or a therapist. Talk to someone.

## OVERCOMING INSECURITIES

**MN:** If you compare yourself to others all the time, you're always going to find things to feel insecure about. Talking to yourself about your insecurities and accepting your flaws is important. I work on that every day. Be honest, and tell yourself you're not perfect, but also start naming things that you like about yourself. Your strengths will outweigh your weaknesses.

## SUICIDE IS NOT AN OPTION

**MN:** Going through my problems made me feel worthless and that life didn't matter. It breaks my heart to know that the thought of ending their lives goes through kids' heads. Suicide is a permanent response to temporary problems. Even though it seems like it will last forever, these challenges are only a small moment in your life.

It's a matter of pushing through and getting beyond that dark place, realizing it's not that bad. I pushed through, and now I am inspiring youth from all over. Your purpose is important. Your life matters, and the world needs you. Follow your calling.

## HOW TO BE BLATANTLY HONEST WITH YOURSELF

**MN:** Being blatantly honest is giving a straight answer and admitting the truth to yourself, even if you don't like it. When we are honest with ourselves, we can solve problems in our lives.

## TOP TAKEAWAYS:

- Don't compare yourself to others. That is how insecurities form.
- If you are being bullied, vocalize it to that person.
- Come forward if you have been sexually assaulted.
- Consent can change at any time.
- Suicide is not an option.
- Your life matters, and the world needs you.
- *Become blatantly honest with yourself.*

# 36
# HOW TO FIND YOUR INNER GENIUS
## *DAVID EDWARD GARCIA*

David is the only motivational comedian who speaks five languages. David empathizes with diverse students who face challenges because he was once considered an "at-risk student" himself before defying the odds and graduating with a bachelor's degree and then earning multiple other degrees. David has motivated children and adults around the world. His upbringing facilitated his multiculturalism/multilingualism, which makes it easy for him to relate to diverse audiences.

## CONNECT:
- Website: www.davidedwardgarcia.com
- YouTube: David Edward Garcia
- Instagram: @DavidEdwardGarcia

## STRUGGLES INCLUDED IN THIS CHAPTER:
- Not good at school and felt dumb
- Troubled and at-risk student
- Challenges from living on the Mexico/Texas border
- Was in a toxic environment

## CONSIDERED AN AT-RISK STUDENT

**David Edward Garcia:** While growing up, I got into trouble constantly. When I was twelve, thirteen, and fourteen years old, I developed a lot of aggression. I didn't have the tools to navigate my anger. I was aggressive toward teachers and other students. When I was in eighth grade, I received an in-school suspension as a result.

In Texas, they were able to paddle kids, so I got paddled. I maxed out the paddling, I maxed out the suspension, and I got kicked off my school bus because I was out of control. Looking back, I put fifty other children in danger because I was running around the bus throwing papers at cars that were passing by. It was a mess.

When I got into high school, things changed. People who I was in school with started causing problems in Mexico, and they got involved in darker violence. The students who I played basketball and football with back then are no longer alive today because they chose another path.

In high school, the punishment was no longer going to the principal's office and getting detention. People my age were facing life-and-death scenarios. When I was sixteen, my parents gave over legal guardianship to me. I moved to Houston, Texas. That was a big turning point in my life. When I moved, I got involved in church and youth groups. That provided structure and positive peer influences in my life. Sports was also a positive outlet for me. When I was sixteen, I started to see a different life. I was working, which provided me with money and gave me the ability to buy things. I realized I could make choices that didn't harm people.

If people didn't do well in school when I was growing up, they were doomed. I failed classes in school. It's not something that I'm proud of. I failed both hard and easy classes. I failed Spanish for non-Spanish speakers, even though I grew up right next to Mexico and heard Spanish all the time. As I went into adulthood, I felt inferior and dumb. I pushed past high school. Now I have three college diplomas, and I'm working on a fourth and fifth master's degree simultaneously. I also speak five languages. I feel like I'm just getting started. When people tell me, "You're so smart. You're so gifted," I tell them that I barely made it past high school.

## WE HAVE THE POWER OF CHOICE

**DEG:** My big turning point was church. Your faith belongs to you. You can share with other people, and you can also learn from other people who believe differently. Many successful people have a purpose and meaning that comes from their beliefs.

Growing up, Latinos in my area didn't have a lot of education or opportunities. Violence was happening four miles from my house on the other side of the border in Mexico. A lot of people got swept into that world.

If people don't have money, they don't have a lot of opportunities for education. If people are just trying to survive and make it to the next day, they're not going to invest in education. If they don't invest in education, then they're going to stay stuck. On the other hand, we are not numbers or percentages; we're individuals. I believe every individual has the power of choice. I didn't have money. I didn't have rich parents to pay for my schooling. I had to work full time while I went to school full time. I had to go on food stamps. I had to wait tables. I couldn't finish my first degree in four years; it took me nine years instead. Yes, the numbers and the percentages were stacked against me, but I worked hard and had faith.

Are you going to look for excuses, or are you going to look for solutions? You can be powerful and strong.

## FINDING YOUR OWN GENIUS

**DEG:** There's a passage in the Bible that says we are God's masterpiece, created to do good works. We're all God's unique design. Every person has something that is unique about them and can do something that nobody else can do. Every person has a unique genetic makeup and a unique personality. When we're able to give that to humanity, that's when the magic happens.

I am the best in the world at what I do. That's not arrogant. I'm the only Hispanic male from South Texas who has the college degrees that I have, who knows the languages that I know, who has gone to the places I have been to, who makes professional standup comedy with a message, and who does motivational speaking. I'm able to package it and do it the way that I do. It's not hard to be the best in the world when you're the only one doing what you do. Every single one of us is the best in the world at what only we can do. Bullying and negativity in society is aimed at stealing your best from the world.

Instead of hiding your uniqueness, bring it out into the open. We need you. We need the next song. We need the next great app. We need the next person who's going to stop a bully. We need more teachers. We need everyone to be the best in the world. When you find your genius, you don't take away someone else's life. There's so much abundance in this world. Success builds success, and we build on each other. When we recognize that we need every person to give their best contribution, that's when life becomes magical.

When you find your genius, you'll be confident because you realize you don't have to be good at everything. You just have to be good at one thing.

It's easy to discount the pain from your past. We go through a sequence from pain to overcoming it to becoming a champion to helping others become champions. You will come to realize that if you hadn't gone through that struggle, you wouldn't be as strong as you are now.

Part of finding your inner genius is facing your struggle, which helps shape your future. What talents and strengths do you have now that can help you shine? Focus on them, and take one step at a time.

## THE PROCESS OF FINDING YOUR UNIQUE GIFT

**DEG:** Finding your unique gift is an evolution. Going back to high school, my life had a purpose. As I've grown, I've developed other skills. I've also had other experiences. There's a moment where you realize that you have a gift, but you also evolve. I knew there was nothing that I couldn't do if it wasn't the realm of my calling and my skill set. No, I can't be a ballerina, an NBA player, or an astronaut, but those things are not my calling. Inside the realm of my calling, there is nothing that I can't do. If I can't do it today, that means I must work toward it, so I can get there eventually.

You might have a moment where you realize your purpose, or it might be more of a gradual evolution. Or it might take several evolutions. Keep on building, don't procrastinate, and take action.

## YOU CAN STILL SUCCEED WHEN NOBODY UNDERSTANDS YOU

**DEG:** A lot of life is being understood by nobody. A lot of life is being alone. A lot of life is hard. You can succeed anyway. If nobody believes in you, but you believe in you, that's all you need. If nobody understands you, but you understand you, that's all you need. You are an unstoppable force. You can choose how far you're going to go, when you're going to go, why you're going to go, and with whom you're going to go. Just because somebody tells you "no" in the beginning doesn't mean it's "no" forever. Just because something is difficult doesn't mean it's impossible. We are living in extraordinary times. You can't control what other people say or do, but you can control your response to it.

## TOP TAKEAWAYS:
- You have the power of choice.
- If you want to get somewhere in life, you must work extremely hard.
- You must have faith.
- You are the best in the world at what you do.
- *Part of finding your inner genius is facing your struggle, which helps shape your future.*
- Your purpose may go through several evolutions.
- You can't control what other people say or do, but you can control your response to it.

# 37
# HOW TO
# OVERCOME PTSD
## *ELENA BREESE*

Elena Breese is the blogger for *Still Blooming Me*, an influencer, and a speaker. She had a normal life until April 15, 2013, when the Boston Marathon Bombing happened. Luckily, Elena did not sustain any physical injuries, but three years after the bombing, she was diagnosed with post-traumatic stress disorder (PTSD) when she was voluntarily hospitalized. At times she couldn't eat, take care of her kids, or carry out the activities of daily life. She had to go to the hospital and undergo years of therapy.

## CONNECT:

- Website: www.stillbloomingme.com
- Instagram: @StillBloomingMe

## STRUGGLES INCLUDED IN THIS CHAPTER:

- Anxiety
- Depression
- Wanted to commit suicide
- Had too much going on and couldn't handle it
- Put a lot of pressure on herself
- Post-traumatic stress disorder

## THE BOSTON MARATHON BOMBING

**Elena Breese:** My husband was running the Boston Marathon, and I was waiting for him at the finish line with my brother-in-law. I was standing in the bleachers directly across the street from where the first bomb went off. Then shortly after, the second bomb went off.

**SS:** What was going through your mind when that happened?

**EB:** I'm one of those people who remembers all of it. It was very, very loud. The bomb exploded, and then we saw waves of air moving toward us. My hair was long at the time, and it flew up and blew all around me. There was a lot of smoke. The most horrific part of the experience was witnessing what was happening with the people across the street. The people were swirling in hysterics. It was very scary. Before I could figure out what I had just witnessed, the second bomb went off. They were about twelve seconds apart. Even though some of those moments seemed frozen in time for us, everything moved very quickly. Before I knew it, we were running from the finish line, and the SWAT teams and big armored vehicles were racing toward us.

**SS:** How long did it take you to reconnect with your husband?

**EB:** He was running with a good friend of his who had his cell phone with him. They were about a mile and a half from finishing, so they didn't hear or see anything, fortunately. Cell phone service was cut quickly there because they were afraid more bombs would be detonated. I was able to get one call out to my dad, but my call was cut while I was talking to him. My husband's friend texted me, and I was able to respond. They knew we were OK, and then we were eventually reunited.

## THE PTSD WASN'T UNTIL YEARS LATER

**EB:** Two days after the bombing, we were back home in Arizona, and I was back to taking care of the kids. I was taking care of everyone else around me, but I failed to take care of myself. A lot of people back home asked me about the bombing. After a while I decided not to talk about it and tried to forget about it.

Around the one-year anniversary of the bombing, I started having bad nightmares. That snowballed into many more symptoms over the next few years, like anxiety and depression.

I wasn't seeing a therapist, and I didn't make the connection that what I was experiencing was tied to the bombing. The anxiety and the panic attacks started to happen in public places and even while I was driving. It became much more difficult to function as a parent and a person. On July 14, 2016, there was a huge attack during Bastille Day in Nice, France, where over eighty people died. I was making dinner for my family, and I sat down to watch the evening news when I caught a clip of a witness recalling what he had experienced that day. Something that man said triggered a downward spiral. It led to a panic attack that triggered weeks of insomnia. I also lost my ability to eat. I was voluntarily hospitalized on August 3, 2016.

## WHAT ELENA HAS BEEN DOING TO GET BETTER

**EB:** I took matters in my own hands and became the CEO of my health and healing. That involved finding the right doctors and therapists to treat me. Not everybody is going to be the right fit, and I wanted a team of people who would educate me about my mental challenges and who had a holistic perspective on treatment, because the medications in the hospital had made me so much worse. I also saw a naturopathic doctor who helped me with supplements and a lot of issues I was having from the trauma. Part of that was using acupuncture. I decided to treat myself naturally. Journaling and meditation have also been a huge part of my recovery.

## EMBRACE THE TRAUMA

**EB:** I can recommend different resources and tools all day long, but what I recommend the most to someone experiencing PTSD is to be open to the different ways that people can heal. You need to embrace your trauma as a possible journey toward growth. It's not easy, but it helped propel me forward and to grow in ways I never thought possible.

## ELIMINATE THINGS FROM YOUR LIFE

**EB:** Sometimes you need to eliminate things from your life in order to heal. It could even be friends or family members. I've had to let some people go. It was hard, but those are some of the decisions that you must make. I also had to eliminate alcohol and caffeine. I was using those substances to cope. I used alcohol in the evenings to bring my stress level down, so I could get my kids fed, bathed, and into bed. Alcohol would make my sleep terrible. Then I would wake up in the morning, and I would drink caffeine to get through the day. It became a cycle, and I felt terrible through it.

## FIND PEOPLE WHO CAN RELATE TO YOUR TRAUMA

**EB:** My husband stumbled across an article in the *Boston Globe* about another survivor. I Googled her, and her website came up. It had great footage of her speaking. She had been in the bleachers as well. I emailed her right away. We met up, and I also met up with some of the other survivors on another anniversary of the Boston Marathon bombing. It was my introduction to the survivor world.

I cried the whole time as the loneliness that I had been carrying for so long melted away. Without having to say anything, I knew these people understood. Now I'm involved in an organization called Strength to Strength International. They support victims of terror and their families. I'm so grateful for this community because it has given me a handful of people who I can call or text any time of the day or night. We are there for each other.

If you're struggling with PTSD, find someone who can relate to you and understand you. They will help you carry that burden.

## FIGHT FOR YOURSELF AND OTHERS

**EB:** Have an open heart, and be gentle with yourself. Do research, so others with PTSD can understand how the trauma affects their bodies. Trauma can come out in physical ways. It's scary. I thought I had a brain tumor or cancer when it was actually PTSD. It came out in a weird way. Get some understanding of what trauma does to you. Your research and your voice can also benefit anyone who is going through it, advocating, fighting for it, and speaking up for themselves.

## TOP TAKEAWAYS:

- Find a therapist who is a good fit for you.
- Sometimes it's best to take matters into your own hands.
- Natural treatments, journaling, and meditation can help you heal.
- Embrace the trauma.
- *Eliminate the things that are holding you back from healing.*
- Find other people who can relate to your trauma.
- Do your own research on PTSD to help yourself and others.

# 38
# HOW TO CREATE YOUR SUCCESS STORY
### *MARISA SERGI*

Marisa Sergi is the winemaker and CEO of Red Head Wine. When she was younger, she was bullied because she had red hair. Many times she felt like an outcast. Fast-forward, and she graduated from one of America's top universities, Cornell. She also named her wine company after what she used to get bullied for and was featured in *Success* magazine's thirty under thirty. Read this chapter to discover how Marisa turned her bullying story into her success story.

## CONNECT:
- Instagram: @MarisaSergi
- TikTok: @MarisaSergi

## STRUGGLES INCLUDED IN THIS CHAPTER:
- Low self-esteem
- Bullying
- Social exclusion
- Fear of failure

## HER BULLYING STORY
**Marisa Sergi:** I wasn't bullied in elementary school. I had a lot of confidence, and I had friends. I was very comfortable being myself, but something changed drastically when I transitioned from sixth grade to junior high. As soon as seventh grade started, a lot of my friends turned on me. I had only fifty-three students in my graduating class. It was a small school. A lot of people who bullied me probably didn't even realize what they were doing. Looking back at it, I just know how much torment, dis-

appointment, and frustration I went through in junior high and high school because of these few individuals.

I was torn apart for everything: being studious, my red hair, not straightening my hair correctly or not styling it to the correct standard, not wearing makeup, not wearing the right clothes, or the fact that I was really into my schoolwork. They picked apart everything. I felt like I couldn't even raise my hand in class because they would make fun of me in the background, spread rumors, or pass notes about me. It was day in, and day out torment for me. I wanted to dye my hair black and be homeschooled.

The group of girls I sat with during lunch would bully me, but I still sat with them because I didn't know where else to go. Then they kicked me out of the lunch table. It was so embarrassing. I rushed into the bathroom crying. It made me angry that some of the other girls who were sitting there watching in silence didn't stick up for me. I was being picked apart for everything and degraded.

I finally found a new group of friends, but then they invited a new person to the group who didn't like me. I was publicly kicked out of my lunch table again by another group of friends. One guy didn't like me, and he had the whole group vote on who needed to be removed from the table because there wasn't enough room for him.

My grades dropped. I was off on the wrong foot in my high school years. Eventually, I looked at myself in the mirror and asked, "What's wrong with me? Why am I a target?" I didn't know how to react. To avoid being bullied, I pretended to be sick, so I didn't have to go to school. It affected my confidence.

It makes me sad that so many people throughout the world are going through the same thing that I did over ten years ago. It's even worse now because social media is more prevalent today than it was in 2006/2007, and kids nowadays get cyberbullied.

I wish I had the confidence back then that I do today because I would have stuck up for myself. My biggest regret is not knowing how to stick up for myself and take control of the situation. Now I take the opportunity to talk to people online, and I prepare them to stick up for themselves because I think that's the best way to help yourself in those situations.

## HOW DO YOU STICK UP FOR YOURSELF?

**MS:** In that moment when I was voted out of the lunch table again, I wish I could have stood up for myself and said, "The fact that we had a vote like this, that you guys are going along with this person and allowing him to be mean to me, is really disappointing. I'd rather be alone than in bad company.

I don't need anyone here. I'm going to find a better place where I deserve to be." Then I would have had the courage to find another lunch table group. I would walk to other lunch tables and ask if I could sit there.

If you find yourself in a similar situation, be honest. Let the new table know you were bullied, got kicked out, and that you want to find better friends. It could feel embarrassing to admit that, but the truth is empowering. I wish I could have embraced that back then.

The way to find new groups of people is to try different activities, go to different clubs, or volunteer outside of school. Try to join groups that have a lot of similarities to you. When you find a group of people who accept you for who you are, that's all you need to build yourself up.

## HAVING THE CONFIDENCE TO PURSUE HER PASSION

**MS:** My family has had a tradition of winemaking for many generations. My grandparents immigrated here from Italy. I enjoyed making wine with my family. Back in 2001, my father cashed in his life savings to start a winery, and four years later, Luva Bella Winery was born. I hung out there a lot.

I didn't have many close friends in high school, but entrepreneurship piqued my interest. I wanted to do the things that I was passionate about, but I didn't have the confidence to do them until college. I found a group of people who accepted me for who I was. I studied winemaking at Cornell University. I was able to embrace my passion but also find the inner confidence that I was lacking.

One summer I decided to take control of my life. Over winter break before that summer, my mom sat me down in her office and told me that she was disappointed because my grades weren't that great. She said that if I applied myself, I could be something. The way she talked made me pay attention and made me believe that I was letting myself down. I was trying to find who I was, and I decided that I was finally going to push myself. I was going to do things that I had always wanted to do but had been afraid to try. I started pursuing random things.

I started to pursue acting and modeling, even though I had been told I was ugly for my entire life. I was also short. That gave me some confidence but while doing those things I also interned at my family's winery, and my parents asked me to redesign our wine labels. They were outdated, and I thought it'd be cool to have my own wine label, called RedHead.

I designed it, and from there my university told me that I needed to create a capstone project to graduate. I asked my professor if I could use RedHead as my capstone to do some research on how I could bring it to

227

market. He agreed. In the beginning it was a fun project, and I didn't think it would go anywhere. After working hard on it for two years, I realized it could be a real business.

It started getting in a couple stores, then 5 and then 20, and now after working on it continually, my wine is in over 2,000 stores. It was just something I wanted to do. I didn't overthink it, and I think that's why it worked.

## HOW CAN SOMEONE START THEIR OWN BUSINESS AT A YOUNG AGE?

**MS:** Finding what you're most passionate about is vital prior to starting a business. Then find how you are going to make money in what you're passionate about. Whether it's video editing, acting, public speaking, or volunteering, find what you love. You don't want to start a business that you don't think about 24/7 because you will get burnt out and regret not going after what you truly desire. That's what I figured out. I really love entrepreneurship. I enjoy connecting with people. I enjoy the game of building something from scratch. I think that's the best advice, to find what you love to do first, and then make a business out of it later.

Embrace your true self, including all your insecurities, and all the positives that you have to offer. The moment you try to change yourself to align with what society wants is the moment that people are going to see that you're not being authentic. It's not going to feel right either. Embrace who you are, and you will succeed.

You must work day in and day out to find your calling. It took me over fifteen years to figure things out, and although I'm very young, I started taking risks at a young age. If you start today, you'll be laying a foundation and have something to stand on. Don't feel like it's ever too late because five years from now you're going to wish you had started earlier. Taking action now is the best decision ever.

## HANDLING FAILURE

**MS:** Any bump in the road is difficult, and those bumps can throw you off. Failures teach you how to appreciate the positives and that you have to learn from your mistakes to keep going. That's where you learn the most.

## TOP TAKEAWAYS:

- Have the confidence to stick up to bullies.
- Find a group of friends who accept you for who you are.
- To find the right group of friends, try new activities, join different

clubs, or volunteer outside of school.
- Take control of your life, and experiment with different types of jobs that you might like.
- Stop overthinking what you want to pursue.
- The best way to start a business is to find what you are passionate about and then figure out how to make money at it.
- *Embrace who you are, and you will succeed.*
- Taking action now is the best decision.
- You learn the most from failure.

# 39
# HOW TO OVERCOME THE STRESS OF APPLYING TO COLLEGES
*WILL HOLDREN*

Will Holdren is the Host of the *WillPower* podcast, author of *Becoming the Best*, a senior in high school, and heavily involved with extracurricular activities and sports. He just scored 1,000 points in basketball. Will comes from a small town in Millville, Pennsylvania. He is still on the fence about what college he should attend.

## CONNECT:
- LinkedIn: linkedin.com/in/will-holdren-019027185
- Instagram: @Will_Holdren

## STRUGGLES INCLUDED IN THIS CHAPTER:
- People pleaser
- Feared being a disappointment
- Put a lot of pressure on himself
- Felt pressured as a high school senior

## THE PRESSURES OF BEING A HIGH SCHOOL SENIOR

**Will Holdren:** Tons of pressure is put on high school seniors, but I'm lucky enough to have a family that supports me in whatever I want to do. As a senior you feel like you must know what you want to do for the rest of your life. You don't want to disappoint the people around you, and you also want to make sure you get good grades. You're also taking harder classes like AP Calculus and AP Physics. Classes get harder, but you must still maintain your grades. You must be ready for the pressure. Realize this is another step on the ladder, and you must do your best to get through it. This is the next stage of your life.

**SS:** Have you looked into different colleges?

**WH:** Yeah, I have. I've been accepted to a couple of colleges already. I plan to major in mechanical engineering and minor in entrepreneurship.

## COLLEGE DECISIONS

**WH:** My brother is three years older than me, so I saw him go through the college application process. I didn't think it was that difficult, and I thought I would know exactly what I wanted to do. That did not happen at all. The first college in the United States was Harvard, which was founded almost 400 years ago. I believe that college is an outdated process, but society still pressures a lot of people to get that four-year degree. Many students go into debt as a result of college and work their whole life trying to pay that off.

There is no one-size-fits-all solution. Sometimes going to a community college first is a better fit for people. For other people, trade school is a better solution. Sometimes not going to college at all is a better fit. College is important if you want to go into certain professions, like becoming an engineer or a doctor, where certification in certain areas is required. If you want to own your own business and master a certain skill, college is not necessary. Plenty of information is available in books and on the Internet. Today, it's easy to learn a new skill. Know what your goals are first. If you still don't know what to do, try taking a semester off to figure it out.

## PICK A COLLEGE THAT REQUIRES THE LEAST AMOUNT OF DEBT

**WH:** If you know what your major is, pick a college that will allow you to graduate with the least amount of debt, no matter what the name of college is. To me, the degree is more important than the college it comes from. Yeah, if an employer has the option to pick between the Harvard kid and you, most likely it will be the kid from Harvard, but that's not always going to be the situation. There are many jobs out there that people don't realize exist. If you have a degree, build a skill that's required in the field, and you'll be able to find a job.

## HAVING A BACK-UP PLAN

**WH:** I feel the pressure to go to college even though I see myself as an entrepreneur because my parents and my brother went to college. I want to major in engineering. Entrepreneurship is my first option, which I can do while I'm going to college. If that doesn't work out, I'll still have a safer route with my engineering background. I can still do other things on the side once I get an engineering job. Since I want to be an engineer, college is the right choice for me because I need to develop those skills, which only college can teach me.

## DEALING WITH STRESS FROM THE COLLEGE APPLICATION PROCESS

**WH:** No matter what you do, stress will be a part of your life. It's part of human nature. To deal with pressure, get down to the root of it. The pressure that you feel is mostly pressure that you put on yourself. The best thing to do is live your life, not the life that your parents or others want you to live. Only you know what is best for you. If you're doing things to please anyone else, you're going to be unhappy. Take those pressures off yourself, and do what you want to do no matter what the consequences are, because you only have one life.

I was watching the movie *Jumanji* with the Rock and Kevin Hart. They had a certain number of lives in the movie. The Rock was on his last life, and he still had to do a courageous act. He said it was a lot harder to do the courageous act with only one life left. That is similar to the real world because you only have one life, so you don't want to mess it up. You also don't want to live a life that's going to leave you with regret when you're older. Only you know what's best for you.

## CONNECTIONS EARLY ON ARE IMPORTANT

**WH:** In my podcast, I get to interview great people and entrepreneurs in all fields. I just talked with an Emmy winner on my podcast. All I did was direct message the guy on Instagram, and he responded to me. It's important to make those connections at a young age. It's also important to help people around you.

On my podcast episode with the Emmy winner, he mentions if a high-schooler direct messages someone in their fifties and up, they would love to help young people because they are not competing with high-schoolers. Most of the time, the adult will respond and give you advice or help you. Once you get older and message someone, it's harder to receive help because they may see you as a threat. If you're on Instagram, I would DM as many professional people in your field as possible because they will most likely reply to you. All you have to say is, "Hey, my name is _____. I see you are a professional in this area. I want to do this in the future. I was wondering if you could give me any tips on what I should do right now."

Get on LinkedIn. This interview between Shelomo and I happened because we met on LinkedIn. Even if you don't own a business or a podcast, get out there, and meet people. That's the most important thing to do right now—build connections.

Message ten to twenty people every day on social media. Even if only a few respond, you will be further ahead than others who are not doing that.

## DEVELOPING CONFIDENCE

**WH:** The best thing you can do to develop confidence is to take action, no matter how small it is or how fearful you are. Fear is a normal thing, and the more you tackle it, the more confidence you will develop.

## SATS DO NOT DEFINE YOU

**WH:** SATs are a standardized test, but they do not define who you are, your intelligence, or what you can accomplish in life. If you're worried that you're not smart enough, you are. Many successful people did poorly in high school, on their SATs, and in college. Have confidence in yourself.

## TOP TAKEAWAYS:

- Write everything that you are grateful for to cheer you up.
- There are no one-size-fits-all solution. Figure out what option is best for you, not what society tells you.
- Pick a college that requires the least amount of debt while allowing you to achieve your educational goals.
- If you want to be an entrepreneur, you can still have side hustles in college. If those doesn't work out, then at least you will have your degree.
- Take the pressure off, and do what you want to do.
- Only you know what's best for you.
- If you reach out to older professionals for advice at a young age, they will respond.
- The best thing you can do to develop confidence is to take action.
- SATs do not define you.

# 40
# DEALING WITH
# TRAUMA IN LIFE
## *ARI GUNZBURG*

Ari Gunzburg is a motivational speaker and a podcast host, helping people feel more connected to each other. When he was ten years old, his rabbi died while out on a hike. This was a catalyst for many struggles due to not addressing what happened at that young age. Ari faced many hurdles over the next ten years, including dropping out of school, depression, drugs, wild partying, nights spent in jail, and more. Ari maintained his positive attitude over the years and now helps to spread hope as a motivational speaker and the creator of the 5 Keys to Greatness.

## CONNECT:
- Website: www.arigunz.com
- LinkedIn: linkedin.com/in/arigunz

## STRUGGLES INCLUDED IN THIS CHAPTER:
- Depression
- Put a lot of pressure on himself
- Wanted to find new friends to fit in
- Was in a toxic environment
- Went to jail
- Death of a loved one
- Dealt with trauma

## THE DEATH OF HIS RABBI

**Ari Gunzburg:** Growing up in an orthodox Jewish school, the Hebrew teachers are called "Rabbi _____." For kids in a particular class, their teacher is called "Rebbe" [reb-bee] which means "my teacher."

Imagine my rabbi, with black pants, white shirt, long beard, and glasses. Each year most Jewish schools have a field trip in late spring. One year he took us to a park in Baltimore City to play baseball and hike in the forest.

After baseball, we went on a hike. None of the seventeen kids on that trip knew how traumatic that hike would be. As we walked through the forest, our rebbe, who loved God and all His creations, told us about different aspects of the wonder of the forest and its Creator.

While hiking, many of the kids spread out along the trail. A few of us found a stream ahead and started playing in it while waiting for everyone to catch up.

Some kids emerged from the trees, and once they saw us, they yelled, "Guys, come quick! Rebbe's hurt!" We thought they were joking. How could our rebbe be hurt? It didn't make sense. We went back to playing in the stream.

They yelled more, telling us to come quickly! We realized something might really be wrong and ran back to the other kids, getting to where our rebbe lay prone on the ground after falling over.

It was surreal. There were dead leaves on the ground in the brown hues common on the forest floor. The sunlight filtered through the trees, casting a golden-green ambiance over the scene. We were seventeen ten-year-old kids in a state of shock as we stood around our rebbe, who was lying on the ground. Nobody knew what to do. One kid fell apart, half-hoping it was a prank, and started yelling, "Get up! Get up! It's not funny anymore. Get up!!"

"I'm going for help," I announced and then left with two other kids. It was a hot day. We worried that the heat had caused our rebbe to fall over, so we took frequent breaks.

Eventually, we heard music in the distance and followed it, hoping to find help. The haunting tunes led us to the edge of the forest, where we saw a man wearing a kilt and playing the bagpipes. I still believe God had him practice there that day to help us find our way out.

We saw buildings and ran for help. We told some rangers what had happened, and two of them grabbed a medical kit and ran with us into the forest to find our rebbe.

When we arrived back at the scene, one ranger immediately started CPR. The other ranger gathered the kids together to lead us out of the forest. They called the school. A few teachers and the principal came to the park to deal with the situation.

They talked quietly, not communicating to us, while we stood around a tree, in shock. After a while, our teacher from the year before told us to get into the van and then drove us home without a word. He only asked where each of us lived.

Later that day, my dad came home, and he wondered what happened. He called the school to find out why I was home early. His face fell as he listened. My father looked at me as he hung up the phone, and said, "He's . . . gone."

It hit me like a ton of bricks. Everything fell apart. My world crashed around me. My dad walked over to me and enveloped me in a hug and cried with me. We stood there crying together for a long time.

## HOW THIS EVENT SHAPED HIS FUTURE

**AG:** This event was a huge catalyst for many negative future events in my life. There were other positive influences as I remembered who my rebbe was and what he stood for.

After that, our class went through a lot together. The school gave us new teachers for the next two years. In seventh grade, we had a lot of problems with the secular studies teacher. The school suspended me right before my thirteenth birthday, my Bar Mitzvah, for getting kicked out of class too many times. That was it; I refused to go back.

After that moment, having a mentor die in a traumatic way, I was never the same. I ended up hanging out with the wrong people to fit in. I still know and love those kids, but we were doing the wrong things together. We were bad influences on each other, and it led to drinking, drugs, dropping out of school, partying, and a night or two in jail.

Much later I developed the 5 Keys to Greatness concept. As kids, we want to find a way to greatness, to elevate ourselves and make something of our lives. Many of us give up on those dreams as we move through life. The goal of the 5 Keys to Greatness is to rekindle that passion, that desire to achieve greatness as you understand it.

Greatness has more than one definition. Everyone defines it in their own way. For most of us, greatness doesn't involve being famous, standing on stage, or anything of the sort. Finding greatness is recognizing how to elevate yourself and taking steps to do so. The 5 Keys to Greatness is an easy-to-remember framework to help everyone achieve their own greatness.

Recently, I recognized that one reason why I created the 5 Keys to Greatness is because of all the amazing things that my rebbe did with his life. Only a fraction of his deeds are recorded in a book that I have.

## JUST SAY NO

**AG:** It is important to recognize your feelings. You can trust yourself! There will be times when the only logical action is to say "no." This may apply to drugs, drinking, crime, vandalism, and more.

If your gut clenches up, and you get a bad feeling that you shouldn't be doing something, don't do it. If you find yourself with friends who are doing something you shouldn't be doing, walk away. Say "no." Gather your strength, and stand up to the peer pressure. You can trust your gut when it tells you that something is not OK.

I could have avoided a lot of trouble if I had just said "no." We all make mistakes, especially when we're young, but our bodies often give us a heads-up, a warning, about the mistake that we are about to make. Listen to that warning!

## EXPLORE WITHIN YOURSELF

**AG:** It is essential to spend time exploring yourself and your mind, especially when you feel lost. You can do this with a therapist, a friend, a mentor, a loved one, or, in some cases, on your own. Often a qualified professional is best. See if you can discover the root cause or your problems, your habits, and your issues. As you discover more, you can choose a healthy way to deal with it.

Some healthy outlets that I like are backpacking, hiking, yoga, meditation, and cycling. Being active is one of the best defenses against depression and lethargy, especially in the age of social media. Exercise also helps instill confidence and raise self-esteem. It also provides quiet time, with no phone, to reflect on your life and to connect with yourself. Giving yourself this time is healthy and helpful for you in the long term.

## THE RIGHT HEADSPACE, THE RIGHT PEOPLE

**AG:** You are the people who you hang out with. I have found this to be true in different ways and in different situations.

When I was nineteen years old and still struggling with things, I moved into a large house with a bunch of Israelis. They were in their early thirties and were in a healthier space in their life than I was. Living with them helped me in so many ways. I am still discovering ways in which they helped me heal and move past negative things in my life. They didn't do anything in particular or give me any specific advice. They were just present as older role models, living a basically healthy life, which changed my life. They showed me without telling me what it meant to be responsible, to be an adult, to live with certain realities in a normal, productive way. Living in that house was a pivotal moment in my life. They took care of me, treating me like a baby brother, and made me feel like I truly belonged. That helped me navigate my own feelings.

If you want your life to change, surround yourself with people who will have a positive effect on you. When hanging out with others, some will go up, and some go down, but people always equalize with those they spend time with.

## INCREMENTAL ACTIONS LEAD TO MONUMENTAL DECISIONS

**AG:** I made a bunch of small bad decisions, took a bunch of small actions, and it led me to bad places, such as having to spend the night in jail on multiple occasions.

On the flip side, when I was pulling myself out of that, when I was in the midst of healing, I made a bunch of small good decisions, took a bunch of small actions, and I transformed my life for the better.

I don't believe that anyone has an epiphany and then, poof! Their life changes. It doesn't work like that. We may have an epiphany and slowly change our lives to align with this thought, but people don't flip a switch and change drastically overnight. Others may see a lightning moment, where someone seems to change their life completely. That's only seeing one part of it! Most likely they've been thinking about changing for a long time and are making small decisions that make an incremental, positive change in their life, which in the long run make a huge impact.

There is no such thing as an overnight success. These people were working toward something for months or years, and then they hit a certain tipping point. To outsiders, it seems as though they were an overnight success.

Remember, it takes years of consistent, small decisions to make a big change.

## FEEL CONNECTED, FIND CENTER

**AG:** Feeling centered and connected is a big part of feeling whole and healthy. It is so important to figure out how to feel centered and a part of your own life. This will help you realize the best way to connect with yourself and to live your best life.

An old story illustrates this well. A king put on a contest, offering a reward for the person who could create the perfect gift for him. He wanted something that would help him back to a normal level when he got too high, and also help lift him up when he got too down. It is hard to function normally in the highs and the lows of our normal emotional system. It is also important to remember that our lives and the world we live in have a beginning and an end.

The contest ended when a brilliant jeweler found the solution to the challenge. This jeweler gave the king a ring. All that the king had to do was look at it to feel centered. The ring helped him feel better when he was sad and helped bring him back to center when he was overjoyed. The ring helped him focus on what was important when he was unable to concentrate due to his highs and lows.

What was so special about this ring that it was able to create this huge transformation in the king? It had a simple inscription on it. It said, "This too shall pass."

These simple words are a reminder that no matter how happy you get or how sad you feel, it is just a moment in a long, healthy life. The worst events ever shall pass and move into memory just as the happiest moments shall pass and move along in the ephemeral winds of time. For the king, wearing that ring became a constant reminder that everything, including the good and bad, shall pass.

You will benefit from finding a way to feel centered throughout the day. Sometimes, bad things happen, and you will feel down. That's OK. Live in the moment, and know that it will pass. Sometimes great things will happen, and you will feel excited. That's great! But this will pass as well.

I am not saying you should never be sad or happy, but don't let it take over your life, distract you from your long-term goals, or stop your day. Don't let a moment define you. You can be more than a moment in time.

## TOP TAKEAWAYS:

- If something is wrong, and you feel it in your gut, just say "no."
- Find the root cause of your problems.
- Find healthy coping mechanisms.
- Remember, this too shall pass.
- If you want your life to change, change your surroundings. Find positive people.
- Incremental decisions can lead us to monumental accomplishments.
- Find a way to feel centered.
- Do not let a good or a bad moment define you.

# 41
# HOW TO OVERCOME DRUG ADDICTION
## *ED KRESSY*

Ed is the author of *My Addiction and Recovery*, and he inspires others to overcome drug addiction. He failed to follow his dreams of becoming a writer. He used alcohol, drugs, and one-night stands to escape the pain of being himself. Through the course of two decades of drug addiction—including eleven devastating years of addiction to methamphetamine--Ed threw away his life savings, his biotecāology career, his home, his relationships, and even his dog.

Ed spent months in jail, including incarceration in a psychiatric ward. Ed got clean in 2008. Amazing people and organizations inspired him to pursue a path of serving his community. Ed may be the only person who was once arrested by the FBI and then went on to receive a community service award from the director of the FBI.

## CONNECT:
- Website: www.edkressy.com

## STRUGGLES INCLUDED IN THIS CHAPTER:
- Social anxiety
- Felt inferior
- Worried too much about people's opinions
- Victim of peer pressure
- Used to be awkward
- Addicted to drugs and alcohol
- Dealing drugs
- Went to jail

## TRYING TO FIT IN LED TO ADDICTION

**Ed Kressy:** I grew up in a small town. When I was a little kid, my life was perfect. I had the woods right behind my home, and we had a big hill for sledding in the wintertime. My dad grew these incredible vegetable gardens. He taught me how to love nature and love plants. Everything was perfect, until I became a teenager.

I discovered that the things that suited me well when I was a young kid, such as reading and escaping through a world of imagination, didn't serve me when I turned thirteen. I was uncoordinated and couldn't play sports. I was also a sensitive kid. I used to cry easily when the teacher yelled or when the bus driver pulled over when the school kids got too rowdy on the ride home. I could not find a way to fit in. I wanted to interact with the kids around me, and I wanted to express myself, but I got bullied all the time. I tried to fit in with the cool kids by listening to the same music as them, wearing similar clothes, and making jokes.

The other kids would have parties and not invite me. I started developing anger and self-hatred. I also started forming negative habits, like drugs and alcohol.

When I was fourteen years old, I was at a wedding at my aunt's house. My cousin was fourteen at the time. He had charisma and swagger while I didn't. Somehow, he had gotten a bottle of champagne and pulled me aside during the wedding reception. He took me to his friend's apartment, which was in the same building. They put on these porno movies. (I had never seen a porno movie before). We drank and watched porno movies. I had never felt a sense of acceptance like I felt on that day. I felt like I belonged, like I fit in. I developed a strong association between feelings of intoxication and feelings of fitting in.

In high school, I started getting drunk and taking drugs to fit in. I also had a girlfriend and hung out with the popular kids. It started off as only a small amount of drugs, which some people might see as harmless. As time went on, I needed more drugs and alcohol for them to work. For my entire life, I had dreamed of becoming a writer, but I didn't pursue my dreams. I never addressed who I was as a person.

In college, I got into cocaine, ecstasy, mushrooms, and LSD, when I could find them. Then when I was no longer a teenager, I got addicted to methamphetamine. That took me down a terrible path and created a false sense of confidence.

## FINALLY PAID THE PRICE

**EK:** I broke the law a lot and got away with it. I never had to pay the price like many people did. I was driving drunk and dealing drugs. The police would pull me over. They would come to my home and search it. Finally, I got arrested. There was a point in my life where I had a lot of things. I had a lot of money, I owned a home, and I had a career at a company that went on to become the best company in America to work for, but I still didn't feel like a worthwhile person. I never pursued my dream of being a writer. That all went away with one moment.

## SELF-EXPLORATION WHEN YOUNGER

**EK:** If I could go back and do things over, I would have explored my true self. Partying and girls made me feel like a worthwhile person temporarily. What would have made me feel more worthwhile was being an artist, a writer, or having some other meaningful pursuit. We all have a spirit within us that expresses itself differently. It could be through writing, music, sports, math, politics, or any number of things. Rather than explore yourself through negative and addictive behavior, I recommend you explore yourself through creative work.

Also, learn as much as you can. When you think you know everything, that's probably the time to start expanding your knowledge.

The danger in life is reaching a point of complacency. French author Marcel Proust once said, "The real voyage of discovery consists not in seeing new sights but in looking with new eyes." To change yourself, you must change your eyes. Maintain a state of constant learning and practice. Never forget that you have what you need inside of you already; it's just a matter of bringing it out.

## "IT'S BETTER TO CONQUER YOURSELF THAN TO WIN 1,000 BATTLES."

**EK:** I read a quote once that said, "It's better to conquer yourself than to win 1,000 battles." I focus my thoughts on love and gratitude instead of fear and what I don't have. I recommend pursuing a spiritual path. It could be faith based, it could be practicing gratitude, or it could be service to others. Going down a spiritual path and getting into personal development helped me overcome my true problem, which was the problem in my mind. I got into drugs because I had an illusion in my mind that if I drank alcohol and did drugs, I would fit in. Now I live a life of fulfillment by giving back. I go into jails and other locations where people don't have direction and provide them with life-skills workshops.

## THE ROAD TO RECOVERY IS DIFFICULT

**EK:** When we use the term "recovery," we mean we are trying to be clean by not taking drugs, and we're improving our lives. Recovery is not for those who need it or for those who want it but for those who are willing to do the work. It's not easy. There's no magic formula. When you need the strength, and when times get tough, you need to push yourself harder than you've ever pushed yourself.

I want you to remember this story. A person was walking through the woods when he ran across a caterpillar. The caterpillar was in a cocoon. The caterpillar started to emerge from the cocoon to become a butterfly, and it was struggling. The person pulled out a knife and cut the cocoon, thinking it would help the butterfly. The person was well-intentioned, but his actions hurt the butterfly because it was the struggle to get free from that cocoon that would give the butterfly strength to fly. When you're struggling in recovery, or you can't find the path, you're like that butterfly. It's a struggle right now, but your struggle and addiction serve a purpose. It's always beautiful on the other side. I've lived it, and so have many others.

## IF A LOVED ONE IS STRUGGLING WITH ADDICTION

**EK:** When we're struggling with addiction, the people whose advice we take are the people who we want to be like. What you can do for someone who is struggling is be a good role model. That means dedicating yourself to improvement and giving back to others. No one is going to listen to you if your life is a mess.

If you are improving yourself every day, say, "Hey, if you want some advice, I'm here for you." That's the best way I've found to help an addicted person. Addicts are looking for self-worth. They are looking for confidence. They are looking for a person who's improving themselves. If you can be that person, the addict is more likely to follow your advice.

## TOP TAKEAWAYS:

- You don't need alcohol and drugs to fit in.
- The drugs and alcohol you take in high school may seem harmless now, but they can lead you down a terrible path later.
- Explore yourself through your creative work.
- Keep learning.

- *"It's better to conquer yourself than to win 1,000 battles."*
- Recovery is not for those who need it or for those who want it. Recovery is for people who are willing to do the work.
- Your struggle with addiction has a purpose.
- Help someone who has an addiction by trying constantly to improve yourself. They will take notice.

# 42

# HOW TO BELIEVE IN YOURSELF WHEN YOUR LIFE IS UPSIDE DOWN

*EVAN CARMICHAEL*

Evan Carmichael is a successful entrepreneur, the author of four best-selling books, and a YouTuber with over 2 million subscribers. At age nineteen, he built and then sold a biotech software company. At age twenty-two, he was a venture capitalist raising $500,00 to $15 million. He wants to solve the world's biggest problem, which is that people don't believe in themselves. Even though he is a successful entrepreneur, he is an introvert and used to lack confidence.

## CONNECT:

- Website: believe.evancarmichael.com
- YouTube: Search for "Evan Carmichael"

## STRUGGLES INCLUDED IN THIS CHAPTER:

- Low self-esteem
- Feared being a disappointment
- Worried too much about people's opinions of him
- Didn't believe in himself

## YOU'RE NEVER GOING TO BE GREAT THE FIRST TIME

**Evan Carmichael:** The hardest day of my life was when I was nineteen years old. It was the end of my teenage years. I had to decide between taking the dream job that I thought I wanted, making $100K a year, and traveling around the world, or being an entrepreneur and making 300 bucks a month with 30 percent ownership of the company. It was the hardest decision in my life because everybody I knew was taking jobs. Nobody was starting their own business. If I failed, I knew within a year I could get a job. I had to at least try to go the entrepreneurship route. When I was older, I didn't want to say, "What if?" I didn't want to live with regrets, so I took action. There are so many ideas out there, and everyone has a lot of potential. Thinking about it alone isn't enough. You must start. You should try, but expect to fail. The first time you do anything, it will not be great. My first YouTube video wasn't great. Fall and then get back up. Through practice and dedication, if you love what you're doing, you can become world class at something. Most people learn that concept way later in life. Hopefully you can learn much sooner.

## HOW CAN YOU START BELIEVING IN YOURSELF?

**EC:** I have two tips. First, find people who come from the same situation as you who have made it. If somebody else has made it, you can make it too. Surround yourself with those people. It's what I did with my YouTube channel. Start by thinking and believing like people who have made it. If you can't be around your heroes, you can still learn from them by reading their books and/or watching their videos. You can even meet people virtually. They can hold you accountable and give you the confidence to keep going. Create a system where you are surrounded by your heroes every day.

Second, act on your ideas. Many people come home and consume Netflix, video games, or even educational content. Take the energy from consuming and use it to make something of your own. Post videos or write a book. Whatever it is, go into creation mode, and your confidence will pick up after you build momentum.

## FEAR IS NOT A GOOD ENOUGH REASON TO GIVE UP

**EC:** Fear is no reason to avoid pursuing your goals. When you create logical or smart reasons why you can't do something, like not posting a video because you don't have the right camera gear, that's fear talking.

The most important skill you can teach yourself is to do the things that you are afraid of even though you can come up with good reasons not to do them. When you run away from fear, you're telling yourself that you play small. All your dreams are on the other side of fear. Instead, tell yourself, "I'm going to do it." Expect to suck in the beginning. That's OK. I posted my first video in April 2009, and it wasn't very good.

Another reason why you may not be pursuing your goals is someone else's opinion of you. If you live based on other people's opinions, you'll never do anything great. Why are you playing small based on their opinions? I'm an introvert, and I still get nervous when I'm making videos for my channel. I'm afraid of disappointing people. I don't want people to watch my videos and feel like it was a waste of their time. I put that pressure on myself every day, but I'm on a mission to do something big. The only way you're going to accomplish the big thing that you're after in life is to do the things that you're afraid of.

## PURPOSE COMES FROM PAIN

**EC:** Your purpose comes from your pain. Whatever you struggled with the most in life is what you want to help other people through. As a teenage entrepreneur, I struggled with not believing in myself, not having anybody to learn from or talk to. I made it hard for myself. I didn't tell my friends that I was struggling. I tried to deal with it all by myself. I'm also a visual learner, so I'd much rather see something than hear it or read it. I thought, *There has to be many entrepreneurs who are like me. I'm going to make some video content to speak to them.* I started my YouTube channel in 2009. At that time, YouTube was not an educational platform. People didn't go to YouTube to learn; they went there to watch funny videos. I was posting educational videos because I wanted to help others who were experiencing the same struggles as I was. It took me five years to get to seven thousand subscribers and then six years to get over 2 million. I was persistent and kept pushing through.

## WHAT'S YOUR ONE WORD?

**EC:** Look at your favorite movie, favorite song, or what you loved about your teacher, and write down one words as to why. You'll see that the things you love have something in common. For me, my one word is "believe." For you, maybe it's "resilience." It's different for everyone. When you pursue that one word, you'll be ninety-five years old and still love helping people pertaining to that one word. If anything, you'll love it even more because you'll be better at it. The only thing that will change is the avenue of how you express that one word. Everyone knows their passion deep inside, so summarize it using one word.

Your one word can become your life's motto. Once you live by it, you will become more fulfilled and confident.

## GETTING YOURSELF OUT OF A RUT

**EC:** I use a big why and a little why. My big why is my big mission. For example, "I want to solve the world's biggest problem." It should be motivating and inspiring for you. The little why is knowing that if you upload a video, you can help at least one person. Yes, maybe you don't have millions of views yet, but your little why is working toward that big why. Tell yourself, "I'm not where I want to be, but the work that I do matters." If you feel every day that the work that you do matters and has an impact even on a small scale, it can be enough fuel for you to go another day.

## STOP BLAMING YOUR CIRCUMSTANCES

**EC:** Blaming your circumstances won't change anything. If you look at your circumstances and say, "Look at the bad life I have," you're going to end up like the people who you don't want to end up like. Other people have gotten out, and you can too. It's easier to get out of a certain circumstance than it was ten years ago. The idea that you can make money from a phone may sound ridiculous to your parents because they didn't have that opportunity. Follow successful people who've come from your circumstances. Surround yourself with their content every day. If you believe you can get out of your circumstances, you're much more likely to do it. If you sit and complain about how rough life is, you're never going to make it.

## TOP TAKEAWAYS:

- *You're never going to be great the first time.*
- Through practice and dedication, if you love what you're doing, you can become world class at something.
- Two ways to start believing are to surround yourself with people who you want to model yourself after and then act on your ideas.
- The only way you're going to accomplish the big thing that you're after is to do the scary things.
- Purpose comes from pain.
- Find your one word.
- Identify your big why and your small why.
- Stop blaming your circumstances.

# 43
# ALLEVIATING THE PRESSURE YOU PUT ON YOURSELF
## *NELSON JIA JUN NG*

Nelson is the founder and CEO of ProjectEd, which strives to tackle education inequality in Malaysia. He's also the host of the *Social Hero* podcast. Nelson was born in Malaysia as the only child. He moved to United Kingdom for college, where he studied aerospace engineering. He put a lot of pressure on himself during those years but eventually found a way to alleviate some of that pressure.

## CONNECT:
- LinkedIn: linkedin.com/in/nelson-nnjj

## STRUGGLES INCLUDED IN THIS CHAPTER:
- Came from another country and didn't speak English well
- Insecure about his accent
- Hated being the only child
- Feared being a disappointment

## THE PRESSURES OF BEING THE ONLY CHILD

**Nelson Jia Jun Ng:** I'm the only grandchild in my family. That is unique and rare in my culture. There are good and bad things about being the only child. The benefit is that I get all the attention, and I get to learn what I want to learn. For example, I learned piano, taekwondo, and drawing. Being the only child also comes with stress. My family put a lot of emphasis on me to make them proud. Because of that, I put more effort in learning every day, and I made sure I was one of the smartest in my class. I would always try to be the best in academics and in sports. I appreciate it and am grateful now, but back then I felt differently.

If your family puts pressure on you, you'll thank them later. Just make sure that pressure is worth it and that you pursue something that you enjoy doing. If not, express that to your parents. When I started learning how to play the piano at five years old, my parents asked me if I wanted to learn rather than force me to play an instrument that I didn't enjoy.

## ALLEVIATING THE PRESSURE FROM YOURSELF

**NJJN:** Figure out if you really like whatever you're going after. Even when you're a child, you'll know if you really like the activity you're doing. For example, when I was learning taekwondo, I was super excited for those classes. As for piano, sometimes I was and sometimes I wasn't excited. I'm a big advocate of doing the things that you like because once you do the things that you like, you'll be doing your best. That's why you and your parents need to have mutual communication. Tell your parents what you love and don't love. Make sure your voice is being counted. Make sure you and your parents are aligned. That way you will alleviate your stress because you get to do what you want, and they get to take off the stress of putting it on you.

## IT'S NOT ABOUT THE ACCENT; IT'S ABOUT THE MESSAGE YOU CONVEY

**NJJN:** Although I learned English when I was young, I didn't have a chance to practice my English while I was in school. I'm from a rural area of Malaysia where people don't speak English. I thought my English was decent until I moved to the UK. I didn't take the initiative to improve until six months into college.

The UK was another part of the world with a different accent. I thought people were going to judge my accent. At first I was shy at meetings to protect myself. Little by little, I knew I had to come out of my comfort zone and put an effort into talking at meetings. Eventually, I realized it's not about the accent but about the message that you convey. That change of mindset opened my world. I would talk to people no matter how broken my accent was. I would talk to people on topics I was comfortable and passionate about.

I was fortunate that I got to travel when I was free. I took the opportunity to go on solo trips. I preferred to do solo trips because it forced me to talk to strangers and gave me the opportunity to improve my English.

## PUT THE PRESSURE YOU ARE FEELING INTO PROPER PERSPECTIVE

**NJJN:** I'm a first-generation college student. Because of that, I put a lot of pressure on myself to get good grades and to become as involved as possible in extracurricular activities. I was happy to have that pressure. I'm proud to be in this family and to be a representation of them.

**SS:** Are you saying it was good pressure?

**NJJN:** Yes. It's all in how you look at it. I used to say, "I have to. I have to get good grades. I have to be involved in extracurricular activities." I changed that mindset to, "I will do my best to make my family proud because they didn't get this opportunity. Let me do that for them." That switch is more of a positive mindset. I don't have to make my family proud; I want to. I should be proud that I get to pursue education overseas. Even though positive pressure is good, it's also important to find ways to de-stress when feeling negative pressure. My favorite way to do this is to play basketball.

## BE OPEN TO OTHER CULTURES

**NJJN:** Be open to other cultures, but at the same time, uphold your own principles and values. When you meet people from diverse backgrounds or when you start conversations with random people, and they talk about something that you don't agree with, be open. Be open to listen to whatever they have to say, process your thoughts, and share them rather than trying to stop the conversation. Be respectful. Later, when you try to share your opinions, they will be more than happy to accept what you say.

## TOP TAKEAWAYS:

- Later in life, you'll be grateful for the pressure that your parents put on you to succeed.
- If your parents sign you up for something, make sure it's something that you enjoy.
- Alleviate the pressure from yourself by communicating to your parents about activities you do and don't enjoy.
- *It's not about the accent; it's about the message you convey.*
- You don't have to make your family proud; you get to make your family proud. You may have the opportunities that they didn't.
- Find ways to alleviate stress.
- Be open and nonjudgmental of other cultures and opinions.

# 44
# HOW TO OVERCOME SEXUAL ASSAULT
*TOVAH MARX*

Tovah Marx runs *HeyTovah*, where people share their stories. She was also a star on *Real World Atlanta*. She inspires others who have been sexually assaulted. She lost her virginity to rape at age sixteen, was diagnosed with bipolar II disorder and depression at age eighteen, tried committing suicide at age twenty-two, and then discovered that her cousin committed suicide sixteen days after Tovah got out of the hospital. Read this chapter to learn what you can do if you have been a victim of sexual assault

## CONNECT:
- Instagram: @TovahMarx

## STRUGGLES INCLUDED IN THIS CHAPTER:
- Anxiety
- Depression
- Low self-esteem
- Death of a loved one
- Wanted to commit suicide
- Sexual assault
- Bullying

## WANTING TO COMMIT SUICIDE AT TWELVE YEARS OLD

**Tovah Marx:** I moved to San Diego in fifth grade. It was a difficult time to move. I went to a new school, and I didn't fit in. I changed schools in sixth grade, but I still didn't fit in. The same thing happened in grade seven. My school had a suicide-prevention assembly. I didn't know what suicide was, but I knew that I was super depressed and that I didn't want to live anymore. Between being bullied and moving was a hard adjustment. I was sad. After that assembly, I went to my nurse who I ate lunch with every day in middle school, and I told her, "I don't want to live anymore. I don't want to be here. Why would I continue to live when all I do is get bullied every day? I cry after school every single day. This isn't a life that I want to live." That's when I started therapy. I was twelve years old at the time.

**SS:** What would people bully you about?

**TM:** I was overweight. I had acne starting at age eleven. I was the new kid. My parents didn't focus on buying expensive clothes, so I was made fun of for my clothes and my hair. I didn't wear makeup, and I did not look like the other kids.

I didn't follow through with my thoughts of suicide because of my mom. I'm her only child. I knew she would not be able to survive if I left her. Every time I had suicidal thoughts, I thought of my mom, and I would push through.

For anyone else struggling with such feelings, I suggest that you find a reason to push through, whether it's a family member or something else in your life.

## WHAT IS SEXUAL ASSAULT?

**TM:** Anything that happens without your consent, whether it's sexual or just touching.

## HER SEXUAL ASSAULT STORY

**TM:** When I was sixteen years old, I began dating. We were not officially boyfriend-girlfriend, and I told him that I did not want to have sex with anybody unless he was my boyfriend, that I wanted my first time to be special. In that moment he decided to go for it and have sex with me. He didn't give me the option to say "no."

When most people think about rape, they picture bruises, someone being held down, fighting, police reports, and hospital visits. None of that happened to me. I did not realize I had been sexually assaulted until I started feeling off. I realized I had told him "no" before, and he didn't give me the option to say it in that moment.

## THE EFFECTS OF SEXUAL ASSAULT

**TM:** After it happened, I didn't talk about it. I was a mess during my junior year of high school. He was the one who defined it as rape. We had a lot of mutual friends, and one of my friends called me over to his house. He said, "I know what happened. I know he raped you. He feels bad. Just don't say anything about it because that's what he wants. He's going to turn it all on you." I didn't say anything, but rumors started getting out of hand, so I changed schools in my senior year. I blocked it out as if it didn't happen. I wasn't brave enough to tell my mom. I didn't want to go to court for it. I couldn't even use rape in a sentence.

People respond to losing their virginity to sexual assault in a couple of ways. Some have sex with a bunch of people. Others shy away from sex and are afraid. I went the multiple partners route. To regain my power, I had sex with a bunch of people. I finally realized a couple of years ago that having sex with a bunch of people is not getting my power back; it's giving my power away. It wasn't until I was twenty-two years old that I finally accepted what had happened to me. I realized it was not OK, and I started to get help for it. I went to therapy after listening to a song by The Weeknd. When I went to therapy, I realized choosing to have multiple partners was not the correct coping mechanism.

## SHE STARTED TO HEAL

**TM:** I started to get help at age twenty-two. I went to Sex Addicts Anonymous. I really had to search around, but eventually, I found a therapist who understood me. For the longest time, I didn't accept the fact that I was raped. I couldn't accept it until my therapist looked at me and said, "You got raped. You did not say "yes." Anything without your consent is a no." I realized how I dealt with my relationships, friendships, and situations from that moment. We finally worked through it. I didn't date for a while, and I didn't hook up with anybody for a long time. I focused on myself. The moment that I was able to accept the truth is when I started to heal from it, and it no longer traumatized me.

## TIPS FOR SEXUAL ASSAULT VICTIMS

**TM:** I found an online support group because I was too embarrassed to talk to anybody else. You should tell at least one person, whether on the Internet or in person. Get your story out, as hard as it is. A big turning point for me was when I started to talk about it.

## MOMENTS WHEN NEGATIVE FEELINGS ARISE

**TM:** When I get feelings of sadness or anxiety, I let myself feel however I'm feeling. Let yourself feel whatever you are feeling instead of pushing away your emotions. If I don't want to have sex, I don't. If I don't want to talk to anybody, I don't. If I want to cry, I cry. Whatever feelings come up, let yourself feel them.

## GIVE YOURSELF SOME TIME TO FEEL SAD

**TM:** When you lose somebody, give yourself ten minutes a day to feel all those emotions. Give yourself all day to feel happy, and assign a daily time where you can feel whatever you want to. That way you won't feel drained all day long.

## WHAT SHE WOULD TELL SOMEONE WHO IS SUICIDAL

**TM:** Talk to somebody. Write down all the things that are going right in your life and all the things that you're grateful for.

When you get into a mindset that everything is wrong, your life sucks, and nothing's going right, start journaling. When you write down things that are going right, your brain will rewire itself, and you will be able see all the things that are going right. I wrote, "I have a great boyfriend. I have a great job. I have a great house. I have great pets. I love my bedsheets. I just got a cool hairbrush. My hair looks good today." If you can't think of things that make you happy, write down things that you did that day. I found my journals from 2014 from when I was suicidal. One of them said, "Today, I woke up. I had coffee, I watched TV, played with my cats, and I went to bed." I would also write a list of all the people who I talked to that day.

## USE GOOGLE AS A POSITIVE RESOURCE

**TM:** Everybody has access to Google. I used to write, "I feel really sad right now. Am I the only one?" or "I'm getting bullied at school. Am I the only one?" in the search window. No matter what you're going through, you are not alone. Many other people feel the same way. I know that middle school and high school can be tough. I changed middle schools three times and high schools twice. I would go on online forums to get help on specific challenges in my life. That's when I realized many people were going through the same thing as me.

## TOP TAKEAWAYS:

- Find a reason to push through.
- Any sexual activity or touching without your consent is sexual assault.
- The moment you realize that you were sexually assaulted is when you can begin healing from it.
- Find at least one person you can tell, whether online or in person, that you were sexually assaulted.
- *Instead of pushing away your feelings, let yourself feel whatever*

258

*you are feeling.*
- Give yourself time each day to feel sad or angry.
- If you are feeling suicidal, write down what you are grateful for, what you did that day, and who you talked to.
- Use Google as a positive resource.

# 45
# OVERCOMING AN EATING DISORDER AND PARENTS' DIVORCE
## *YVETTE MYSTAKAS*

Yvette Mystakas is the founder and owner of *She is Sacred*, a blog that embraces womanhood, sisterhood, and motherhood. She writes raw, from the heart, heartbreaking, yet empowering words of her struggles with mental health, the importance of self-care, and identity. Yvette has brought together women from across the globe who share each other's stories. Her parents divorced when she was fourteen, she suffered from bulimia at age sixteen, and her grandfather died when she was seventeen.

## CONNECT:
- Instagram: @YvetteMystakas
- Facebook: www.facebook.com/sheissacred

## STRUGGLES INCLUDED IN THIS CHAPTER:
- Depression
- Anxiety
- Death of loved one
- Parents got divorced
- Put a lot of pressure on herself
- Worried too much about people's opinions of her
- Eating disorder

## PARENTS GOT DIVORCED

**Yvette Mystakas:** At age fourteen, when my parents divorced, it wasn't that hard for me. It was more of a relief because I saw so much pain in their relationship. What was more painful than the divorce was the process of their relationship falling to bits. My mom spoke harshly about my father, and it took my dad a couple years to speak to me. I think he just wanted to step back from the situation.

It was so sad. I have other friends whose parents are divorced, and their parents have always been there for them, whether the parents speak to each other or not. I felt abandoned, and I felt sorry for myself. I became an angry teenager. I stopped caring about everything and didn't put effort into school.

## OVERCOMING AN EATING DISORDER

**YM:** When I was fifteen, I started getting picky about my body image. I don't know if it was the result of my parents' divorce or my boyfriend at the time, who was a gym junkie. I started going to the gym with him, and then I started to look in *Vogue* magazines and comparing myself to the models. I started cutting out pictures of bony, skinny models and putting them on my walls as my inspiration board. I strived to look like them. I started cutting out certain foods. I'd wake up at 5 a.m. to work out before school and only have a cup of milk or water for breakfast. I would do another workout after school and another one before bed. I would start feeling guilty about eating certain foods. I started getting bulimic. I got tiny for my height. Because I wore baggy clothes, no one noticed how skinny I was until my family started telling me that I needed to start eating more, or they would put me in a hospital. Then they started showing me pictures of others with eating disorders. That's when I realized I needed to change.

Instead of looking at the mirror and pointing out flaws about yourself, do affirmations in the morning. Tell yourself, "I'm worthy. I'm sacred. I'm lucky I have this body. I'm unique." I still get self-conscious about my weight when I compare myself to how I looked as a teenager, but then I snap out of it. I have an eight-year-old. I don't want him to get obsessed with his body.

## LIVING A HEALTHIER LIFE

**YM:** My husband and I want to get healthier. It's not only about looking better; we want to live a healthier life as we get older. Instead of being conscious about everything we eat, we are more mindful of what we eat. We choose foods that are satisfying to us and nourishing to our bodies. It's a win-win situation. We eat healthy, and we satisfy our cravings.

It's about finding a diet that's right for you. My diet might not be what you would like. I like to have a lot of Mediterranean food. I love Greek salads, pomegranates, watermelon, figs, and seafood. You might not like that. My husband doesn't like seafood. On those days, he will have ham or chicken.

When you start restricting yourself and say, "I can't eat that. I'm on a diet today. I'm watching my calories," you're eventually going to binge eat. Then you'll start getting sick and feeling sorry for yourself, and then you'll start giving yourself hate talk.

## BEING HEALTHY IS ALSO ABOUT YOUR ACTIVITIES

**YM:** Having a good laugh every day is healthy. I also love meditating because I've suffered from depression and anxiety. I love to meditate morning and night. It gives me clarity. I love reading. I love to read a classic novel or something that's enriching. I love going outside in nature. I also love spending time in my garden and going to the beach. Doing the activities that you love to do will help you live a happier life.

## HOW SHE COPED WITH HER GRANDFATHER'S DEATH

**YM:** I had to do counseling because I was not coping with my grandfather's death. I spent time with my family. We celebrated his life and never left him out of a conversation.

I still do that today. I keep him in conversation. I show photos of him to my son, even though he never met his great-grandfather. I was fortunate we got to go to my grandfather's country. Last year was my first time going to Croatia. We went to his village, which is located on an island. That was a proud and healing moment for me, to show my son where our family began. We got to meet some family members who we had never met before.

Every time we go to church, I make sure to light a candle for my in-laws who have passed away, including my grandfather. My son does that too. It's important to know our loved ones are not forgotten and to keep them in conversation.

## ADVICE FOR THOSE WHOSE PARENTS ARE GOING THROUGH A DIVORCE

**YM:** Don't be afraid to talk about it with your friends because you're going to find that you may have a couple friends who have gone through or are going through the same struggle.

I had some friends who already went through it in their early teens, and I could talk to them about it anytime. We had something in common.

Tell the right people. You don't want to end up doing drugs, drinking, or falling into an addiction that will ruin you.

Don't let your parents' divorce define your journey in life. Just because it happened to them does not mean it will happen to you. I used to think, "Oh, gosh, no one's going to love me because my parents are divorced. I'm going to carry that burden when I get married." I never ended up carrying that burden with my husband. We've been married for nine years and have been together for thirteen years.

## UNFOLLOW PAGES THAT MAKE YOU FEEL INSECURE

**YM:** If you're going through an eating disorder, go to your social media pages and unfollow people or pages that make you start questioning your worth or make you feel insecure. Out of sight, out of mind.

## TOP TAKEAWAYS:

- Instead of pointing out flaws in the mirror, do affirmations.
- Instead of being super conscientious about what you eat, become mindful of what you eat.
- Find a diet that is the right fit for you.
- Doing the activities that you love to do will give you a happier life.
- A good way to cope with the loss of a loved one is counseling and making sure their memory is never forgotten.
- If your parents are going through a divorce, tell your friends about it. You may find that some of them have experienced the same thing.
- Don't let your parents' divorce define you.
- *Unfollow social media pages that make you feel insecure.*

# 46

# DEALING WITH FRIENDS SAYING, "YOU'VE CHANGED"

## IZZY NGOV

Izzy Ngov, a.k.a. Izzy.soo.dizzy, is a high school senior in Philadelphia who is about to graduate and is pursuing her dreams of becoming an Asian American Influencer. Nearly two years ago, after she started building a brand online, many of her friends told her that she had changed. This affected her mental health, and she didn't post for a while. In this chapter she talks about her journey toward becoming a high school influencer and what you can do to take care of your mental health while in high school.

### CONNECT:
- Instagram: @Izzy.Soo.Dizzy
- YouTube: Izzy Ngov

### STRUGGLES INCLUDED IN THIS CHAPTER:
- Depression
- Worried too much about people's opinions of her
- Friends turning against her

### BEING PROUD OF HER HERITAGE

**Izzy Ngov:** I'm Chinese and Cambodian. There weren't a lot of Asian people in my school. I wasn't treated badly because of it, but the feeling of oppression was constant. I knew I was different.

I've always been very confident about my culture because it's my history and my background. I bounced between two cultures. I was never ashamed of one culture, but I always knew I would have to flip flop, depending on where I was. Whatever culture you are, you shouldn't be ashamed of it. It's who you are.

Since the media lacked Asian American influencers, I wanted to be that inspiration for future generations.

## TRANSITIONING INTO HER JUNIOR YEAR OF HIGH SCHOOL

**IN:** The summer before junior year, I was working a lot, and some of my videos were on Instagram's explore page. I started gaining traction on my brand. I didn't see my friends as much as a normal teen would.

My junior year was a bit rough. Most of my friends during my freshman and sophomore years were older, so they graduated from high school. Once they were gone, I isolated myself, so I could work.

I had a different drive going into junior year, and I was already an independent person. Since the other kids recognized my brand, in school other kids would start yelling "Izzy so Dizzy!" in the hallways or at the gym.

A lot of the friends who I grew close to during sophomore year from a club I was in started to dissipate because I wasn't as present as I was before. I was working on my brand. They started to spread rumors about me. Others would say, "Izzy's changed. Izzy's a horrible person. She's no longer who she was. She thinks she's a big shot." Those words hurt. They were engraved in my mind. Online hate doesn't bother me. Hate in real life from people I care about and consider family hurts.

That's the consequence for growing online. Some people will not understand and will not be on the same wavelength as you. I consider myself a nice person. I don't go out of my way to hurt people or talk poorly about them. I questioned why they would do that to me if I had never done anything to them. It affected me so much that I took a month off from posting content, which was hard to do because I loved doing that.

## GETTING OVER HER FUNK

**IN:** My growing point took place in my senior year. I decided that I needed change. Everything in life seemed like it was going day by day. It felt like the same motions. On my birthday I woke up and told myself, "I'm not doing this anymore." I heard about a place in Philadelphia called REC Philly, a place for creators. I went to check it out and took a tour. I fell in love with it and got a membership.

Some days after school, I went into the city because I had a job in film production at REC Philly, I met some cool people there. We helped each other grow, and sometimes we would talk about life.

It's important to find a community where you can help others grow and spend time with people who have similar goals.

## YOU DON'T NEED TO BE GLOBAL TO SUCCEED

**IN:** My parents see how disciplined I am in what I am doing and my mission. I want to see where my passion for film production takes me. For me, it doesn't feel like work.

You don't need to be global to have a strong following. You just need a group of people who support you and impact some people's lives. That's the overall goal. If you are doing that, you are living your best life.

## HOW CAN SOMEONE FIND THEIR PASSION?

**IN:** I found my passion in something that I didn't believe should be the way it was. When I was younger, I watched a lot of Asian influencers, and they would always talk about how they were taking a step for the next generation. There's a lack of Asian influencers in media, and it shouldn't be that way. I asked myself, "How can I help other people with that same mindset? How can I be an inspiration?" If you want to find your passion, find something that you don't believe should be the way it is, and try to change it.

## HOW TO BE IN A BETTER MENTAL SPACE

**IN:** Think optimistically, and don't rely on stimulants to make you happy. Stimulants will make your bad moods worse. When I was in my depressive phase, it was hard to stay positive. I found positivity in the things that I was doing, whether helping spread a message or making a video. I found a great friend group too.

Stay away from people who drag you down. Put yourself in situations that you want to be in. If an event is happening and that means you have to be around people who you don't want to spend time with, don't go.

## HOW TO FIND A MENTOR AT A YOUNG AGE

**IN:** You can find mentors in a lot of different ways. I consider a lot of people in school mentors, such as my math teacher and my music teacher.

My boss is another mentor. I work for a video production company. He teaches me a lot. I even look up to some of my friends. A mentor is anyone who has something that you don't but which you want to develop.

**SS:** Another great way to find mentors is through Instagram. I have interviewed over fifty people for my podcast, and I have learned from all of them. They gave me a different perspective. Direct message people. If you send twenty DMs, and one person responds, that one person can change your life. It's crazy.

**IN:** Everyone who you meet has a direct influence on you. REC Philly has influenced me because it's a spot for creatives. It's had a huge impact on my life. My best friend influences me to become a better person due to her support for me. Anyone who influences you can be a mentor regardless of age. Learn from people of all ages.

## GO FOR BROKE

**IN:** The following three words guide my life: go for broke. Go all in, and take the risk on your dreams. Do whatever it takes to make it happen no matter the consequences.

## TOP TAKEAWAYS:

- Be proud of your culture.
- Find a community of people who share your goals and where you can help one another grow.
- You don't need to be global to have a strong following.
- If you want to find your passion, find something that you don't believe should be the way it is.
- Think optimistically, and don't rely on stimulants to make you happy.
- Find positivity in the things that you love to do.
- Avoid people who drag you down.
- *Anyone who influences you is a mentor regardless of age.*
- Go for broke.

# 47
# HOW TO ESCAPE FROM ABUSE
## *LADY MICHELLE AUSTIN*

Lady Michelle Austin is a survivor of childhood abuse, which continued into adulthood. Because of the trauma that she experienced, she started a nonprofit organization called Heal and Rebuild – Unbreakable Spirit, Inc. to give back to victims of abuse. She is also the author of *Pieces of Me*, in which she shares her abuse story.

## CONNECT:
- Website: www.healandrebuild.com

## STRUGGLES INCLUDED IN THIS CHAPTER:
- Low self-esteem
- Abusive parents
- Being in abusive relationships
- Substance abuse

## BACK THEN THE ABUSE WAS CONSIDERED DISCIPLINING YOUR CHILDREN

**Lady Michelle Austin:** I endured a lot of abuse as a child. The problem was, no one helped, and no one intervened. It had a lot to do with the fact that it was the 1970s. Everybody was more concerned about disciplining their children. It wasn't considered abusive to beat them or curse them out in the street. It was called disciplining and keeping your children in line. I experienced a lot of that from my mom. She was my primary abuser. My father didn't step in. He never hit me or said anything bad to me, but he did not do anything to stop it, and he knew what was going on, which made him my secondary abuser. To the naked eye, it did not look like I was being abused. My home was clean. I had all my shots, my hair and clothing neat every day, and I did well in school. Behind closed doors though, there was a lot of verbal, emotional, and physical abuse. My mom was a great provider, creating an illusion that everything was going great in our home. That's what people saw. They thought she took good care of me, which she did on some levels.

At one point, a couple of adults stepped in. The sad part is, my mom beat them up for stepping in and then beat me up more to show me that she could control everybody in the room. I began telling people not to intervene or do anything. I ran away once, but the world outside my home wasn't any better. I went to live with my dad, but he couldn't provide for me like my mom did, so I ended up going back to her house and her abuse.

As a result of the abuse, I developed low self-esteem. Later, I started getting into bad relationships with other people who abused me. I also started substance abuse, taking prescription pills.

## WHAT ARE THE SIGNS OF ABUSE?

**LMA:** There are many signs that indicate a child is being abused. Some of these signs include unexplained or repeated bruising and/or injuries. Also look for behavioral problems, such as withdrawn or clingy behavior, silence, constant anger, running away, or truancy. If you notice excessive fear of parents or caregivers or even going home, these are major signs of child abuse. Another sign that is often overlooked is substance abuse. You may also see eating disorders or bed wetting. This list goes on and on. Children who are abused also display numerous challenges with everyday life skills.

## HOW SHE HELPS OTHER CHILDREN WHO HAVE BEEN ABUSED

**LMA:** When I was a child, I didn't know that what I was experiencing was abuse, but I knew I didn't like how I was treated or how it made me feel. With that in mind, I can help adult survivors of child abuse today. I assist them through my organization's confidential support group, Courageous Conversations. Through the support group, I help them realize they should not blame themselves for what happened. Many times, we blame ourselves, and we feel shame. I tell those who have been abused that they did nothing wrong. The person who abused them is the one who did something wrong. I also tell them to seek professional help. That was the best thing that I ever did. I wish I would have known that when I was younger.

Seeking professional help and going to support groups helped me so much that I started my own support group for victims of abuse and their families to help deter the continuation of the abuse cycle. Child abuse is preventable. If you're experiencing it, ask for help.

## INCREASING YOUR SELF-WORTH

**LMA:** Believe in yourself, listen to motivational people, and spend time with positive people. Do not surround yourself with negative people. Learn how to say "no"! Do something for yourself each day. Forgive yourself! Face your fears. Conquering them will give your self-esteem a boost. Enroll yourself in support groups with people who are in similar situations, so they can help you cope. Exercising and self-care are also super helpful. Other things that you can do are take a walk or light a candle and spend a quiet moment with yourself. Do whatever will make you feel better during rough times.

## NATIONAL ORGANIZATIONS THAT CAN HELP YOU

**LMA:** The National Domestic Violence Hotline (1-800-799-7233) is a great resource, and they're twenty-four hours a day, seven days a week. There is never a moment when you can't get the help that you need. Here is the website: www.thehotline.org. Everything you tell them is confidential.

## SAFETY PLANNING

**LMA:** According to the National Domestic Violence Hotline, "A safety plan is a personalized, practical plan that can help you avoid dangerous situations and know the best way to react when you are in danger. This plan includes ways to remain safe while in the relationship, planning to leave, or after you leave." Safety planning depends on the situation. Make sure you have all your important documents. Sometimes the abuser will keep things like birth certificates and Social Security cards. You may want to take them to a family member's home or keep a suitcase in your car, if you have one. A safety plan for a child who is being abused looks very different than an abused adult's safety plan. If a child is being abused, he or she needs to find a trusted adult and tell them what is happening. Silence hides violence. As adults, we can do our part by reporting any abuse that we suspect. Call 911 if safety is of immediate concern. Learning how to recognize possible signs of family violence, responding appropriately, and referring to community resources will save many children from abuse. We can also promote education and awareness on the topic of family violence in our churches, schools, and community. A huge one that I wish was done for me is to teach young people about healthy relationships (and that is *not* just for intimate relationships).

Some safety plans to use during an argument:
- Stay in an area with an exit, and avoid letting the other person get between you and the exit.
- Practice getting out of your home safely.
- Avoid rooms with weapons, such as the kitchen.
- Keep your cell phone on you, so you can call for help, or have emergency phones hidden in the home.
- Devise a code word or signal to use with your children, family, friends, and trustworthy neighbors when you need the police.

Some safety plans for when you are preparing to leave:
- Leave money, extra keys, copies of important documents, extra medicine, and clothes with someone who you trust, so you can leave quickly.
- Determine safe people you can stay with.
- Review and rehearse your escape plan.
- Keep a packed bag at a trusted relative or friend's home.
- Plan where you will go if you must leave.

You may want to figure out how to make money online before you leave, so you can be financially stable and support yourself. Make sure the abuser doesn't know you're trying to get money, or he or she might try to stop you. I also recommend seeking help for that. Call the hotline listed above, so they can help you create an appropriate safety plan.

Never let your abuser know what's going on. Leaving an abusive and/ or toxic relationship is the most dangerous time for a victim.

## JUDGE LESS, HELP MORE

**LMA:** Decide what taking care of yourself looks like. Some people will judge you for the actions you take. They will blame you for what's going on or think you are letting this happen. This includes adults and kids. A lot of young people live on the streets because they don't want to stay in an abusive home. They don't have anybody to help them. We must stick together to help each other. What does that look like for you? Maybe you want to start a shelter or an organization that helps people in your situation. We should do less judging and more helping.

272

## TOP TAKEAWAYS:

- Pay attention to kids' behavior and marks, so you don't miss signs of abuse.
- *If you've been abused, understand that you did nothing wrong.*
- Seek professional help.
- Increase your self-worth by spending time with positive people, listening to motivational talks, spending time alone, and exercising.
- Call the National Domestic Violence Hotline, or visit their website if you need help. They are confidential.
- Have a safety plan in place.
- Judge less, and help more.

# 48
# OVERCOMING PORNOGRAPHY ADDICTION
## *YAMILEXIS FERNANDEZ*

Yamilexis Fernandez is a Christian leader who inspires people to walk in freedom through her life and her social platforms. She was introduced to pornography at age six, experienced sexual abuse trauma and depression, got into drugs, and had low self-esteem. Through her ministry and her business, she shares her story to help others move forward and overcome their challenges.

## CONNECT:
- Instagram: @YamilexisFernandez
- TikTok: @YamilexisFernandez

## STRUGGLES INCLUDED IN THIS CHAPTER:
- Anxiety
- Depression
- Low self-esteem
- Parents got divorced
- Felt alone
- Moved to a new country
- Pornography addiction
- Was sexually abused
- Was in an emotionally abusive relationship

## HER STORY
**Yamilexis Fernandez:** I was new to this country; we came from

Cuba. My dad stayed behind to take care of his parents. I didn't speak the language, and I was struggling with insecurities about who I was. I went through a lot as a child, including sexual abuse, and I was introduced to pornography at age six.

By the time I was twelve, I had the courage to tell my mom about the abuse. I felt like I had no self-worth or beauty because that was all I heard. Pornography was something that I went to because it felt normal. I didn't know any different.

I got into a relationship at age thirteen, and I was with that guy for five years. He was emotionally abusive and would constantly reaffirm everything that I was already insecure about. That turned into drugs and hanging out with the wrong friends. I got good grades in school and looked perfect from the outside, but nobody knew that my life behind the scenes was a mess. I would look for ways to numb the pain. I had no sense of purpose or identity. I didn't have anybody to guide me in the right direction. I didn't trust anybody. I felt alone, angry, depressed, and anxious.

## DIFFERENT LEVELS OF PORN ADDICTION

**YF:** There are different levels to porn addiction, just like any other addiction. Some people watch porn every single day, and others do it periodically, whether it's weekly, monthly, or every few months. An addiction is something you want to stop because it's affecting your life, but you can't.

My addiction was periodic. I couldn't stop. I told myself that I was not going to do it anymore, and then a couple of months would pass, and I would do it again. I didn't think it was a problem until I became a Christian.

Once I gave my life to the Lord, it got harder because I knew looking at porn was wrong, but I didn't know if I could stop it. It became a cycle until I finally talked to my Bible study group leader. I was in a Bible study for two weeks, and I knew I had to tell her about it. If I didn't, I would never be able to overcome it.

It's important to realize the ways that we numb ourselves in life. Once you realize the impact an addiction is having on you, you need to talk about it because you are not meant to overcome it alone.

## OVERCOMING PORN ADDICTION

**YF:** Overcoming my porn addiction started with talking to somebody. Then I started going to counseling. Then I set goals and created a plan. I had to take steps like setting up content blockers on my phone. I would also talk to people to have accountability. I also stopped listening to certain types of music and stopped following certain people on social media. Most of my friends thought I was crazy. It took me two years, and then I ended up going to a Christian conference. I felt something shift in me. I realized I had to make a commitment, or things would never change. I couldn't go half in because then I would keep making exceptions.

Even if you follow these steps, sometimes temptation still creeps in, especially when porn is normalized in culture. Don't beat yourself up too much. I would have to remind myself, "I am pure. I am holy. I am not going to go down that route. I am not going to think about somebody like that." It was hard to stop. Before, I would entertain it and allow myself to stay there mentally. I was stuck in that cycle because I was OK with it. If you are in that cycle, you are not alone, and you can overcome it.

## THE NEGATIVE FACTORS OF THE PORN INDUSTRY

**YF:** I got educated about the porn industry. I realized that most of the women who are part of it are forced, drugged, and they're not enjoying it. Many of the people who get into the porn industry are sexually abused and are sex trafficked. I do not want to support that. These people could be my sisters, my brothers, or my future children. It breaks my heart. Pornography makes people suicidal. It also leads to drugs, loneliness, and low self-esteem.

## OVERCOMING INSECURITIES

**YF:** I'm still learning. Every day, I must be intentional and speak life into myself. Every day, I must get to know myself and see myself the way that God sees me. What's helped me is scriptures about who God says I am. I tell myself, "If he says that about me, why don't I believe that about myself?" It's easy to compare yourself to other people. What I've learned is that the more that I compare myself, the less beautiful and less worthy I feel. Now if I look at another girl on social media, I say, "Wow, she's so beautiful, but so am I." I say that over and over again every single day. I do this for my physical appearance and my characteristics. It also helps if you have other awesome people around you who are always speaking life into you and saying those affirmations.

## MASTURBATING WHEN SINGLE

**YF:** Masturbation is like playing with fire. You are entertaining your sexual desires. You may be single, and you may have needs, but if you can't control yourself now, what makes you think you'll be able to control yourself when you're married?

You may think, "When I'm married, I'm going to be having sex every day." But when you're married, that doesn't mean you won't have temptations. People might still hit you with direct messages on Instagram. Temptations will always exist. If you can't say "no" to yourself now, what makes you think you're going to be able to say "no" later? By not masturbating, you're building up that discipline, so you can be faithful when you're married. If you build discipline now, it will be much easier to say "no" to someone later because your sexual desire will be under control.

## TOP TAKEAWAYS:

- There are different levels of addiction. It's important to realize how heavy your addiction is.
- Tell someone about your addiction to help you overcome it. Accountability is important.
- To overcome your porn addiction, you must make a commitment and deal with the trauma that is leading you there.
- *If temptation creeps in, don't beat yourself up; ask for help.*
- There are a lot of negative factors in the porn industry.
- You can overcome insecurities by reading scriptures and having a personal relationship with Jesus.
- Discipline yourself in sexual purity.

# 49
# HOW TO ESCAPE NEGATIVITY IN A BAD NEIGHBORHOOD TO FOLLOW YOUR PASSION
## *LUIS QUINTERO*

Luis Quintero went from living in a Venezuelan neighborhood surrounded by negativity to creating soundtracks for games with over 10 million installs, creating a YouTube channel that got over 1.2 Million views and achieving over 115,000 Spotify Streams since the age of thirteen. Now Luis is nineteen years old. He is making music for games with over 10 million downloads and impacting millions of people around the globe through music.

## CONNECT:
- Website: www.linktr.ee/luisquinteroco
- LinkedIn: linkedin.com/in/luisquintero-co
- YouTube: youtube.com/c/bitonallandscape

## STRUGGLES INCLUDED IN THIS CHAPTER:
- Family was poor
- Lived in a dangerous neighborhood

## GETTING INTO MUSIC

**Luis Quintero:** I grew up in a small neighborhood in Trujillo, Venezuela. Back in the day, my family didn't have much financial support. My passion for music started around five years old. I wanted to do something music related in the future, but I didn't know what. I didn't know if I wanted to be a rock 'n' roll star or a rapper. My brother was in a band. He made a friend in an electronic music group. I started to investigate electronic music, but I was nine years old, and I didn't have a computer. The only computer that was at my home was the one that my brother used for college. Later, I discovered artists like Tiesto and Daft Punk, which were awesome, and soon I started producing my own music.

At age thirteen, I got tired of making trance music and wanted more growth. My brother and I decided to make video game music. That's how my video game music journey started, with me making music for popular games with millions of downloads. It wasn't an overnight success. I went through multiple evolutions to find out what I was good at and passionate about. To reach success, you must go through several evolutions.

## NOT GETTING INVOLVED IN THE NEIGHBORHOOD MESS

**LQ:** I was focused on music, so what was going on in my neighborhood didn't affect me much. For example, in my neighborhood, there was gun violence and drugs. It was the most dangerous neighborhood in Trujillo. I didn't care. I loved to be super positive. There was a lot of negativity, pessimism, and drugs in my neighborhood, but I didn't see or touch any of it because I was focused on my goals. When you focus on yourself and your goals, you don't care about your surroundings.

I kept my passion for music a secret from everyone. People didn't know I was making music or producing music. I kept it a secret until I was eighteen. The other kids would party and drink. I attended a few parties, but I didn't like it. I preferred to be in my studio.

## HOW TO GET OUT OF YOUR SITUATION AND PURSUE YOUR PASSION

**LQ:** Spending time alone is super important because it helps you discover yourself. When I was fifteen, I isolated myself from people. During that time, I had a spiritual awakening. When you spend time alone, ask yourself, "What do I like? What is the thing that helps me deal with my pain? What do I want? What do I love to do?" Then invest in yourself. Don't try to change yourself for other people; change yourself to grow. When you discover yourself, you will start loving yourself. Then find friends who you can truly be yourself around. I was depressed at one point because I was hiding who I was. I was afraid of judgement. Then I realized I needed to be myself. Self-awareness is key.

## TAKE FULL RESPONSIBILITY

**LQ:** Take full responsibility for yourself and your life. Don't say it's your parents' fault, blame your environment, or blame anyone else for your failures. If you do that, you will never be successful.

## TOP TAKEAWAYS:

- *To reach success, you must go through several evolutions.*
- When you focus on yourself and your goals, you won't care about your surroundings.
- Spend time alone to discover who you are.
- Surround yourself with people who allow you to be yourself.
- Take full responsibility for your life.

# 50
# HOW TO THINK IN ABUNDANCE WHILE FACING ADVERSITY
## *DAVID MELTZER*

David Meltzer's dad left his family when David was five years old. His single mother had a hard time supporting the family financially. Despite these struggles, he was always grateful for the life he had. Now he is the co-founder of Sports 1 Marketing, a three-time international bestselling author, a top-one-hundred business coach, the executive producer of Entrepreneur's number-one business show, *Elevator Pitch*, and the host of the top entrepreneurs' podcast, *The Playbook*. His life's mission is to empower over one billion people.

## CONNECT:
- Website: www.dmeltzer.com
- Instagram: @DavidMeltzer

## STRUGGLES INCLUDED IN THIS CHAPTER:
- Family was poor
- Divorced parents
- Became rich and then lost everything

## HIS VIEWPOINT ON HIS CHILDHOOD

**David Meltzer:** I'm probably different than a lot of people. Besides the financial stress, I had a great childhood. My dad left me at five years old, but my mom was so extraordinary. We didn't always have the best food or enough food, and we had a lot of financial stress, but my mom pushed us to have character and value as well as to be happy and educated. She wanted us to pursue our potential.

## LESSONS HE LEARNED FROM HIS FINANCIAL STRESS

**DM:** During those times, I learned two main things. One is to find what you love to do. My grandpa and my mom were super optimistic. They wouldn't let me come downstairs if I had a negative attitude. Mom would say, "We're not starting the morning. Go pray, and give thanks to God. Ask for ten people who you can help." My mom would always have us volunteering. Even though we didn't have enough, we were always volunteering to help other people. She made me say "thank you" before I went to bed. Gratitude became a cornerstone to everything that I did. My mom also taught me accountability from the time I was very young. She would always tell us to ask two questions, "What did you do to attract this to yourself?" and "What are you supposed to learn from it?"

She told us to learn the lesson associated with the negative event. Lessons keep coming in life. Negative events only result in pain when you don't learn the lesson. If you're experiencing pain right now, seek to learn the lesson through these experiences, or ask others for help.

## YOU DON'T HAVE TO TAKE EVERY PIECE OF ADVICE GIVEN TO YOU

**SS:** You went to law school, and then you reached the point where you had two options: either sell legal research online or become a lawyer. What path did you take to make your first million dollars within nine months?

**DM:** I respect my mother, so I went to her for advice, but I always take her advice (even if I don't ask for it) with a grain of salt. I listen to it, and I'm grateful for it. I tell her, "I understand. I never thought of it that way." My mom told me that the Internet was going to be a fad and that I should be a real lawyer. That was in 1992.

For the first time, I didn't blindly listen to her. She said, "Doctor, lawyer, or failure." I finally told myself that I was to appreciate my mom's advice, but she was a second-grade teacher. I was going to mitigate my risk from what my mom said. I was going to take the bar exam, but then I was going to sell legal research online. I was going to vote for what I wanted. I was going to elect what I wanted in my life. I decided to sell legal research online. My goal was to become rich for my mom. I wanted to buy her a house and a car. I always say, everybody already knows their why.

Just because someone loves you doesn't mean you should follow their advice. You have to evaluate what the advice is and who is giving it. Is the person giving the advice an expert in that subject?

## REVERSE ENGINEERING

**DM:** I reverse engineered by looking at the power of sixty-four in a book called *Connected to Goodness*. Anybody can help produce and be successful. Most people work, on average, eight productive hours a day.

I got focused and told myself that I was going to work sixteen productive hours a day. Then I was going to create systems of efficiency, so my sixteen hours of productivity turned into thirty-two hours of productivity. Then I was going to be consistent and persistent in that efficiency and discipline to practice what I did to get better at it. That thirty-two hours of productivity became sixty-four hours of productivity in one day. Then I decided to take the word "work" out of my vocabulary and start focusing on calling it "activity I get paid for."

I had more activity in my life that I got paid for than activity I didn't get paid for. In nine months, I made $1 million. People gave me all these awards for being the top sales guy and making so much money, I was laughing on the inside because I just beat people with math. I worked ten years in nine months. I was productive, which was equal to what most sales guys took ten years to do. I did it in nine months through sixty-four hours of production a day, seven days a week.

**SS:** How do you stay so productive without burning out?

**DM:** There is no burnout in what I do because I have this idea of shifting the paradigm of motivation. Motivation is temporary. I believe in inspiration. I believe I'm consistently connected to the greatest source of energy that exists. I'm focused strictly on clearing the interference or corrosion that I've created through that connection. This is how I work, so with that perspective, I am "on vacation" every day.

I don't think burnout exists. People who get burned out are just creating too much interference and corrosion to what they're already connected to, an incredible source of light, love, and lessons.

## ABUNDANCE ATTITUDE

**DM:** I wake up every morning with an attitude of abundance toward everything coming through me in a world of more than enough. I lost everything in the 2008 crash. When money was limited, I received my first paycheck from Leigh Steinberg Sports and Entertainment. I wrote (with my wife's permission) a big check to provide a scholarship to help kids go to college. With everything that I do, I continue to give back to charitable causes.

## THE THREE BEST LESSONS TO THOSE WHO ARE STRUGGLING

**DM:** First, ask for help. Whatever is bothering you, someone in your life has situational knowledge, experience, and relationships that can help you. You are not alone.

Second, learn and practice gratitude. Before you go to bed each night, list everything that you are grateful for. Every morning when you wake up, do it again. Program your conscious, subconscious, and unconscious mind to have a mindset of gratitude.

Finally, be of service. If things aren't going well for you, help somebody else who is struggling. Open a door for someone. Help someone cross the street. Volunteer at the homeless shelter. Whatever it is, you will feel much better about yourself when you help others.

## TOP TAKEAWAYS:

- Find the light in what you love to do.
- Negative events only result in pain if you fail to learn the lesson.
- *Be grateful for receiving certain advice, but don't take every piece of advice given to you.*
- To get more done, find ways to work harder and be more productive and efficient.
- There is no such thing as burnout if you clear interference and corrosion from your head.
- You have more than enough.
- Ask for help, practice gratitude, and be of service.

# 51
# HOW TO FACE AN
# IDENTITY SHIFT
## *ANTHONY TRUCKS*

Anthony Trucks is an international speaker, bestselling author, and successful entrepreneur, and he is happily married with three amazing children. He is also a former NFL athlete whose career was cut short by injury and the first NFL athlete to hit the American Ninja Warrior buzzer. From the outside his accomplishments are spectacular. His struggles included being put into foster care at age three with three of his siblings. He was abused and tortured by some of his foster parents until he was finally adopted by a family at age fourteen.

## CONNECT:
- Website: www.anthonytrucks.com
- Instagram: @AnthonyTrucks

## STRUGGLES INCLUDED IN THIS CHAPTER:
- Depression
- Family was poor
- Was in foster care
- Wanted to commit suicide
- Abusive foster parents
- Family didn't have much money
- Felt like a failure
- Had a hard time trusting people

## STUCK IN FOSTER CARE

**Anthony Trucks:** I was put into the foster care system in 1986. I bounced around a lot of homes, tortured to earn meals, and abused by some foster parents. It was a messed-up system. My foster parents would receive a paycheck as long as I didn't die in the system. By age six, I had experienced what no one should experience in their lifetime. I was finally adopted at age fourteen by the same family I had been with since I was six years old. I was the only African American male in an all-white family, so I was trying to figure out where I fit in and how to find myself in this world. We were poor. My adoptive father was an alcoholic and abusive. Eventually, my adoptive mom got remarried to a good guy, and life got better. I started playing football at age fourteen, and I was horrible.

## HOW TO STAY POSITIVE

**AT:** Positivity comes from a place of perspective. Before when I saw something that could not be any better, I ended up living in that negative emotional place. I used to think that nothing positive would come from this, so why try? Positivity comes from seeing something that gives me a bit of hope. That gives me a purpose to work toward. If I'm striving toward something, I might do poorly at first, but once I get a small win, I get more joy. I seek more of those experiences. During dark times, I always seek small wins, so it can spark the next one and eventually lead to something bigger.

## WHEN THE MENTAL SHIFT HAPPENED

**AT:** When I played football during my first year in high school, I wasn't very good, and in the second year, I was just OK. I told myself, *I'm never going to be good at this. I'm just this foster kid who's not going to do much with his life.* My mom was sick, my brother, who I was close to, joined the military. I was one of six children, and no one cared about school in my family, so I decided not to care either. I slept during class all the time.

In one class I overheard a girl say the reason she was so bad was that she was in foster care. I got to hear my own excuse spoken out loud. That didn't sound right, and I was uneasy about it. This whole time I was making an excuse not to be great because I was in foster care. One day I looked at myself in the mirror, and I told myself that I was going to be great. I chose to be great at football, and then I went to work. I started doing what other great football players do: eating right, hitting the weights, and putting in overtime. After a year of that, I was unstoppable. My mentality was that no one could beat me. I had put in too much work in the dark that people didn't see. I changed my beliefs, my thoughts, my actions, my habits, my character, and my pride to make an everlasting change. Now it was my identity that I was a great football player, and I was going to fight for that.

## DARK TIMES AFTER THE NFL

**AT:** In my third NFL season, I suffered an injury that ended my career. I had an identity crisis, and I had to figure out who I was without football. In doing so, I ruined my marriage, I ruined my business, and I ruined my parenting. I reached a point where I wanted to take my own life. I was hanging out with multiple women, drinking, and I distanced myself from my faith. I had a moment of reflection where I realized I needed to change my life. I stopped drinking and partying, and I no longer hung out with multiple women. I sat and looked at a wall and asked myself some hard questions to discover who I was. Eventually, I put in the work to change for the better.

## TAKE THAT WALL DOWN TO LET PEOPLE IN

**AT:** Many times foster kids like me put up a wall. We don't want anyone hurting us anymore. I did that to feel safe. Unfortunately, by blocking out the bad things, we keep out the good things too. We also develop a gut instinct for who is genuine and who is not. I started letting people in, but I had a rule: if they betrayed me, I would kick them out immediately.

## THE THREE PHASES OF AN IDENTITY SHIFT

**AT:** My identify shift involved three phases. The first is "see." Get clear on the actual thing that is holding you back. Find the direction you need to go.

The second phase is "shift." Create a structured process of the work that you need to do to shift your life. Only actions can make shifts happen.

The third phase is "sustain." You need to be able to sustain the traction and make progress from where you are now. Also, you need to sustain perspective on what the next level of life is.

## ASKING PEOPLE WHO WILL KEEP IT REAL

**AT:** Talk to three people (two people who you know will keep it real and one person you have had a problem with), and ask them, "Based on how you see me, what do you think I should work on?" Don't interrupt them as they talk, and don't try to defend yourself. Just listen, and don't take it personally. It's an opportunity for improvement. If all three people say the same thing, maybe you need to work on that.

## TOP TAKEAWAYS:

- Positivity comes from a place of perspective.
- *During dark times, seek small wins, so it can spark the next win and*

*eventually lead to something bigger.*
- Tell yourself that you're going to be great.
- To change your identity, you must change your beliefs, thoughts, actions, habits, character, and pride.
- Ask yourself some tough questions to change.
- Take down the wall, and let people in.
- The three phases of an identity shift are, see, shift, and sustain.
- Ask people what you should work on, and then let them talk.

# WHY I WROTE THIS BOOK

## *SHELOMO SOLSON*

You've heard everyone's story, but I have yet to share my story. So, here it is.

I have been battling an inner game for as long as I can remember, as far back as the first day of kindergarten. My mom packed me a sandwich and juice for my first day. I had a red Power Rangers lunchbox. It was my first time away from my mom, who had stayed home and taken care of me for five years.

After lunch, we could take out our pillow to take a nap. I remember being the last one to finish my lunch and the last one to take a nap. When I put my head down for the nap, tears fell down my face. I told myself I was slower than everyone else, and I was always going to be slower than everyone else.

I carried that thought until after college. Occasionally, it still appears in my head. Most of our limitations and negative self-talk start at a young age. Unless we recognize what those thoughts are, it is difficult to eliminate them.

What struggles have I gone through that affected my mind? I've been bullied, I've battled depression and anxiety, lacked confidence, been self-conscious, shy, and awkward, I've had troubles getting a girlfriend, friends have passed away, and I've had a difficult time reading and paying attention.

As difficult as these challenges have been, I'm grateful for them because they have led me to a career of inspiring people and changing their lives.

## MY STORY ON BULLYING

I knew from a young age that I was different. I have had glasses since I was six years old and would wear a strap in the back of the glasses, so I wouldn't lose them.

Bullying has been a big part of my life and one of the reasons why I wrote this book. I was bullied pretty much from eight years old until my early twenties. I was the typical story of a kid who got bullied. I was bullied for four main reasons.

## 1. How I Spoke

English wasn't my first language. I went to speech therapy and enrolled in an ESL (English as a Second Language) program for seven years. I had a hard time pronouncing words, I had an accent, and many times other people had a difficult time understanding me. Other kids started noticing that. As they started noticing, they would say some harsh stuff, like: "Can you speak proper English?" and "Shelomo has a speech impediment."

This left me self-conscious about how I spoke. Throughout middle school, high school, and college, any time I was with a group of people, I wouldn't speak because every time I spoke, they made fun of me. People told me I was a horrible storyteller, I wasn't good at telling jokes, and half the time they didn't understand me when I spoke.

## 2. I Was Bad at Sports

I would always play football and basketball with the neighborhood kids. I wasn't fast, I wasn't good at catching, I wasn't good at throwing, I wasn't good at dribbling, I wasn't good at running, and I wasn't good at shooting. I was always the last one to be picked, which hurt. It also hurt to know I didn't have an ounce of athletic ability. I even got last place in a couple of races in high school out of a lot of people. Looking back, I had a chance to be athletic if I worked toward it, but no one told me to keep trying.

## 3. My Religion and Etāicity

My mom is from Bombay, India, and my dad was born in Karachi, Pakistan. My siblings were born in Israel. I was born in the United States and brought up Jewish. In my teenage years, I was always the token brown kid and the token Jew. I got made fun of for both things, being Jewish and being Indian.

I reached a point where I didn't want to associate myself with my roots. It was causing me more trouble than good. I wanted to either be Hispanic, Black, or White (not knowing that every race is discriminated against somehow).

Real friends should embrace diversity in their friend group and not push it away.

## 4. Never Having a Girlfriend or Kissing Anyone

I thought no girl would ever like me. It started in the fifth grade when a girl who I had a crush on told me that she would never go after someone like me. After that I thought I was ugly and would never have a girlfriend.

In middle school, other girls and boys started dating. Boys made fun of me for never seeing a girl's body parts before. In high school, the relation-ships got more serious. A lot of people were losing their virginity. Mean-while, I never had a girlfriend, never kissed a girl, and never had a girl who liked me. Other boys would make fun of me for it. They would call me ugly, say I had a small penis, that I would never see any girl's body parts, that I would always stay in the friend zone, and girls would never date me because I was not a real man. They would even tell me to say inappropriate things to girls (I had no idea what they meant) for their entertainment. I was a late bloomer, and I used to be ashamed of it.

Every morning I dreaded going to school for these reasons. I always wondered, why me? I only saw my struggle and thought I was the only kid who was getting bullied. I was an easy target. The fact is, even my bullies had bullies. People usually bully to make themselves feel better. They either have confidence issues or have problems at home. They don't know any better. Back then I didn't know that. I thought bullies were mean, cruel kids.

Even I was a bully at times. Any time I saw an opportunity to make myself feel better, I did it. If I saw someone name calling or laughing at another kid, I participated. For once it wasn't me getting picked on. It made me feel better about myself. Later in life, it made me feel guilty. I never apol-ogized to those kids.

Bullies are often victims themselves. I talked to people who were bullies in middle school, and I realized what they were going through back then. Even though bullying is unacceptable, I had no idea of the challenges that they were facing. Those who have confidence in themselves will not put others down. The next time someone says something bad about you, remember that it has nothing to do with you and everything to do with the other person.

## MY STORY ON ANXIETY

I didn't realize I had anxiety issues until I was twenty-six years old. I al-ways put unnecessary pressure on myself about the future without realizing the damage it was doing. I have been outcome oriented since I was five years old, which isn't a bad thing unless you are constantly worrying about the outcome (which I was).

I mentioned the story about the first day of kindergarten and how I was the last one to finish lunch, and from then I always thought I was going to be last. I had other incidents in my early days that led to my anxiety build-up.

- Reading assessments – I got anxious thinking about reading exams.
- School grades - I got anxious when I didn't do as well in school.
- Behavior – I got anxious when I let people down.
- Running – I got anxious I didn't hit my running times.

- Leadership – I got anxious in my leadership positions.

This anxiety was a mix of trying to please people, worrying about outcomes, and not accomplishing my goals. I have always set the bar high for myself and didn't give myself a fair shot.

I was constantly fighting this internal battle, and I know many others are doing the same thing. This book is not only a way for me to give back to teens and parents; it is also a way to figure out solutions for myself.

Life is a long-term game. You may see many teens and adults who seem like they have everything together. Let me tell you a secret: *no one has everything together.* We are all on our own path trying to figure out life.

## LOSING MY BEST FRIENDS

I remember it so clearly. There was a hangout with my fraternity brothers one Saturday evening. I went there after work to join them. We were doing what guys like to do. We played video games, board games, ordered pizza, and joked around with each other. I was invited to a birthday party but decided to pass because I was tired after a long day at work.

I went home and fell asleep on the sofa with the TV and the lights still on. I woke up at 3:00 a.m., turned off the lights and the TV, and then went to my room to charge my phone because it was dead. After I brushed my teeth, I turned on my phone and saw several missed calls and voicemails.

I called back and was notified that four of my fraternity brothers (Jobin, Dammie, Ankeet, and Jim) had been driving back from the birthday party when a drunk driver going the wrong way collided with them head-on while driving 120 miles per hour. He and my fraternity brothers died on impact.

It was one of the toughest things I had to go through. I had just seen them hours before, and all I could think about was the memories I had with them. I was close to all of them. My fraternity brothers and I went to four funerals in a matter of two weeks. We saw four parents bury their children. We had to hear the painful cries of their siblings and parents.

It was the first time that I lost someone that close to me who didn't die from old age. There were nights when I couldn't sleep because I couldn't stop thinking about them. With time, my wounds started to heal. I learned how precious life is and how it could end at any moment.

Why spend life worrying about the stuff we don't have control over? Why spend life being annoyed about what someone said about us? Why spend life stressing about a negative event that won't matter ten years from now.

Life is too mysterious and too short not to enjoy it. Embrace life as it comes, the good and the bad. It's not about the destination; it's about the process. Things happen to us for a reason, but we won't know that reason until later, so have faith.

## MY STRATEGY ON HOW TO OVERCOME ANY CHALLENGE OR ACHIEVE ANY GOAL

The key question is what should you do if you're being bullied, have anxiety, confidence issues, or never had a girl or boyfriend? Everyone's experience is different. What has worked for me might not work for you. What I do know is everyone has problems; they're unavoidable. As you eliminate one set of challenges, another set of challenges will arise. Below is a three-step process that I use when I'm facing problems. Even if you are experiencing a challenge that is not listed in this book, you can use this three-step solution to overcome it.

### 1. Acknowledgement and Acceptance

The first step to overcoming any issue is to acknowledge what you're going through. I knew I had anxiety and low confidence, but I didn't want to admit it because I was worried about what other people would think of me. As soon as I accepted the fact that I needed help, the closer I was to getting better by creating an action plan. Do you struggle with depression, anxiety, suicidal thoughts, or family problems? Whatever you are facing, write down the following: "I accept that I am going through (name the struggle)." Getting it out of your head and defining your problem on paper (or a computer screen) is the first step toward tackling it.

### 2. Get into Personal Development, and Become a Problem Solver

Personal development changed my life. Personal development means you are constantly trying to improve yourself. When you focus on improving yourself, you don't care what happens to you. You focus on trying to make the situation better.

I got into personal development during the summer before my fifth year of college. I was at one of my lowest points. I was going through a break-up, and I had no idea what I wanted to do with my life. I started improving my skills and learning what I needed to do to get over that hurdle. I started reading books, taking courses, and finding mentors who could help me get over my current situation.

I learned that I wanted to inspire people and become a speaker. I started pursuing new goals. Suddenly, all the problems I had no longer mattered because I knew I could overcome the challenge.

295

Personal development will not fix your problems, but they can help you start figuring out ways to fix them. Personal development is a lifelong journey. It gets you thinking consistently about how to fix certain problems in your life.

### 3. Write Down a Plan, and Put It into Practice Immediately

Nothing gets better if you don't create a plan to fix it. If you keep all your thoughts in your head, that means you are not serious about what you want. Harvard University did a study that found the 3 percent of students who wrote down their goals made 10 times more than the 97 percent of people who either didn't write down their goals or had no goals. Follow the plan consistently, but be flexible if the plan isn't working out. Act on your plan immediately because if you don't act right away, you might lose excitement about the plan and procrastinate. By starting right away, you can build momentum.

For example, here is the action plan that helped me overcome low self-esteem.

1. Join Toastmasters – September 2014
   - Complete my Competent Communicator manual by May 2015 by completing ten speeches
   - Find a mentor in Toastmasters, and follow his footsteps
   - Read one book per month on public speaking/confidence
   - Win 3 speech competitions
2. Take Dale Carnegie (eight-week sales program) – End of 2014
   - Do all assignments
   - Learn from mentor
   - Win sales presentation championship
3. Talk to three new people every week
   - Befriend one new quality person per month who I can hit up anytime
   - Have one conversation per week where I talk for over an hour

Doing this skyrocketed my self-confidence. I took programs, I found mentors, and I stepped outside my comfort zone when talking to people. Treat your personal struggles, like depression and anxiety, the same way. It won't get better instantly, but it will get there eventually.

## MY TOP TAKEAWAYS FROM ALL FIFTY-ONE INTERVIEWS

Everyone has gone through their fair share of struggles. It's tough when you feel like everything in your world is falling apart. You want to give up. You think no one understands you. Many of the people in this book attempted suicide or thought about suicide, but they found a better solution, and you can too.

The majority of the people in this book took the following ten actions to overcome adversity and become resilient.

1. **Find a positive outlet or find meaning in your work.** Viktor E. Frankl once said, "Life is never made unbearable by circumstances, but only by lack of meaning and purpose." You may not know what you want to do for the rest of your life, which is OK. A positive outlet is a way to express yourself, whether it is through music, writing, painting, or any other creative means. When you find meaning in your work, that means you are doing something that makes you fulfilled. I am finding meaning by writing this book because I am inspiring you. Inspiring people makes me fulfilled. Find activities that help you forget about the negative situations you are going through. Happiness is a byproduct of pursuing something that you enjoy.

2. **Tackle your fear to grow.** When you are pursuing your meaning or purpose in life, you will find yourself in uncomfortable situations. The more you do the things that you fear or make you uncomfortable, the more you will progress in your life. The more progress you make, the more your confidence will grow, and you will feel better about yourself. It's scary to post a YouTube video or to give a speech if you are insecure. You don't know if others will make fun of you. In the end though, it will be rewarding. Tackling your fears will increase your chances of success. You will not succeed all the time, but every time you fail, it is an opportunity to learn.

3. **Be honest with yourself.** When you are going through difficulty in your life, like depression or anxiety, it takes a great deal of courage to tell yourself, "I'm depressed" or "I'm anxious." No one wants to admit that because they are afraid of judgement. I couldn't help my anxiety until I admitted that I had it. It takes a lot of alone time and reflection to realize what challenges you need to tackle. Once you are honest with yourself, you can overcome any challenge.

4. **Reach out for help.** This book is based on the idea that you shouldn't—and you can't—fight alone. We may be hesitant to reach out for help because we are afraid of how people will respond. We are afraid it will make us look weak or that people won't care. Having a group of people who support you and help you makes it ten times easier to overcome a challenge than if you try do it yourself. You can talk to your parents, guidance counsel-

or, friend, friend's parents, uncles, aunts, teachers, coaches, online communities, or professional hotlines. There are people out there who have gone through what you have. Take that wall down, and let them help you.

5. **Gratitude.** Lots of research says that gratitude rewires your brain. It helps with any challenge you are going through because instead of feeling sorry for yourself, you feel thankful for what life has given you. Practice gratitude as soon as you wake up and before you go to sleep. Say out loud what you are grateful for, write it out, look at yourself in the mirror and tell yourself what you're thankful for, or tell another person. Being grateful doesn't have to involve something big like a house or clothes. It can be the smallest thing, like a compliment someone gave you or talking to your best friend.

6. **Change your perspective on your situation.** I would have never known that being bullied for the way I spoke would lead me to become a speaker and inspire people. If I had never been bullied, I don't know if I would have become a speaker. It may not seem like it now, but eventually, everything that is happening will make you a better person. Steve Jobs, co-founder of Apple, once said, "You can't connect the dots looking forward; you can only connect them looking backwards. You have to trust that the dots will somehow connect in your future. You have to trust in something—your gut, destiny, life, karma, whatever. This approach has never let me down, and it has made all the difference in my life." The situation you are going through is not happening to you; it is happening for you.

7. **Stop blaming other people, and take full responsibility for your life.** Whether it is the death of a loved one, your parents got divorced, you were raised poor, or you were a foster kid, the moment you stop blaming outside circumstances is the moment you take charge of improving your life. It's not your fault that your dad left you, but you can't blame him for you acting out in school. What happened to you is in the past. All you can do is look forward to how you are going to overcome your situation. Many of the most successful people in the world have overcome extreme hardships because they took full responsibility for their response to their situation.

8. **Other people's opinions of you don't matter.** People will always have opinions about you, even when you get older. I used to be the biggest people pleaser. I didn't want to offend anyone. Your self-worth is only defined by you, not by someone else, not

even family members or friends. Cyberbullying is a big deal these days. If you let what others say about you online or in person bother you, you give up your power. No matter what decisions you make in life, someone will always be offended. As they say, if you want to make everyone happy, serve ice cream.

9. **Surround yourself with the right people.** I used to wake up not wanting to go to school because I knew I would get picked on by my "friends." I would be the target for the day. As soon as I found a solid group of friends in college, I began to grow as a person because they supported me no matter what. They pushed me to be better. If you get drained when you hang out with someone, either you need to talk to that person because sometimes they don't know the negative effect they are having on you, or you need to avoid that person and find positive people to hang out with. If necessary, find a trusted adult to help you get out of that situation.

10. **Positive rituals like journaling and meditation can change how you feel.** Do something every day that helps you find peace in the midst of chaos. I do twenty minutes of walking with music, ten minutes of meditation, and ten minutes of journaling every morning to help me start my day. You should have at least a fifteen-minute morning ritual to start the day. It will put you in a positive mood, so you can be more productive and focus on your day.

## CLOSING REMARKS

I'm going to close with a story from the ninth grade. I ran cross-country (a 3.1-mile race) all four years in high school. The first year, I was horrible! Our boys' team had nine runners, and I was the eighth fastest. Our team wasn't very good either. The top seven were varsity runners. Districts was the last race of the year if we didn't make it to regionals or the state finals, and that was only for varsity runners. One of the boys didn't show up, so the coach put me in at the last minute.

I was extremely nervous. The district race was a three-lap course, one mile per lap. I stretched and got ready with the team. Then the race started. By the time I was starting my last lap, some of the runners were already finishing the race. Midway through the last lap, I realized no one was behind me, and the person in front of me was finishing the race. It was embarrassing. To make it worse, when I finished the race minutes after the second-to-last person, people gave me a standing ovation.

I could see some people hold back their laughter. I wanted to go to the car and cry. I didn't want to run anymore. However, as the weeks went by,

I continued to run, and I ran track in the spring. I placed last in my first two-mile run too. Two last-place finishes in a row!

How embarrassing, right? In that moment I knew I was an underdog, and I had to work hard to get better. That's exactly what I did. I didn't miss a practice, and I ran all summer.

When my sophomore year came around, we had several more boys on the team, our team was stronger, and I ran varsity for every race. In the district race, I placed closer to the middle, which was far from a win but still a huge improvement from dead last.

When track season came along, I received the Most Improved Runner Award at the end of the year.

During my junior year, our team was unstoppable. I ran varsity in every race except districts because someone beat me out. We made regionals, and I got to run regionals again because someone couldn't run. I got my best time then!

Then, at age twenty-three, I ran my first half-marathon (13.1 miles). At age twenty-six, I ran my first marathon (26.2) miles.

This is a typical underdog story of someone experiencing hardships and embarrassment and then working hard to become a success.

Was I a star runner? No, and you don't have to be to write your own underdog story. Many times we only hear the rags-to-riches story, someone who completely sucked at something and then became a winner and celebrity. No one hears about the kid who got last place, got significantly better, ran a marathon, and went on to use running as a pastime, even though he never became a star.

Neither do we hear about someone who flunked high school, went to a community college, and then became an accountant.

Or someone who didn't like socializing with people but went on to become a salesperson.

Each of us can write our own underdog story. How do you do that? It's simple.

1. Ask yourself, what are you really bad at, or what problems are you facing?
2. Make a goal and a plan to achieve it.
3. Work extremely hard toward that goal.

It doesn't matter if you become famous for it. You accomplished something, and you should feel proud of it. Life is filled with moments that we should feel proud of.

These fifty-one beautiful stories are a perfect example of proud moments and creating underdog stories. Each person in this book encountered challenging moments in their life, but they were able to overcome them without giving up. If they can do it, so can you!

I hope you were able to find inspiration to face your challenges head on, to be more open about your mental health struggles, and motivated to make an impact on your community.

Life is not easy, but it is worth it. The struggles we face are a gift. So are the people in our lives. Life itself is a gift.

We were made to do great things. You may be the next doctor who saves many lives or the entrepreneur who creates the next big app, or the next speaker who inspires people to overcome their struggles, or the next athlete who changes history.

You will never know what life has in store for you if you don't reach out for help. I wish you the best of luck. Whatever you're going through, take that first leap of faith to overcome it. Your future self will thank you.

## HAS THIS BOOK MADE AN IMPACT ON YOU, OR DO YOU WANT TO SHARE YOUR STORY?

I want to hear about it. Email me at shelomo@shelomosolson.com, or share your story with the world on Instagram and tag me @shelomosolson. Or you can make a TikTok out of it and tag me @shelomosolson. Nothing brings me greater joy than hearing about people's lives changing.

## DO YOU WANT TO CONTINUE YOUR GROWTH, LEARN HOW TO BECOME MORE RESILIENT, AND MAKE AN IMPACT LIKE THESE FIFTY-ONE INDIVIDUALS?

Over the past decade I have invested over $35,000 to learn from the best in the world, read over seventy-five books in a span of a few years, and taken many programs, workshops, and seminars for growth. I am a strong believer in constant learning.

I provide a lot of free resources that will teach you how to implement the tools to become resilient, so you can overcome challenges, pursue your purpose, and become more excited about life. Visit www.shelomosolson.com for more information.

## FURTHER RESOURCES

1. National Suicide Prevention Lifeline: https://suicideprevention-lifeline.org

2. National Institute of Mental Health: https://www.nimh.nih.gov
3. National Association of Anorexia Nervosa and Associated Disorders: https://anad.org/
4. National Eating Disorders Association: https://www.nationaleatingdisorders.org
5. Other resources: https://teenhealthandwellness.com/static/hotlines

# ABOUT THE AUTHOR

Shelomo Solson is one of the top youth motivational speakers. His mission is to inspire teens to overcome adversity in life, so they can make an impact.

Shelomo wasn't always positive. He was bullied from elementary school all the way to college. He lacked confidence and self-esteem in every area of his life.

He made it his goal to become more confident. He held over fifteen leadership positions from age seventeen to twenty-eight, including being the Florida regional director for his fraternity, overseeing seven schools; the chief executive officer of the fraternity's first national alumni association; the University of South Florida's College of Business Senator; Director of Corporate Relations for the International Business Board; and the president of his Toastmasters group. He has also held executive roles for the startup he worked for after college. He graduated from the University of South Florida in 2014 with a double major in management information systems and business management. He joined a Toastmasters club, which is a public speaking organization, where he won multiple speech competitions and became the district finalist twice. He has been trained and certified by prestigious speakers and organizations. This includes a Dale Carnegie Sales Certification (where he also became the sales presentation champion for the group), the Brian Tracy Speaker Academy, and Joe Yazbeck training certification. He is also certified to teach John Maxwell's content.

Shelomo wants to help as many people as possible because he knows what it's like to feel alone. He hopes you can spread his mission and his message.

## SHARE HIS MISSION TO OVERCOME ADVERSITY AND MAKE AN IMPACT.

Follow Shelomo's social media channels to receive free positive content, share your favorite tips, and tag Shelomo to help him spread the

mission of the book
- Podcast: https://shelomosolson.com/podcast/
- Instagram: @ShelomoSolson
- YouTube: Teenage Impact
- Twitter: @Shelomosolson
- Facebook: @ShelomoSolson
- TikTok: @ShelomoSolson
- Website: www.shelomosolson.com

Contact Shelomo Solson if you are interested in:
- Hiring him to be a speaker at your school or organization
- Ordering *Never Fight Alone* in bulk
- Purchasing his online video series for your students
- Having him on your podcast or show

Made in the USA
Middletown, DE
06 July 2023

34659409R00176